LAND, SEA & AIR

LAND, SEA & AIR

THE ULTIMATE BOOK OF MILITARY MACHINES

Bath • New York • Cologne • Melbourne • Delhi
Hong Kong • Shenzhen • Singapore • Amsterdam

This edition published by Parragon Books Ltd in 2015 and distributed by

Parragon Inc.
440 Park Avenue South, 13th Floor
New York, NY 10016
www.parragon.com

ISBN 978-1-4723-7154-6

Printed in China

CONTENTS

▲ World War I artillery
One of the howitzers most widely used by the Germans during the Great War. Photograph taken in Armentières (France) in 1914.

INVENTIONS FOR WAR

Whether or not our zeal for conquest is part of human nature remains a contentious issue, but it is undoubtedly this characteristic that has driven humankind to create the tools and mechanisms that make achieving this goal simpler and faster. We know that war machines existed and were in use in the most ancient of known cultures, and their appearance is often associated with major milestones in human history. Among the earliest and most groundbreaking inventions are the wheel and domestication of the horse, a combination of which led to the first chariots. These machines were highly sophisticated, which is hardly surprising if we consider that throughout history we have employed the most effective and state-of-the-art technology within our grasp to create new machines with which to accomplish major objectives, outclass the enemy's weapons, or counteract their effects.

Warfare in antiquity consisted of localized, open-field battles, mostly aimed at gaining settlements on fertile and well-connected territory. Very soon, however, exploration—and indeed conquest—would set its sights on large rivers, along coastlines, and then on to the seas. Across the Great Green, as the Egyptians called the Mediterranean 3,500 years ago, sailed some of the first warships: machines with which man would reach practically all corners of the Earth and which, over the centuries, would become symbols of strength among the ruling powers. Finally, with the conquest of the skies, first with balloons and aerostats and then, in the early twentieth century, with airships and propeller-driven aircraft, war machines would take their penultimate step in the dominion of the elements. The "ultimate" step takes us beyond the boundaries of our planet, into outer space, where the most sophisticated systems of observation, communication, navigation, and weapons control are already in place.

Great Siege Engines

As well as chariots, which reached high levels of sophistication with the Hittites and Egyptians but were no longer used in battle by the Roman Empire, an array of remarkable war machines can be found in fourth century BCE Macedonia. Before the times of Alexander the Great (356–23 BCE), armies had already made use of ladders fitted with hooks, battering rams, and structures

▲ USS *Constitution*
Launched in 1797, this U.S. frigate equipped with 44 cannons became famous during the war of 1812 against Great Britain. It is still in active service.

that protected attackers as they approached city walls and fortresses. It was during the Hellenistic period, however, that some of the most sophisticated machines for launching arrows, stones, or incendiary projectiles were developed, like the onagers—similar to catapults—and the ballistae—capable of hurling one or several projectiles great distances. These siege engines were effective against the highest of fortifications, but, in terms of complexity, were no match for the period's mighty helepolis. This enormous wooden tower, complete with different levels interconnected by stairways, was ideal for surmounting enemy walls, although it required the force of hundreds of men to operate it. Many were clad in metal plates, and it is said that the armor of one such machine was melted down to make the Colossus of Rhodes in the third century BCE.

Such towers were also deployed by ancient Rome, although smaller and equipped with drawbridges at the top. The Romans refined the workings of their siege engines and the way in which their legions employed them, which together with their conquest strategies and tactics, became models that would be followed for centuries. In fact, until well into the Middle Ages, the basic principles of the war machines used varied very little from those used by the armies of Julius Caesar. Counterweights and torsion mechanisms continued to operate weapons up until the fourteenth century.

The Age of Gunpowder
The slow evolution of artillery (mechanisms like the mangonel, counterweight trebuchets, or the springald, were machines designed to fire projectiles long distances, a principle of artillery that remains unchanged to this day) would take a very different turn once gunpowder came into common use. Invented in China in the ninth century, it was introduced into Europe by Arab traders between the twelfth and thirteenth centuries, and in the fourteenth was produced throughout Britain and Germany. Used as an explosive to propel projectiles, this substance

would forever change the workings of war machines. By this time the first cannons had already been manufactured and incorporated into armies, a situation that determined the design and construction of armor and fortresses. Very soon, there would be dramatic improvements in ranges and firing techniques, along with developments in the calibers and materials used to make the projectiles. The first of these were spherical and made of stone, although these would later be replaced by hollow, metal versions, capable of incorporating explosive substances. From the fifteenth century, during the Age of Discovery, until the eighteenth century, slow but constant progress was made in artillery, as well as in naval engineering. Throughout this time, great fleets of ships were built, which could each carry up to a hundred cannons. The enormous firepower these guns offered would soon turn navies into a key element for the ruling powers, allowing European empires to spread through the globe, establishing safe trade routes across the oceans.

From Steam Engines to Nuclear Reactors
The Industrial Revolution, which completely transformed society, first in Great Britain and then in Europe and the United States between the second half of the eighteenth century and the early twentieth century, brought with it new and dizzying changes. The steam engine, a new milestone in technology, led to the development of the railroad and the first self-propelled vehicles and ships, prompting a switch in how warfare was waged, with mechanized forces playing a key role, and spelling the end of sailing ships in naval forces. Ships were fitted with engines, had their masts removed and their wooden structures replaced by metal ones. Two further developments in the mid-nineteenth century—the invention of the internal combustion engine and the generation of electricity—would change everything. It is precisely here, between the nineteenth and twentieth centuries, when new and increasingly astounding war machines would start to appear, once again transforming warfare and marking the beginning of an unbridled race to improve ranges,

▲ **Yugoslav Wars (1991–2001)**
From March to June 1999, NATO bombed Yugoslavian territory with around a thousand aircraft, which flew 38,000 combat missions.

capabilities, and characteristics. During World War I, the first armored combat vehicles came into operation, and in the sea, submarines reached new depths and longer ranges, while in the skies, aircraft were making their first flights. The latter would become as important for the European armies of the twentieth century as horse-drawn chariots were for the Egyptian armies of Ramesses II more than 3,000 years before.

With more effective and faster aircraft, and unmasted metal ships propelled by powerful engines, aircraft carriers would soon become a reality. The structures of already existing ships were used for the first carriers, but before long shipyards would be producing specially designed models: gigantic vessels which, as well as carrying a large number of fighter aircraft, also served as capital ships. Their role remains as such today, assisted by a large fleet, or battle group, consisting of destroyers, frigates, and many other ships, which either perform a supply role or complement the offensive or defensive measures of the main ship. Although, during World War I, aircraft already played a major role, it was not until World War II that they became fully integrated into the world's armed forces.

By that time, almost ten years had passed since the first radar systems (an acronym for RAdio Detection and Ranging) had been built, based on the theories of electromagnetic-wave frequency and power developed by the great engineer and inventor Nikola Tesla (1856–1943). The British aircraft that fought in the Battle of Britain in 1940, the first waged entirely in the air, already had this new machinery, which gave them a strong advantage over their adversaries. From the forties on, Germany and many other countries employed different radar technologies and developed advances in their own systems that would finally converge into a single model of radar for detecting ground targets, missiles, and artillery, used by practically all armies in the ensuing decades.

After 1942, with the Manhattan Project and the construction of the first nuclear reactor in the United States, everything would change once again. Beside being used to create devastating arms, as demonstrated in the bombings of Hiroshima and Nagasaki, this new form of energy was soon employed to power the engines of huge war machines, which saw their capabilities increased to previously unimaginable limits. In 1954, USS *Nautilus*, the first nuclear submarine, was launched, and in 1960 USS *Enterprise* entered service, the world's first nuclear-powered aircraft carrier. Since then, armies across the globe have continually improved, producing ever more sophisticated ships, vehicles, and aircraft.

Satellites, Computers and Drones

From the 1970s to the 1990s, with the development of satellites and computer-assisted technology, extraordinary progress was made in communications, an area of vital importance for the coordination and control of war machines. Whether on land, sea, or in the air, communications systems are an asset for all armies, essential for the operation of today's highly sophisticated war machines. In our digital age, when military action has a greater impact on the information society than ever before, war is also changing.

The maneuver warfare of World War II, Germany's "lightning war," and the irregular warfare of the Vietnam War have now been succeeded by a new model called "hybrid warfare," which combines conventional warfare with so-called asymmetric warfare (such as antiterrorist operations, guerrilla warfare, counterinsurgency, or warfare with no specific fronts). This has led the armed forces to incorporate robots and attack and defense systems with unmanned vehicles, popularly known as "drones." Computer-operated remotely in real time and guided by satellites, their latest operational versions are—and will continue to be for some years yet—a jealously guarded secret.

▲ International troops in Afghanistan
Dutch troops in Afghanistan as part of the UN
International Security Assistance Force (ISAF), in 2009.

CHAPTER 1
LAND

▲ Roman siege
Roman troops using siege engines to begin their assault on a walled city.

INTRODUCTION

The evolution of land-based war machines, for the main part, has been determined by the different combat models employed over the course of history. One of the first such devices, which reached a high level of sophistication, was the chariot, used by the Sumerians as far back as 2500 BCE. The Standard of Ur (British Museum, London), dated from this period, displays what is considered to be the oldest depiction of an army and features images of four-wheeled carts. These are no comparison, however, to the agile chariots of the Hyksos, the inventors of the spoked wheel, evidence of which appears from around 1800 BCE. The course of history tells us that these were adopted by the Egyptians and were also used, in different variations, in Mesopotamia, Syria, Babylon, and Persia up until the fifth century BCE. As crucial elements in the Battle of Kadesh between the Hittites and the Egyptians (circa 1275 BCE), the earliest battle in recorded history, chariots were highly effective in fighting on open terrain, but of little use in the attritional battles to besiege and conquer walled cities. As a consequence, during the Roman Empire, their use as war machines was phased out in favor of cavalry.

By that time, many other less complex but equally ingenious machines had been used in ground warfare, the first of which, including ballistae and onagers, derived from the use of bow and torsion technology. These incorporated mechanisms capable of firing arrows, stones, or incendiary devices remarkable distances. In the time of Alexander the Great (356–323 BCE), ballistae were used on land and mounted on chariots, and they also used battering rams and mobile wooden structures lined with animal hides, which served to protect raiders during siege maneuvers and approaches to city walls. This was when one of the most astounding war machines of ancient times reached its zenith: the helepolis, a siege tower of colossal dimensions, such as the one erected in 305–04 BCE, with metal-plate armor and nine floors equipped with ballistae, torsion catapults, and armed men.

Until the Middle Ages, though with many different variations, siege machines and ingenious pieces of artillery would maintain their basic function from the time of the Roman Empire, such as weapons like the mangonel, counterweight trebuchet, and springald from between the fifth and fourteenth centuries. Europe only began to develop firearms and other war machines with the arrival of gunpowder. In this area, the Arab peoples had a strong influence, having already used highly accurate machines since the twelfth century, such as the arrow-firing *jarkh* or the *manjaniq*, a piece of counterweight artillery with highly sophisticated mechanisms, both of oriental origin.

Between the thirteenth and fourteenth centuries came the first use of gunpowder, and the development of cannons and warfare with firearms marked the evolution of war machines in Europe, which would now be capable of reducing previously indestructible city walls to rubble. Leonardo da Vinci, the genius of the Renaissance, as well as siege towers, mortar shells, the scythed chariot, and giant crossbow, designed, in the fifteenth century, a tortoise-shaped vehicle with metal armor and armed with cannons, often viewed as a precursor to the first tanks. It even included a kind of machine gun, an artillery device comprising multiple cannons. For two centuries, the destructive capability of artillery improved, and firing systems and ammunition were made more sophisticated. The birth of modern warfare in the eighteenth century saw

armies, which already had rifles and flintlock pistols for the cavalry, equipped with small-caliber cannons known as falconets, and field artillery came to the fore. Projectiles at this time were still spherical, but very soon would be given a cylindrical body, conical head, and explosive interior. Between the second half of the eighteenth century and the early nineteenth, with the development of the steam engine and the iron industry, war machines began to be fitted with armor. It is worth noting how, three whole centuries after Leonardo's designs, it took just a few decades for large warships to be armored—like the French *Gloire*, in 1859—and the American Richard J. Gatling to patent the first machine gun, in 1862, which was capable of firing 350 rounds every minute.

At the end of the nineteenth century and the start of the twentieth century, the invention of the torpedo and the incorporation of aircraft into the armed forces were key factors in an unbridled race to improve and

surpass enemy armor and artillery. For ground forces this was when tanks came into action, like the British Mark I, the world's first, which entered service in 1916. Its armor was between 0.24 and 0.47 in (6 and 12 mm) thick and, as it had no gun turret, it had weapons fitted only on its sides. The first to incorporate a turret was the French light tank, the FT-17, in 1918, whose design was key in the manufacture of later tank models, and which came to dominate World War I. During World War II, the Germans organized their tanks into panzer divisions and used them to support the infantry during their "lightning war" (*blitzkrieg*) offensives, while the allied forces used different models in combat, including constantly upgraded versions of the British Churchill Mk IV and Soviet T-34.

Between 1946 and 1990 tanks of a new generation came into service, like the British Centurion, which did not enter combat in World War II and whose initial versions could withstand a direct hit from the German 3.46 in (88-mm) missiles, were armed with a 4.13 in (105-mm) gun and could reach 21 mph (34 km/h). Not only did this tank inspire many others, but also, until very recently, its chassis served as a base for antiaircraft gun turrets, antitank vehicles, and armored vehicles for emplacing bridges. Nowadays, despite the questionable effectiveness of large tanks in armed conflicts, many armies continue to use models like the German Leopard, of which more than ten upgraded versions were made between 1979 and 2008, the French AMX-56 Leclerc, which entered service in 1992, or the Israeli Merkava, active since 1979, and whose latest versions are at the forefront of Western tank design. The future of these war machines points toward their invisibility to radar, while armies are stepping up their use of light armored vehicles for transporting troops and artillery, which can be easily transported in cargo aircraft and are suitable for security missions in urban environments, where large armored tanks lack the necessary maneuverability.

▲ Panzer divisions
A unit of German Panzer V Panther tanks advances on the eastern front during World War II (1944).

Chronology

The use of war machines has been documented for over 4,500 years, practically since the beginning of history. Since the dawn of their age, humans have called upon their ingenuity and inventive capacity to design and construct machines that help to fulfill their goals of conquest. The first such machine began a race for military superiority, in which nations across the globe are still competing today.

2500 BCE
Standard of Ur, featuring the first known depictions of war chariots.

305–04 BCE
Use of the largest helepolis, a Macedonian siege engine, in the siege of Rhodes.

1275 BCE
Battle of Kadesh between the Egyptians and Hittites, involving 5,500 horse-drawn chariots.

70 CE
The Romans lay siege to and conquer Jerusalem.

539 BCE
Cyrus the Great conquers Babylon, which subsequently becomes part of the Persian Empire.

72 CE
The Roman army besieges the Masada fortress.

711 CE
The Arabs initiate their conquest of the Iberian Peninsula.

800 CE
Charlemagne is crowned emperor of the Holy Roman Empire.

1066
First recorded use of the crossbow in Europe.

1099
The crusaders break through the city walls of Jerusalem with siege engines and towers.

circa 1200–40
The Muslims bring gunpowder into Europe.

1260
Battle of Ain Jalut, between the Egyptian Mamluks and the Mongols in Galilee, in which explosive hand cannons are used for the first time.

1300
One of the first European formulas for gunpowder appears in Marcus Graecus's *Liber Ignium*.

1346
In the Battle of Crécy (Hundred Years' War) waged between the English and the French, a bombard is used for the first time.

1453
The Ottomans besiege Constantinople. Sultan Mehmed II orders the construction of the largest cannon ever built, measuring more than 26 ft (8 m) in length.

circa 1480
Leonardo da Vinci designs various war machines, among them a multibarreled piece of artillery.

1522
The troops of Charles V make use of harquebuses to clinch victory at the Battle of Bicocca, in Italy.

1618
The Thirty Years' War begins in Europe.

1777
Battle of Saratoga, in which the North American riflemen outclass British musket volleys.

"The time has passed when the Russians had no instinct for technology; we will have to reckon on the Russians being able to master and build their own machines, and with the fact that such a transformation in the Russians' fundamental mentality confronts us with the Eastern Question in a form more serious than ever before in history."

Heinz Guderian, Chief of Staff of the German Army. *Achtung-Panzer!* **(1936)**

1983
U.S. President Ronald Reagan approves the Strategic Defense Initiative against a possible Soviet nuclear attack.

1803
Beginning of the Napoleonic Wars which would end in 1815.

1940
The first German tank destroyers enter into action.

1950
Start of the Korean War.

1860
The first breech-loading rifled artillery appears.

1962
Cuban missile crisis.

1990–91
Gulf War, during which the Iraqis fire 88 Scud missiles.

The United States Army uses GPS for the first time in warfare.

2011
U.S. Special Forces shoot dead al-Qaeda leader, Osama Bin Laden, in Pakistan.

The UN authorizes foreign military intervention in the Libyan civil war.

1916
The world's first combat tank enters service, the British Mark I.

1942
The Germans Wernher von Braun and Walter Dornberger successfully fire the V-2 rocket, although it would not be deployed until 1944.

1964
Intervention of the United States in the Vietnam War.

1862
Richard J. Gatling patents his multibarrel machine gun.

1922
Creation of the Soviet Union.

2003
Saddam Hussein is captured by U.S. troops after the invasion of Iraq.

1866
The Whitehead torpedo is developed, a predecessor of those used today.

1926
The North American engineer Robert Hutchings Goddard fires the first liquid-fuel rocket, the Goddard 1.

1943
Battle of Kursk between German and Soviet troops, involving more than 7,000 tanks—the largest tank battle in history.

1979
The Soviet Union invades Afghanistan.

2013
North Korea conducts a nuclear test, sparking an international crisis.

2000 CE

Military Leaders

They commanded great armies, won the respect and loyalty of their men, and played crucial roles in some of the most significant events in military history. Expert strategists, master tacticians in combat, and highly knowledgeable of the technological possibilities of their time, they all had one thing in common: whether siege towers or modern artillery pieces, they all made use of sophisticated war machines.

356 BCE–323 BCE

Alexander III of Macedon

Disciple of Aristotle and King of Macedonia for just thirteen years, between 336 BCE and the day of his death, Alexander the Great extended his empire to the Indus. His armies, even after his death, used the most breathtaking war machines of their time, like the 47 ft 6 in (14.5-m) high helepolis.

100 BCE–44 BCE

Gaius Julius Caesar

As brave and skillful in strategy as he was ambitious, he was Prefect of the Morals, supreme commander of the army, high priest, perpetual dictator, and Roman Emperor with the right of hereditary succession. He conquered almost all of what would become modern Europe and the Mediterranean. He was assassinated.

742–814

Charles the Great

Also known as Charlemagne, history considers him to be one of the architects of a common European identity. King of the Franks and Lombards and Emperor of the West, he extended and strengthened the Carolingian Empire, becoming a legend shortly after his death.

1138–1193

Saladin

This was how Yusuf ibn Ayyub was known, one of the most admired governors and strategists of his time and unifier of the Islamic World. He conquered Jerusalem, sparked the Third Crusade, and fought Richard I of England. He was buried outside the Umayyad Mosque in Damascus.

Alexander the Great   Julius Caesar   Charles the Great   Saladin

"Lightning war (blitzkrieg) is the art of concentrating strength at one point, forcing a breakthrough, rolling up and securing the flanks on either side, and then penetrating like lightning deep into the enemy's rear guard, before he has time to react."

Erwin Rommel, German Field Marshal during World War II

1769–1821

Napoleon Bonaparte

General in the Republic during the revolution and then Emperor of the French, he was one of the greatest military minds in history. In barely a decade his armies took control of nearly all of Western and Central Europe. He died in exile on the island of Saint Helena.

1769–1852

Sir Arthur Wellesley

The First Duke of Wellington went down in history after defeating Napoleon—whose army he had already driven out of Spain—in the Battle of Waterloo in 1815. Of Irish origin, as well as commander-in-chief of the British Army he was twice prime minister of the United Kingdom.

1885–1945

George Smith Patton, Jr.

Four-star general, he was one of the military leaders most feared by the Germans during World War II. His successes in North Africa and in the Normandy campaign gave him command of the United States Third Army, which played a decisive role at the Battle of the Bulge in December 1944.

1934–2012

Norman Schwarzkopf

U.S. Army general, at the head of the United States Central Command, he led the coalition forces in Operation Desert Storm (1991), during the Gulf War, winning a fast and comprehensive victory. His strong character earned him the nickname "Stormin' Norman."

Napoleon Bonaparte

Sir Arthur Wellesley

George Smith Patton, Jr.

Norman Schwarzkopf

▲ Assyrian war chariot
Bas-relief of the palace of Ashurbanipal in
Nineveh, which depicts the campaign against
the Elamite kingdom circa 654 BCE.

CHARIOTS

War chariots are the result of two milestones in the history of humanity: the invention of the wheel and the taming of the horse. The first took place in Mesopotamia during the fifth millennium before the common era, and the second around 3500 BCE. Although the Standard of Ur (a Sumerian artwork from 2500 BCE, in the British Museum, London) already features four-wheeled chariots, historians have found evidence that the Hyksos were the first to use them in battle, around 1800 BCE, when the lighter spoked wheel came into use. Of Syrian Palestinian or Canaanite origin, the Hyksos, who are credited with introducing these machines to Egypt, lived in the center of Anatolia (modern Turkey) and brought together city-states and different cultures, like that of the Hittites, which between the eighteenth and twelfth centuries BCE became the third power of the East, after Babylonia and the land of the pharaohs. The Hittites possessed magnificent iron war chariots and had the technology to make them light and agile. Found in the ruins of Hattusa, the old capital, was a manual written in 1345 BCE by a Hittite named Kikkuli, in which he outlines a series of rules for looking after and training horses for chariots, which are still considered to be relevant today.

Seventy years after the writing of this manual was one of the last great battles of the Bronze Age—and one of the first recorded battles in history—in which chariots were key. In Kadesh, circa 1275 BCE, a battle took place between 35,000 and 55,000 men and some 5,500 chariots, 2,000 from the army of Ramesses II and 3,500 from that of the Hittite king, Muwatalli. Victory is said to have gone to the Egyptians, whose chariots could reach over 22 mph (35 km/h), were equipped with arrow-filled quivers, and could turn more tightly, thanks to their spaced wheels. Like those of their enemies, their chariots were pulled by two horses, but carried two men, while the Hittite chariots carried three: a charioteer, an archer, and a shieldbearer.

Thanks to its speed, the power and driving force of the horses—which pulled from a single drive axle and were free of saddles and weight—and spoked wheels with metal tires, the chariot was the most powerful war machine for over a millennium. Used since ancient times in Asia and China, they were present in Mesopotamia, Syria, Babylon, and Persia between the ninth and fifth centuries BCE and there is evidence of their use by armies of the Maurya dynasty (320–180 BCE), whose empire extended through modern India, Afghanistan, and Pakistan, and by the Chinese Qin and Han dynasties (220 BCE–220 CE). Recently, remains of much older chariots have been found in chariot burial sites from the Shang dynasty (1766–1046 BCE), the first recorded in Chinese history, and even in tombs excavated in the north of Central Asia, corresponding to the Andronovo culture (2000–1200 BCE). Effective in fighting on open terrain, but also useful for conquering fortified positions, their use in combat came to an end during the Roman Empire.

The First War Chariots

Chariots were first used in warfare around the middle of the third millennium BCE in Mesopotamia. However, it was not until the eighteenth century BCE, with the appearance of lightweight two-horse chariots, that they acquired the speed and agility needed for battle. Their development by the large ancient empires, like the Hittites, Egyptians, and Assyrians, soon made them a key element in combat.

SUMERIANS

It is believed that around 2500 BCE, the Sumerians were already using chariots in warfare. These primitive versions were robust, and comprised a car and four solid, very heavy wheels. They were most likely used as platforms for archers.

Wheel type ▸ Solid, wooden

Number of wheels ▸ 4

Power ▸ 4 wild asses

Crew ▸ 2

Wheel type ▸ Spoked, wooden and metal

Number of wheels ▸ 2

Power ▸ 2 horses

Crew ▸ 3

HITTITES

Around the eighteenth century BCE, the use of the spoked wheel and horses made chariots more agile and faster, gradually turning them into the main strength of the Hittite army.

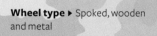

EGYPTIANS

It was probably the Hyksos that introduced the war chariot in Egypt around the sixteenth century BCE. The Egyptians built chariots that were lightweight (about 65 lb/30 kg) and fast. Additionally, the car was moved forward of the axle, which made it more maneuverable and capable of making extremely tight turns without losing stability.

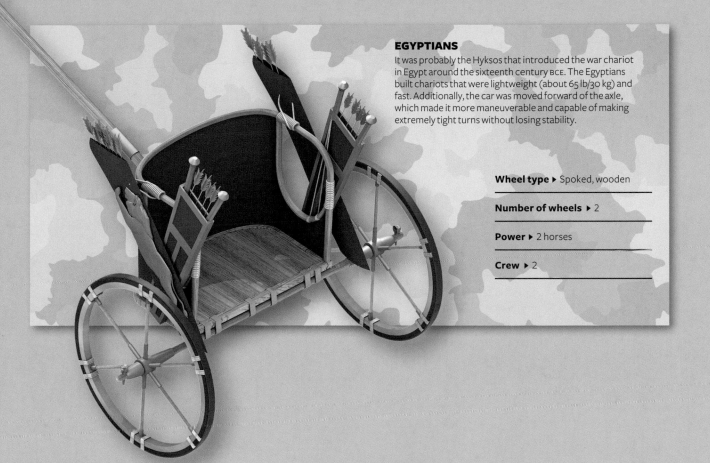

Wheel type ▶ Spoked, wooden

Number of wheels ▶ 2

Power ▶ 2 horses

Crew ▶ 2

ASSYRIANS

From the fourteenth or thirteenth century BCE, the Assyrians used chariots drawn by up to four horses and with a crew of as many as four men. They were robust vehicles with large, eight-spoked wheels and metal tires, and were possibly used as a shock force.

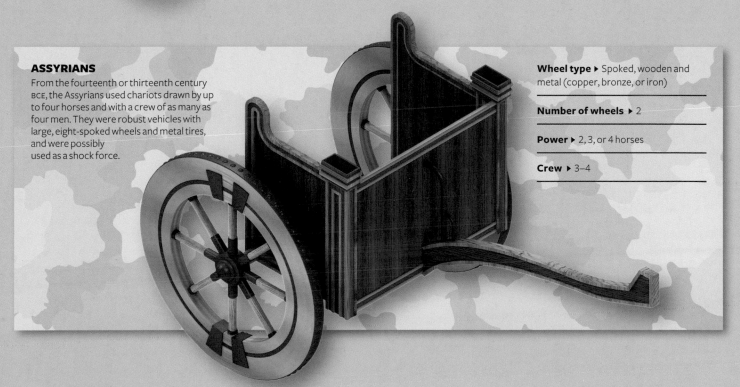

Wheel type ▶ Spoked, wooden and metal (copper, bronze, or iron)

Number of wheels ▶ 2

Power ▶ 2, 3, or 4 horses

Crew ▶ 3–4

The Hittite Chariots

The Hittites, from Anatolia (modern Turkey), extended their empire throughout the Middle East between the eighteenth and twelfth centuries BCE. Chariots were a fundamental piece of their powerful army. At the height of its power, the Hittite army had more than 3,000 combat chariots in its ranks. With a crew of three men—charioteer, shieldbearer, and warrior—their heavy chariots served as powerful shock forces, breaking the enemy's infantry lines.

Charioteer
He drove the chariot, and the success of an attack depended largely on his skill.

Horses
The introduction of horses, instead of the asses used by other peoples, gave the chariots greater mobility and power than those of their enemies.

THE HITTITE TACTIC
The Hittite chariots were designed to carry out powerful charges at the enemy infantry. Their effectiveness increased on flat, open terrain, where their power and speed significantly increased. The warrior began by firing arrows, and during the charge used spears, axes, or swords.

Shieldbearer
He protected the warrior and charioteer. He could jump from the chariot to give support in battle.

Warrior
He wore plate armor and an iron helmet. He could throw spears and fire arrows.

Chariots
They had a solid structure with a centered axle, which allowed them to transport up to three men.

War Chariot Tactics

With their increasing sophistication, chariots gave the armies of antiquity greater mobility and changed the way they did battle. An example of this is the Battle of Kadesh in modern Syria (circa 1275 BCE), between two of the era's great empires: the Egyptians and the Hittites. This is the first recorded battle involving the use of chariots, in which they played a decisive role in the fighting.

Chariot-to-chariot attack tactic
Combat between chariots relied on approaching the enemy, firing, and then retreating to allow the archer to reload before attacking again.

Hittite chariots
These were larger and heavier than those of the Egyptians; effective in open terrain, but less maneuverable in smaller spaces.

THE PHARAOH'S GLORY
The Battle of Kadesh is extensively documented since, although there was no clear winner, the Egyptians commemorated it as a great victory, with poems and reliefs about the pharaoh's bravery. Left is a reproduction of a relief representing Ramesses II in battle.

EGYPTIANS

Men ▸ Approx. 20,000

War chariots ▸ Approx. 2,000

HITTITES

Men ▸ Between 15,000 and 40,000

War chariots ▸ Approx. 3,500

Infantry attack tactic
The chariots charged the infantry, thereby dispersing them before turning around and attacking again.

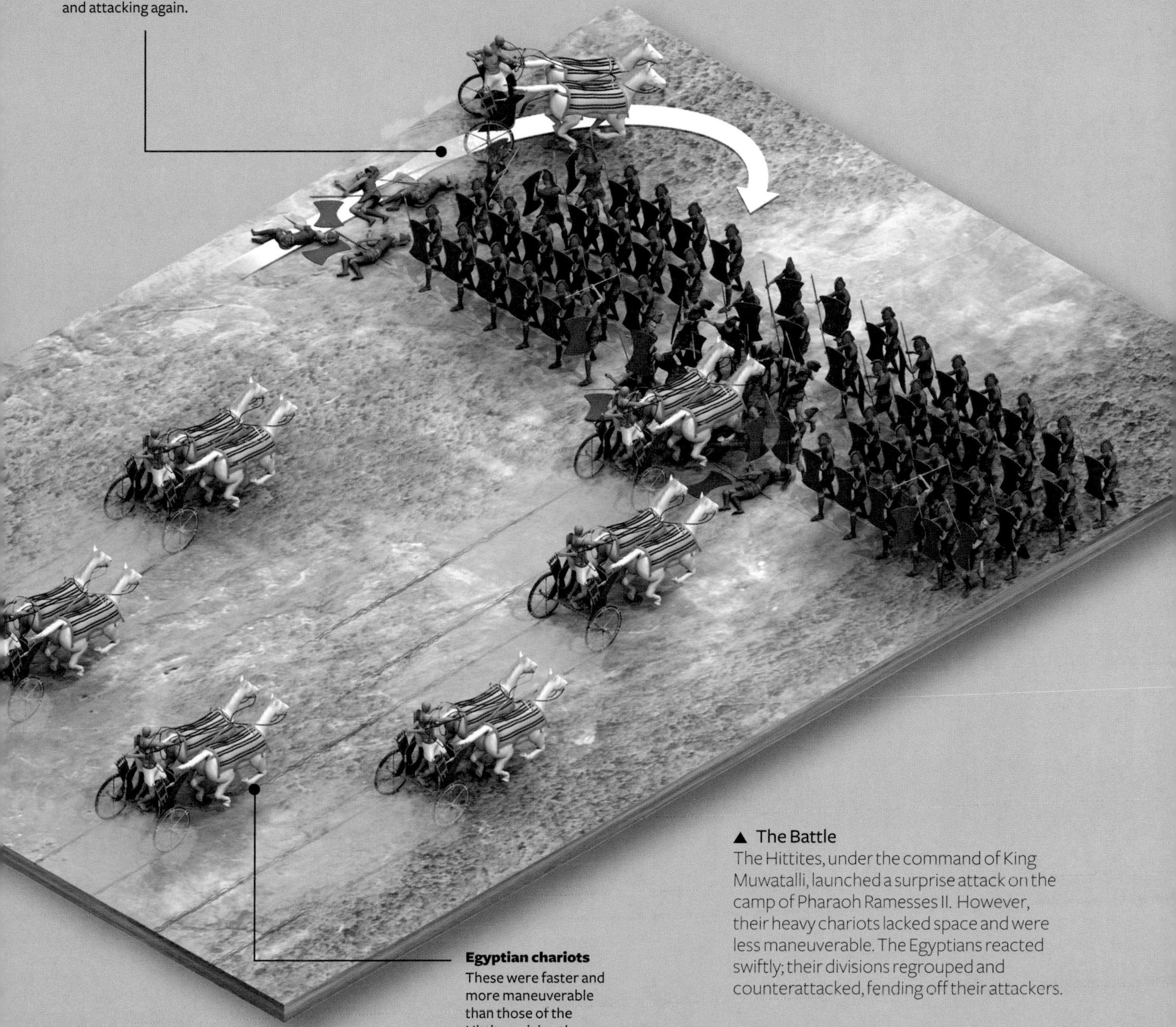

Egyptian chariots
These were faster and more maneuverable than those of the Hittites, giving them the advantage in the counterattack.

▲ The Battle
The Hittites, under the command of King Muwatalli, launched a surprise attack on the camp of Pharaoh Ramesses II. However, their heavy chariots lacked space and were less maneuverable. The Egyptians reacted swiftly; their divisions regrouped and counterattacked, fending off their attackers.

▲ Medieval siege
Image of an illuminated manuscript from the
fourteenth century depicting the siege and
capture of the French city of Rouen.

SIEGE MACHINERY

The appearance of walled cities and fortifications in ancient times gave rise to the design of machines to besiege them, which, over the centuries, became increasingly complex and effective. As well as fighting the enemy in open field, armies had to be capable of capturing fortresses, and consequently began to develop wheeled ladders, hooks, rams, and widely varying mobile structures, clad in wood or metal plates, used during approaches to protect against enemy projectiles. Battering rams and large siege towers in the Mediterranean were first used by the Carthaginians against the Greeks in Sicily, in 397 BCE. They were also used during the reign of the tyrant Dionysius I of Syracuse (405–367 BCE), though it was under Alexander III of Macedon (356–323 BCE) that siege towers, whose origins date back to the ninth century BCE, reached the height of their development. Macedonian engineers created versions of the helepolis (literally "taker of cities"), extremely solid towers with levels interconnected by internal stairways, which carried armed men, catapults, ballistae, and smaller machines for firing stones. They were built to a height of 66 ft (20 m), some even higher, and were probably the largest siege engines in history. The Macedonian armies also used and developed artillery capable of firing arrows, stones, or incendiary objects, like ballistae or onagers, machines based on torsion mechanisms that fired projectiles with great force. The former could be operated on the ground and from chariots, and the latter could hurl huge stones distances of up to 875 yd (800 m).

In ancient Rome, siege towers did not have the immense dimensions of those of the Macedonians, and their construction was often undertaken in situ and adapted to the measurements of the city or fortress walls. Specialists in conquering by force and by attrition through military blockade, the Romans built smaller constructions that were easier to handle, whose structures in many cases could be dismantled. They were also extremely skillful in attacking with a combination of catapults, onagers, and ballistae, together with the use of the *testudo* (tortoise) formation and mantlets to protect their men, who also employed ramps and towers equipped with drawbridges.

In Europe, battle towers, trebuchets (stone launchers of Asian origin with counterweight mechanisms), battering rams, and different versions of catapults and ballistae remained in use until the mid-fourteenth century. Most were imitations of twelfth-century machines employed by the Muslims, who brought them from the east in the eighth century through their alliances with the Chinese dynasties, which were highly advanced in the development of combat and siege mechanisms. In the thirteenth century, when the European kingdoms began to use the springald, considered to be the only Christian-developed piece of torsion artillery with a trigger and winch, China had already been using an effective triple crossbow system for a hundred years; it featured three bows and a seven-piece triggering mechanism and was as complex as it was accurate.

The Macedonian Helepolis and Catapult

The Macedonians built devices designed to break down a fortified city's defenses and penetrate its walls, while minimizing the number of casualties. The helepolises were known for their remarkable structures and mechanisms, while catapults could fire stones or incendiary missiles over many yards.

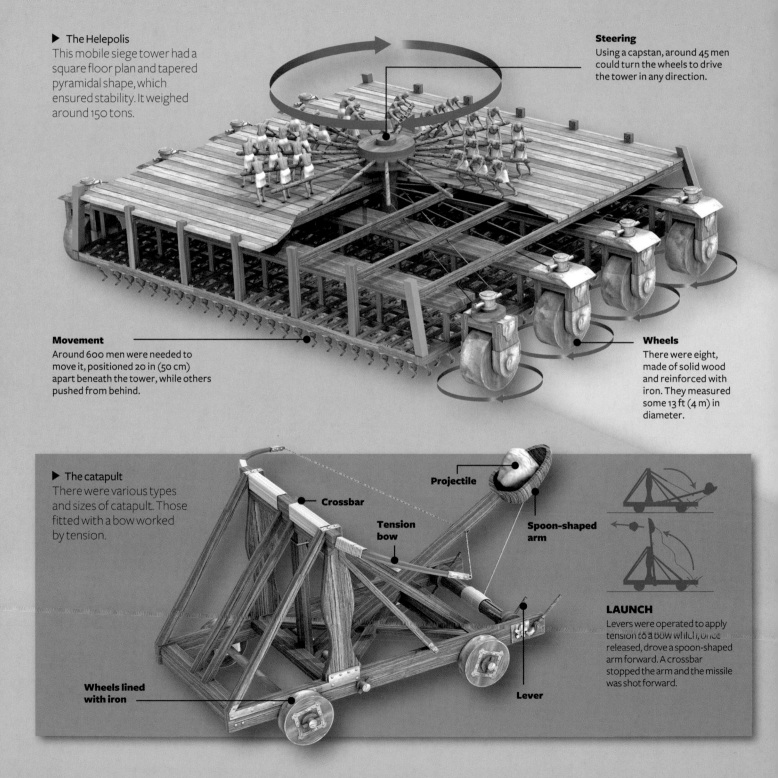

▶ The Helepolis
This mobile siege tower had a square floor plan and tapered pyramidal shape, which ensured stability. It weighed around 150 tons.

Steering
Using a capstan, around 45 men could turn the wheels to drive the tower in any direction.

Movement
Around 600 men were needed to move it, positioned 20 in (50 cm) apart beneath the tower, while others pushed from behind.

Wheels
There were eight, made of solid wood and reinforced with iron. They measured some 13 ft (4 m) in diameter.

▶ The catapult
There were various types and sizes of catapult. Those fitted with a bow worked by tension.

Crossbar

Tension bow

Projectile

Spoon-shaped arm

Wheels lined with iron

Lever

LAUNCH
Levers were operated to apply tension to a bow which, once released, drove a spoon-shaped arm forward. A crossbar stopped the arm and the missile was shot forward.

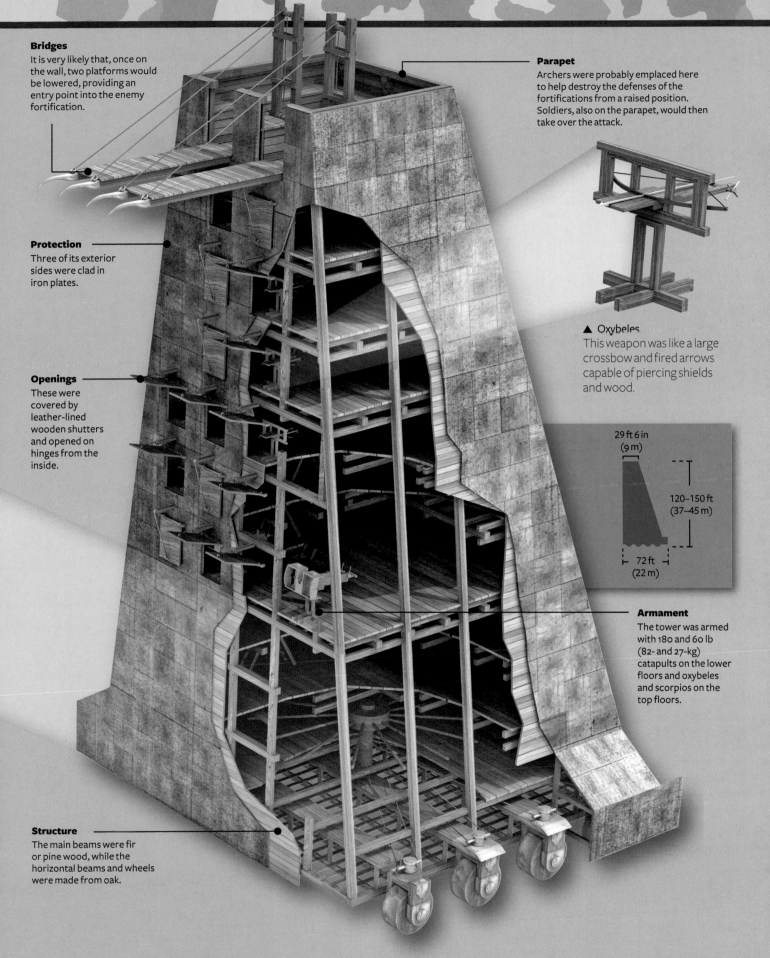

Bridges
It is very likely that, once on the wall, two platforms would be lowered, providing an entry point into the enemy fortification.

Parapet
Archers were probably emplaced here to help destroy the defenses of the fortifications from a raised position. Soldiers, also on the parapet, would then take over the attack.

Protection
Three of its exterior sides were clad in iron plates.

▲ Oxybeles
This weapon was like a large crossbow and fired arrows capable of piercing shields and wood.

Openings
These were covered by leather-lined wooden shutters and opened on hinges from the inside.

29 ft 6 in (9 m)

120–150 ft (37–45 m)

72 ft (22 m)

Armament
The tower was armed with 180 and 60 lb (82- and 27-kg) catapults on the lower floors and oxybeles and scorpios on the top floors.

Structure
The main beams were fir or pine wood, while the horizontal beams and wheels were made from oak.

Roman Siege Engines

The Romans showed their practical genius in the different devices they created and their combined use for laying siege to fortifications. They used towers and battering rams to penetrate the walls and various machines for launching missiles, like the ballista—a highly maneuverable, medium-range catapult—and the onager, which took four men to operate it.

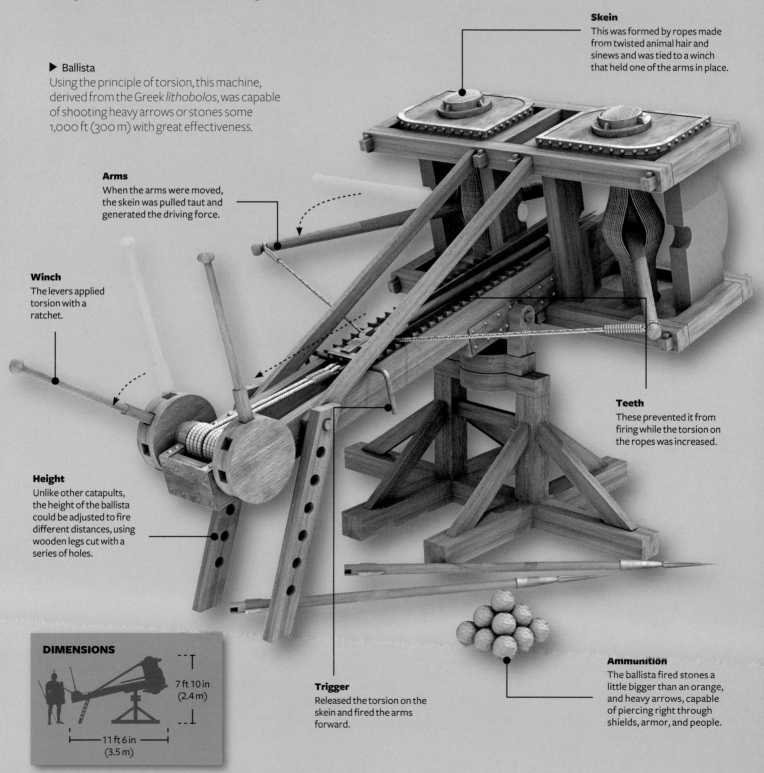

Skein
This was formed by ropes made from twisted animal hair and sinews and was tied to a winch that held one of the arms in place.

▶ **Ballista**
Using the principle of torsion, this machine, derived from the Greek *lithobolos*, was capable of shooting heavy arrows or stones some 1,000 ft (300 m) with great effectiveness.

Arms
When the arms were moved, the skein was pulled taut and generated the driving force.

Winch
The levers applied torsion with a ratchet.

Teeth
These prevented it from firing while the torsion on the ropes was increased.

Height
Unlike other catapults, the height of the ballista could be adjusted to fire different distances, using wooden legs cut with a series of holes.

Trigger
Released the torsion on the skein and fired the arms forward.

Ammunition
The ballista fired stones a little bigger than an orange, and heavy arrows, capable of piercing right through shields, armor, and people.

DIMENSIONS

7 ft 10 in (2.4 m)

11 ft 6 in (3.5 m)

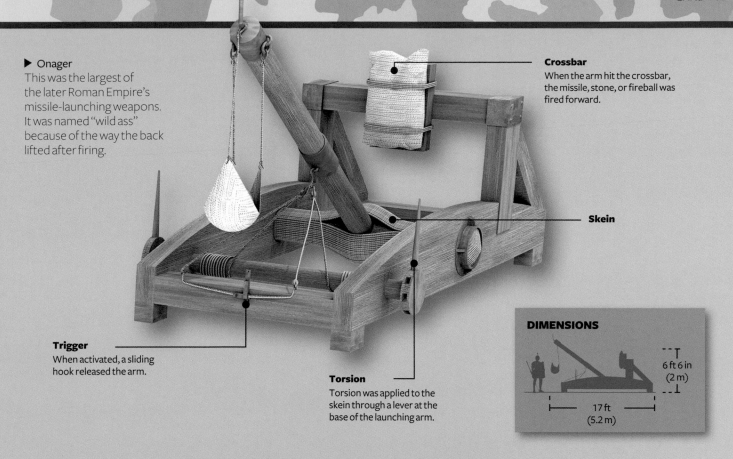

▶ **Onager**
This was the largest of the later Roman Empire's missile-launching weapons. It was named "wild ass" because of the way the back lifted after firing.

Crossbar
When the arm hit the crossbar, the missile, stone, or fireball was fired forward.

Skein

Trigger
When activated, a sliding hook released the arm.

Torsion
Torsion was applied to the skein through a lever at the base of the launching arm.

DIMENSIONS

6 ft 6 in (2 m)

17 ft (5.2 m)

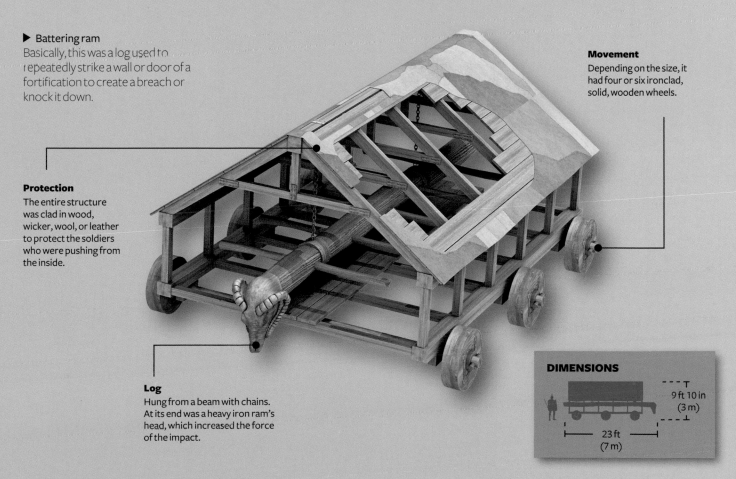

▶ **Battering ram**
Basically, this was a log used to repeatedly strike a wall or door of a fortification to create a breach or knock it down.

Movement
Depending on the size, it had four or six ironclad, solid, wooden wheels.

Protection
The entire structure was clad in wood, wicker, wool, or leather to protect the soldiers who were pushing from the inside.

Log
Hung from a beam with chains. At its end was a heavy iron ram's head, which increased the force of the impact.

DIMENSIONS

9 ft 10 in (3 m)

23 ft (7 m)

Roman Towers Against City Walls

In the Roman era, taking a fortified city was a task that could take months of intense work. Most walls could withstand hits from catapults. To attack a fortress the soldiers had to avoid the projectiles and stones fired by the city's defenders and reach the city walls, which they either scaled or broke down using siege towers or battering rams.

▶ **The Siege of Masada**
In 72 CE, the Romans besieged the fortress of Masada, next to the Dead Sea, which was giving refuge to the survivors of the Jewish revolt against Rome. The siege lasted almost two years, until the Roman troops led an attack on the fortress and were able to open a breach in the west wall.

PREPARATION FOR THE SIEGE

The siege of a fortified city began by creating a circumvallation around it to stop help from the outside. To do this, camps, towers, pits, and walls were built around the city. Machines like catapults, onagers, and ballistae launched projectiles at the defenders and protected the soldiers as they approached the city walls. The image shows an eighteenth-century engraving depicting the siege of Masada.

The fortress of Masada

Located on a 900-ft (280 m) high cliff, the site had several palaces and an aqueduct. When the siege began, there were 960 inhabitants, and they had enough resources to resist for years.

Walls

The fortress was surrounded by walls that were 16 ft (5 m) high by 13 ft (4 m) thick and incorporated dozens of towers, from where the Roman besiegers were continually harried.

Siege tower

This stood at around 100 ft (30 m). Soldiers fired ballistae from the upper floors, while the lower part housed a battering ram to breach the walls.

Agger

This was a long ramp built from the base of the hill by the Romans to bring the tower close to the walls.

Medieval Siege Engines

Until the arrival of gunpowder, the siege engines of the Middle Ages were, in essence, an evolution of those inherited from ancient times: ballistae, catapults, battering rams, and mobile towers. But the most significant innovation of this period was the trebuchet, introduced into the West by the Arabs around the twelfth century, which had a longer range than a catapult and was capable of demolishing walls.

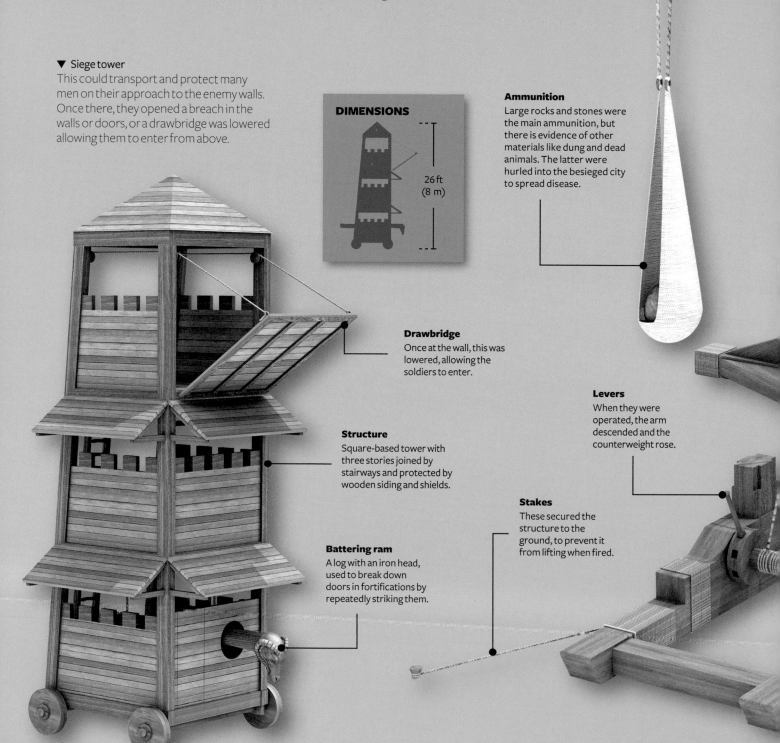

▼ Siege tower
This could transport and protect many men on their approach to the enemy walls. Once there, they opened a breach in the walls or doors, or a drawbridge was lowered allowing them to enter from above.

DIMENSIONS

26 ft
(8 m)

Ammunition
Large rocks and stones were the main ammunition, but there is evidence of other materials like dung and dead animals. The latter were hurled into the besieged city to spread disease.

Drawbridge
Once at the wall, this was lowered, allowing the soldiers to enter.

Structure
Square-based tower with three stories joined by stairways and protected by wooden siding and shields.

Levers
When they were operated, the arm descended and the counterweight rose.

Stakes
These secured the structure to the ground, to prevent it from lifting when fired.

Battering ram
A log with an iron head, used to break down doors in fortifications by repeatedly striking them.

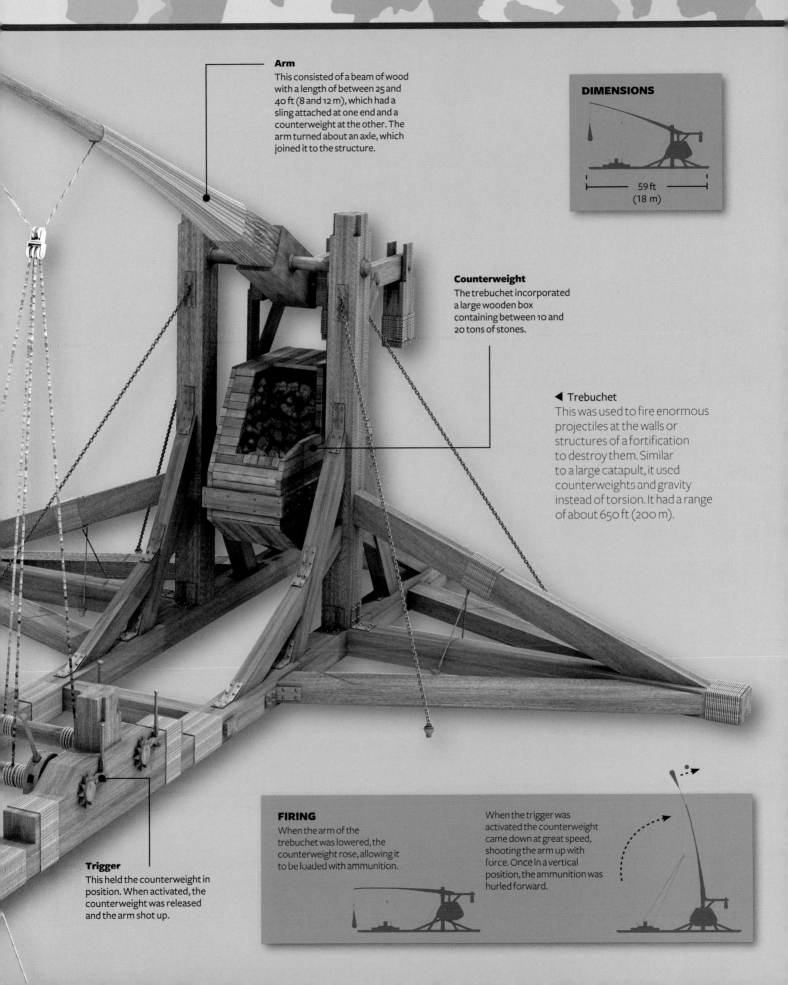

Arm
This consisted of a beam of wood with a length of between 25 and 40 ft (8 and 12 m), which had a sling attached at one end and a counterweight at the other. The arm turned about an axle, which joined it to the structure.

DIMENSIONS

59 ft
(18 m)

Counterweight
The trebuchet incorporated a large wooden box containing between 10 and 20 tons of stones.

◀ Trebuchet
This was used to fire enormous projectiles at the walls or structures of a fortification to destroy them. Similar to a large catapult, it used counterweights and gravity instead of torsion. It had a range of about 650 ft (200 m).

Trigger
This held the counterweight in position. When activated, the counterweight was released and the arm shot up.

FIRING
When the arm of the trebuchet was lowered, the counterweight rose, allowing it to be loaded with ammunition.

When the trigger was activated the counterweight came down at great speed, shooting the arm up with force. Once in a vertical position, the ammunition was hurled forward.

Attacking a Fortress

In the Middle Ages, the siege was the most common tactic in warfare. Besieging a fortified city or castle took thousands of soldiers and it could be months before the besieged population surrendered, due either to attrition or intimidation. If the enemy did not surrender, the next stage was to launch an assault on the fortress. This was when the siege engines—catapults, towers, and battering rams—came into action.

▶ The capture of Jerusalem
In July 1099, the armies of the First Crusade conquered the city of Jerusalem, at the time in Arab hands. The crusading army had just 1,200 knights and 12,000 foot soldiers, but were able to capture the fortress and slaughter its inhabitants.

Ladders
This was the simplest system for scaling the walls, but also the most dangerous.

City walls
Jerusalem was surrounded by 2.8 miles (4.5 km) of walls measuring between 16 and 50 ft (5–15 m) high, with 43 lookout towers and 11 gates.

Mantlet
This was a kind of wooden mobile shield, sometimes fitted with wheels, which the soldiers used as protection while approaching the walls.

Battering rams
Protected with wet hides, these were used to open breaches in the city walls.

Catapults
These hurled stones and burning projectiles into the city.

Towers
Being wooden they burned easily. Nevertheless, the crusaders were able to take them up to the walls and penetrate the city.

TECHNIQUES FOR BREACHING THE WALLS

Battering rams or even simple picks were used to open a breach in the wall. The sapping method was also used to destroy the foundations of the walls: this consisted of a hole dug into the base of the wall, or even a tunnel beneath it, propped up with wooden beams, which were then set alight.

▲ **German gunners in the Soviet Union**
German soldiers fire a howitzer sFH 18 close
to Zemloslaw, during Operation Barbarossa
(invasion of the USSR).

ARTILLERY

odern artillery—in other words, heavy machinery designed to fire projectiles across large distances using an explosive charge—originated in China. This was the birthplace of gunpowder in the ninth century, which was subsequently taken to Europe by the Arabs between the twelfth and thirteenth centuries. Shortly after, in the mid-fourteenth century, Europe began to develop cannons. Both technologies completely revolutionized the art of war, first on land and later at sea and in the air. The Arabs made use of primitive artillery in the fourteenth century, but it was the army of Charles VII, the French king in the mid-fifteenth century, that first used artillery in Europe. During this period, city walls became more vulnerable and soldiers went to battle clad in armor. It was also around that time when a small firearm was invented in Spain that could be transported and fired by a single man, known as the harquebus. Although it was heavy and had to be mounted, the harquebus marked the beginning of light firearms and was succeeded in the sixteenth century by the matchlock musket. Originally classified as "portable artillery," this gun could fire lead bullets capable of piercing armor.

From 1600 onward, new types of explosive ammunition were invented, and cannons and mortars were further developed so that the missile trajectory could be inclined, allowing bombs to reach the interior of fortifications. Improvements were also made in mobility with the introduction of limbers and caissons, carts on wheels that supported cannons and carried ammunition respectively, allowing the artillery to be more easily managed. When, in the eighteenth century, the use of field artillery in battle became more widespread, grooves were incorporated in the interior of the barrels to improve their accuracy. Barely a century later, cast iron came into use in artillery production and, in the second half of the nineteenth century, steel. Breech-loading artillery and recoil systems were other major advances. In World War I, with the arrival of highly developed mortars and fragmenting, incendiary, and explosive ammunition, artillery attacks were carried out at ranges of up to 60 miles (100 km).

In 1870, Krupp modified a 1.46-in (37-mm) cannon, creating the first antiaircraft gun (to shoot down balloons), and in 1916 the first antitank guns appeared, whose improved versions were used in World War II, along with assault guns mounted on armored vehicles and rockets, like the German V-2. The technology behind the latter was used by the United States after the war to make missiles, guided rockets self-propelled by jet engines. Today, missiles are manufactured in all sizes and ranges, incorporate computerized targeting, guidance, and flight control systems, and can carry one or more heads with armaments of all kinds. On the ground they are fired from multiple rocket launchers mounted on self-propelled armored vehicles, and their use relies on military satellite networks, like the United States' Milstar, which provides its armed forces with a jam-resistant communications system, designed to survive nuclear warfare.

Exploding Projectiles

It is not known with certainty when gunpowder was first used in China for military ends, but there was possibly already a kind of flamethrower in the ninth century that used gunpowder to project fire a distance of 10 ft (3 m). In the ensuing centuries, and until the development of cannons in the fourteenth century, the Chinese made use of the properties of gunpowder to manufacture a wide variety of explosive devices: from incendiary projectiles launched using catapults, to various types of bombs, grenades, and rocket launchers.

▲ Fire Arrows
These were probably rockets tied to a bamboo arrow. They are first mentioned in texts from the first half of the thirteenth century.

▼ From China to the Mongols
In the Battle of Mohi (1241) against the Hungarian army, the Mongols likely used gunpowder brought from China for the first time. In the chronicles of the battle "flaming arrows" are mentioned, which were fired by the Mongols. Evidence also suggests that they fired incendiary grenades using catapults.

Explosions
The rockets lacked accuracy but their whistles and explosions brought chaos and fear to the enemy lines.

ROCKET LAUNCHER

The Chinese infantry had soldiers in its ranks that shot several rockets at once. There were also fixed launch platforms and mobile ones mounted on carts, which were loaded with hundreds of projectiles. The Mongols and Koreans produced devices of this nature using knowledge acquired from China.

Chinese rocket launchers

Mongol rocket launcher, 13th century

Korean arrow launcher or *hwacha*, circa 1400

World War I Artillery

Trench warfare put the basic principle of artillery to the test: fire on the enemy from farther and farther away and with greater power. With huge guns and howitzers, heavy artillery would be essential on the Western Front to achieve victory in numerous battles, since only these weapons had the range, caliber, and power needed to destroy the fortified positions of the enemy lines.

DIMENSIONS

19.3 ft
(5.88 m)

▶ "Big Bertha"
German siege howitzer, manufactured by Krupp and used on both the Western and Eastern fronts. Weighing in at 48 tons, it reduced the Belgian forts of Namur and Liège to rubble.

Barrel
16.5 in (420 mm) in diameter, it fired 1,825-lb (830-kg) shells a distance of around 5.8 miles (9.3 km) at a speed of 1,300 ft/sec (400 m/second).

Loading
It used the sliding-wedge breech mechanism.

Mobility
It had very limited mobility and was transported in pieces on four trailers towed by two Daimler Benz tractors.

Logistics and operation
Over 200 people were needed to move, set up, and operate this howitzer. Its assembly took six hours and it required 12 men just to operate it.

Aiming arc
It was fitted with a wedge, which was buried in the ground to anchor the gun, and a guide used to direct it.

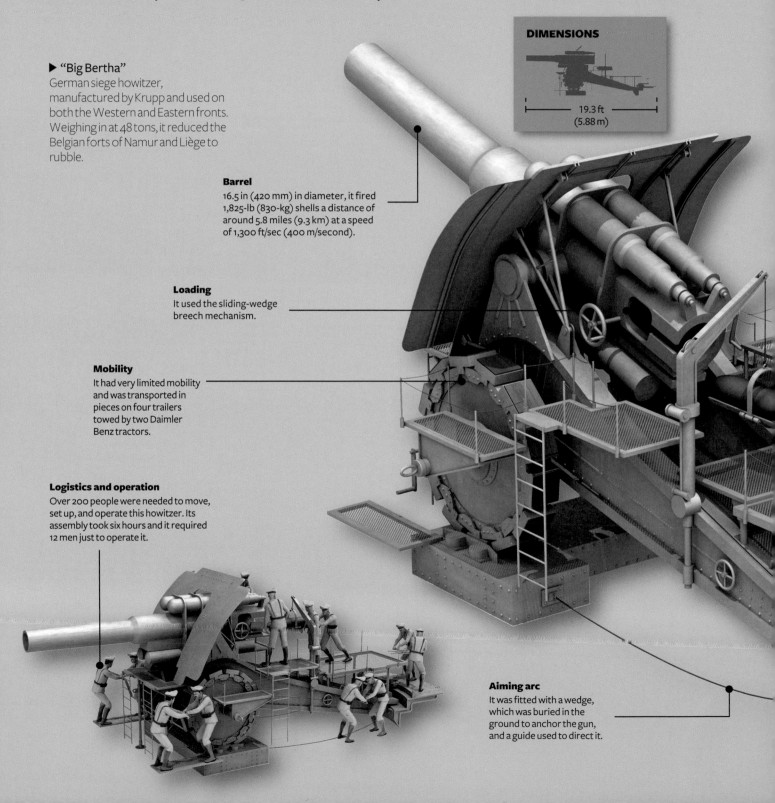

► **Canon de 194 mle GPF**
The first of its kind, this French self-propelled gun entered service around the end of the conflict. Powered by a Panhard SUK4 M2 engine, it could reach a speed of 6 mph (10 km/h).

Ammunition
Its 7.64-in (194-mm) Filloux barrel fired 173.7-lb (78.8-kg) shells a distance of over 12 miles (20 km).

DIMENSIONS
21 ft 7 in (6.57 m)

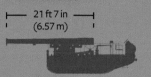

► **Paris gun**
Used by the Germans to bomb Paris between March and August in 1918 from Crépy and the forests of Corbie and Bruyère, 75 miles (120 km) from the capital. Its 125-ton barrel meant it could only be transported by rail.

8.27-in (210-mm) gun
It could fire 265-lb (120-kg) shells with 15.5 lb (7 kg) of explosive a distance of 82 miles (132 km).

Shell
This exploded once inside the enemy fortification, producing shock waves that destroyed the foundations. Given its weight, a crane was needed to put it in place.

DIMENSIONS
50°
111 ft 7 in (34 m)

Barrel
Made with two steel "tubes," one inside the other.

Loading
It used the screw breech system.

◄ **Ordnance QF-18 Pounder**
British field gun introduced in 1903. It had an effective firing range of 5.3 miles (8.5 km), weighed 3,035 lb (1,380 kg) and was operated by six people.

DIMENSIONS
7 ft 8 in (2.34 m)

Antitank Artillery

With the arrival of tanks on the battlefield in World War I came a need for weapons capable of dealing with them. However, it was in the interwar period, and especially during World War II, when specific artillery was developed, designed to destroy armored vehicles. To defend against tank attacks, antitank artillery was combined with airstrikes.

ANTITANK GUNS

▸ **M3**
United States, 1940

This light 1.46-in (37-mm) gun could be towed by a jeep. In 1943, it went out of production and was replaced by more powerful guns.

▸ **Type 1**
Japan, 1942

This 1.85-in (47-mm) caliber gun was effective over short distances and had a semiautomatic breech block that gave a firing rate of around 15 rounds a minute.

▸ **Ordnance QF 6-pounder**
United Kingdom, 1942

A 2.24-in (57-mm) caliber gun, which was small and easy to transport. It was first used in the North African Campaign and remained in use even after the war had finished.

▸ **Pak 43**
Germany, 1943

This heavy 3.46-in (88-mm) gun was designed as an antiaircraft gun and converted into an antitank gun. It could pierce armor up to 7.2 in (184 mm) thick.

▸ **SU-100**
USSR, 1944

This self-propelled tank destroyer was equipped with a D10S 3.94-in (100-mm) gun mounted on the chassis of a T-34 tank. It was kept in service after the war in several countries allied to the Soviet Union.

▶ **Antitank warfare**
Until the appearance of guided missiles in the 1950s, tactics for antitank warfare combined the use of guns (static and self-propelled) with other infantry weapons like mines, grenades, and aircraft.

Artillery
Static antitank guns were camouflaged and embedded in defensive hollows, protected by minefields.

Aircraft
In general, dive bombers and ground-attack aircraft (capable of destroying moving ground targets) were used when the tanks were still at a distance and had not yet entered into combat.

Tanks
The increase and improvements in armor forced armies to also increase the power of the tanks and antitank ammunition.

Ammunition
Ammunition also developed throughout World War II. Hollow-point shells emerged that were capable of piercing tank armor and exploding once inside.

World War II Artillery

World War II was a conflict of great mobility, which meant that, unlike in the Great War, field guns dominated over heavy artillery on the battlefields. Because of the widespread use of tanks and aircraft, antitank and antiaircraft artillery also played a fundamental role.

▶ **3.46-in (88-mm) Flak 18/36**
Designed as an antiaircraft gun, this was Germany's most famous piece of World War II artillery. It was also used with great success against tanks, thanks to its high level of effectiveness. It included many innovations, including a modern fire-control system.

DIMENSIONS

7 ft 10 in (2.4 m)

25 ft 3 in (7.7 m)

Range-finding mechanism
Equipped with a clinometer (to measure slope angles), panoramic sights, and handwheels.

Ammunition
The different types of shell were distinguished by color, number, and initial. For example, yellow indicated a high explosive charge; the number 1 indicated a TNT charge; the initials NG or NGL stood for nitroglycerine.

DIMENSIONS

5 ft 9 in (1.75 m)

21 ft (6.4 m)

▼ **3.46-in (88-mm) Pak 43**
The war's most lethal antitank gun. Thanks to its high quality and power it was mounted on the biggest German tanks of the conflict: the King Tiger, Jagdpanther, Nashorn, and Elefant.

Power
With a tungsten projectile it could penetrate armor up to 7.2 in (184 mm) thick, at an angle of 30° and at a distance of 1.6 miles (2.5 km).

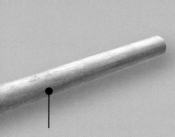

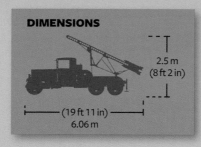

Range
Its long muzzle gave a horizontal range of 9.2 miles (14.8 km), and more than 29,500 ft (9,000 m) vertically.

DIMENSIONS

2.5 m (8 ft 2 in)

(19 ft 11 in) 6.06 m

▶ **Katyusha BM-13**
This Soviet rocket launcher entered service in July 1941 and was an economic and easily produced artillery piece. Mounted on a ZiS-6 truck, although not very accurate, it could fire a large amount of explosives in a short period of time.

M-13 rocket
It could fire all 16 rockets simultaneously, whether 3.23 in (82 mm), 5.2 in (132 mm) or 11.8 in (300 mm).

Protective shield
Fitted to protect the gunners on the antitank version.

Circular firing platform
Allowed a single operator to quickly and easily change aim.

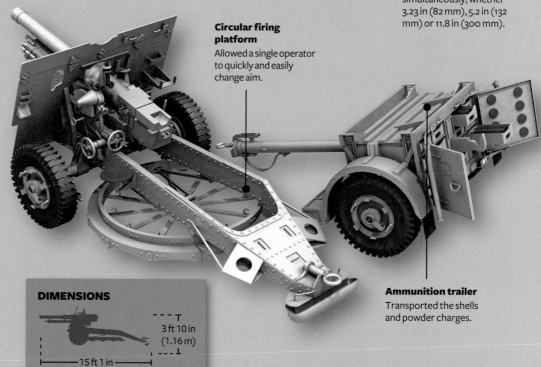

▶ **QF 25-Pdr Mark II**
Used in all theaters of operation during the war and with a caliber of 3.45 in (87.6 mm), this was the British Army's primary artillery field piece. Its development combined the best features of a howitzer with those of field artillery.

DIMENSIONS

3 ft 10 in (1.16 m)

15 ft 1 in (4.6 m)

Ammunition trailer
Transported the shells and powder charges.

Block breech
Easy to handle and with a range of 7 miles (11.3 km) and elevation/depression angles of +66°/-5°.

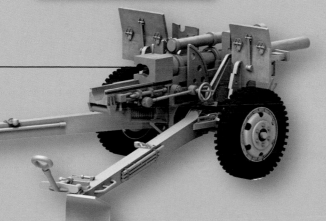

DIMENSIONS

5 ft 7 in (1.7 m)

19 ft 4 in (5.9 m)

◀ **4.13 in (105-mm) M2A1 howitzer**
Introduced in 1941 as the standard howitzer of the United States's field artillery, it fired high-explosive 4.13-in (105-mm) semifixed ammunition.

Military Vespa Scooter

The continual adaptation to changing scenarios and needs in war has, throughout history, produced an array of machinery with military applications, both diverse and curious, much of which has failed, but some enjoying success in their time. An example of the latter was the Vespa 150 TAP, a scooter modified for the French paratroops (TAP), which was used in the Suez Crisis and the Algerian War in the 1950s and 1960s. It could be parachute-dropped and carried an antitank gun capable of piercing 4 in (100 mm) of armor with HEAT munition (high-explosive antitank warhead).

Manufacturer ▸ Atelier de Construction de Motocycles et Automobiles (ACMA), licensed for Vespa

Produced ▸ 1956–59

Number built ▸ More than 600

Weight ▸ 253 lb/115 kg (1959 version)

Top speed ▸ 41 mph/66 km/h (1959 version)

Range ▸ 125 miles (200 km) with 2 fuel tanks

Engine ▸ 2 stroke, 125 cc (1956 version) and 146 cc (1959 version)

Gun

It carried a recoilless, U.S.-made, 2.95-in (75-mm) M20 gun. To fire it, the rider had to get off the vehicle and mount the gun on a tripod.

Ammunition
Each scooter carried six ammunition cartridges. Sometimes they would work in teams of two, one Vespa carrying the gun and the other the ammunition.

DIMENSIONS

5 ft 7 in
(1.7 m)

2 ft 7 in
(0.78 m)

3 ft 5 in
(1.04 m)

OTHER STRANGE DEVICES

During World War II all sides looked for innovative ideas that would surprise the enemy and defeat their defenses, although not all worked as planned.

The Great Panjandrum

This British-designed 10-ft (3-m) high wheel was designed to be used in Normandy. Propelled by rockets and loaded with more than a ton of explosives, it was meant to be rolled at its target where it would explode. However, it failed in tests and was never used in combat.

Leichter Ladungsträger "Goliath"

This was a German-made demolition vehicle, a 2-ft (60-cm) high device with an explosive charge that could be activated from a remote terminal. Around 7,500 units were produced and it could reach speeds of up to 22 mph (35 km/h). They were used on almost all fronts.

DD Duplex Drive tank

This British-made system could be installed on various tanks, providing them with a kind of flotation screen that enabled them to reach the shore after disembarking. It was used in the Normandy landings in 1944 and later allied operations.

Missile Launchers

Missiles (guided rockets) are highly effective, long-range weapons. Some can be fired from small, shoulder-carried launchers, while others need larger platforms. During World War II, rocket launchers were mounted on wheeled and tracked vehicles. Today, armies have light trucks capable of accessing difficult terrain, firing several missiles in just a few minutes and rapidly changing position.

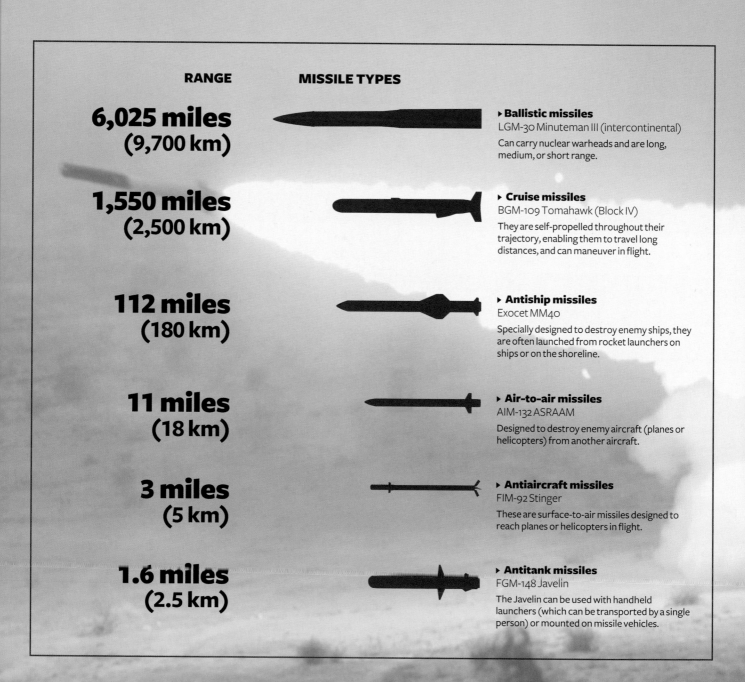

RANGE **MISSILE TYPES**

6,025 miles
(9,700 km)

▸ **Ballistic missiles**
LGM-30 Minuteman III (intercontinental)
Can carry nuclear warheads and are long, medium, or short range.

1,550 miles
(2,500 km)

▸ **Cruise missiles**
BGM-109 Tomahawk (Block IV)
They are self-propelled throughout their trajectory, enabling them to travel long distances, and can maneuver in flight.

112 miles
(180 km)

▸ **Antiship missiles**
Exocet MM40
Specially designed to destroy enemy ships, they are often launched from rocket launchers on ships or on the shoreline.

11 miles
(18 km)

▸ **Air-to-air missiles**
AIM-132 ASRAAM
Designed to destroy enemy aircraft (planes or helicopters) from another aircraft.

3 miles
(5 km)

▸ **Antiaircraft missiles**
FIM-92 Stinger
These are surface-to-air missiles designed to reach planes or helicopters in flight.

1.6 miles
(2.5 km)

▸ **Antitank missiles**
FGM-148 Javelin
The Javelin can be used with handheld launchers (which can be transported by a single person) or mounted on missile vehicles.

◀ V-1, the first
This was the first German missile used in the war. Developed during World War II, it was fired from fixed land-based platforms and had a range of 155 miles (250 km).

▼ HIMARS
This vehicle of the United States Army is fitted with a multiple missile launcher. The HIMARS (High Mobility Artillery Rocket System) has capacity for six MLRS (Multiple Launch Rocket System) rockets or an ATACMS (Army Tactical Missile System) tactical missile.

Manufacturer ▸ Lockheed Martin (missiles) and BAE Systems (vehicle)

Entry into service ▸ 2005

Range ▸ 43 miles/70 km (MLRS) / 185 miles/300 km (ATACMS)

Weight ▸ 23,950 lb (10,886 kg)

Missiles and Satellites

After *Sputnik* became the first satellite launched into orbit in 1957, the USSR and United States invested huge resources in developing satellite systems whose military applications opened a new era in warfare. One of the most ambitious projects in this area was the U.S. Strategic Defense Initiative (SDI) approved in 1983 and developed from its predecessors, the Sentinel and Safeguard programs. Nicknamed "Star Wars," this was a sophisticated system that used satellites, lasers, and missiles to halt a possible full-scale nuclear attack from the Soviet Union. Because of its high costs it was never finished.

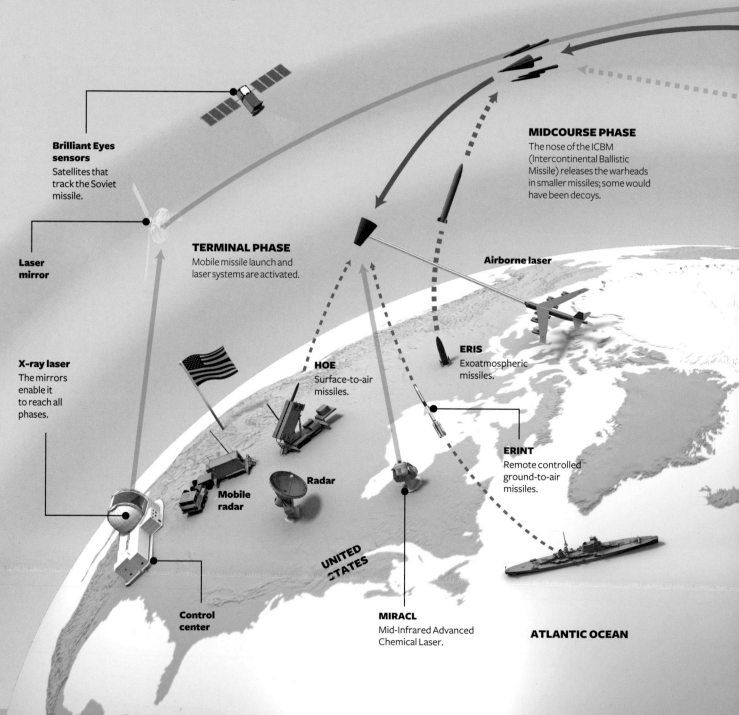

Brilliant Eyes sensors
Satellites that track the Soviet missile.

MIDCOURSE PHASE
The nose of the ICBM (Intercontinental Ballistic Missile) releases the warheads in smaller missiles; some would have been decoys.

Laser mirror

TERMINAL PHASE
Mobile missile launch and laser systems are activated.

Airborne laser

X-ray laser
The mirrors enable it to reach all phases.

HOE
Surface-to-air missiles.

ERIS
Exoatmospheric missiles.

ERINT
Remote controlled ground-to-air missiles.

Mobile radar

Radar

Control center

UNITED STATES

MIRACL
Mid-Infrared Advanced Chemical Laser.

ATLANTIC OCEAN

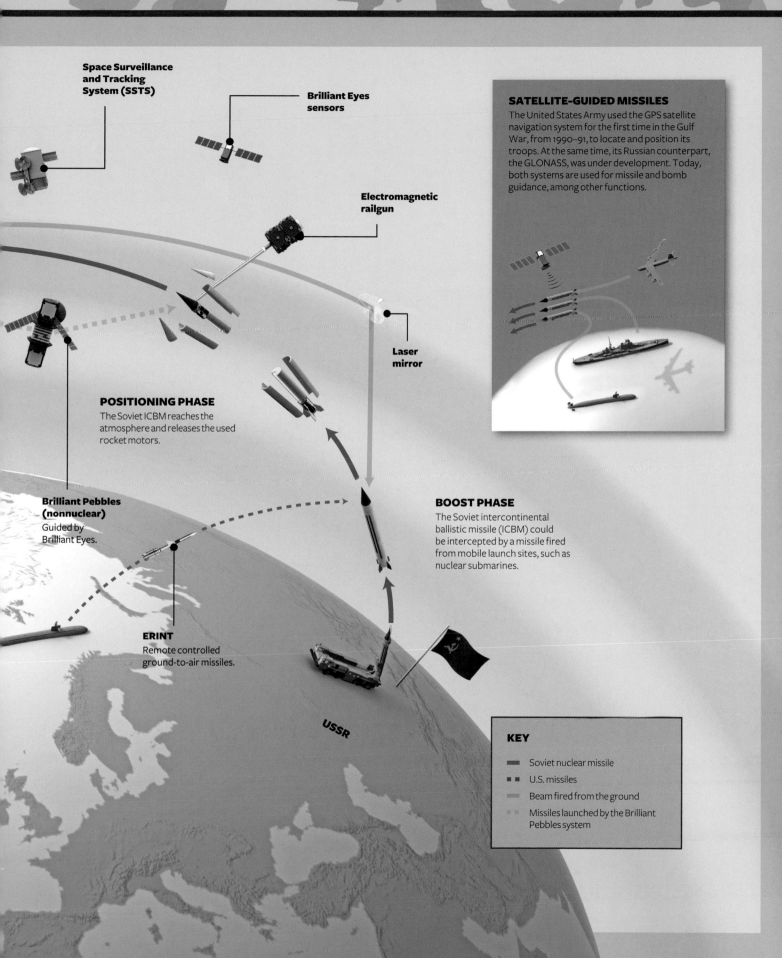

Space Surveillance and Tracking System (SSTS)

Brilliant Eyes sensors

Electromagnetic railgun

SATELLITE-GUIDED MISSILES

The United States Army used the GPS satellite navigation system for the first time in the Gulf War, from 1990–91, to locate and position its troops. At the same time, its Russian counterpart, the GLONASS, was under development. Today, both systems are used for missile and bomb guidance, among other functions.

Laser mirror

POSITIONING PHASE

The Soviet ICBM reaches the atmosphere and releases the used rocket motors.

Brilliant Pebbles (nonnuclear)
Guided by Brilliant Eyes.

BOOST PHASE

The Soviet intercontinental ballistic missile (ICBM) could be intercepted by a missile fired from mobile launch sites, such as nuclear submarines.

ERINT
Remote controlled ground-to-air missiles.

USSR

KEY

▬ Soviet nuclear missile

▪▪ U.S. missiles

▬ Beam fired from the ground

▬ Missiles launched by the Brilliant Pebbles system

▲ **M3 Bradley**
Combat vehicles from the U.S. Army cavalry units, armed with 0.3 in (7.62-mm) guns, after intervening in Operation Desert Storm.

ARMOR

In the mid-nineteenth century, improvements in torpedoes and increased artillery calibers prompted the armies of Europe to armor their war machines. Soon, in the early twentieth century, armored vehicles were developed that, as well as being capable of flattening and crossing enemy lines to allow infantry to pass, could fight their adversaries with direct firepower. This was the origin of the modern tank, which between 1940 and 2000 became one of the most effective of all war machines. The name "tank" came from the British factories where the first Mark I was built, and where, to safeguard the secret, it was claimed they were manufacturing large mobile water tanks. It was designed in 1915, built between 1916 and 1919, and entered combat in World War I. It was rhomboid-shaped and had no gun turret, transported eight crew members, moved by way of metal tracks and its armor could withstand shells of up to 0.315 in (8 mm) caliber. After the Germans developed the armor-piercing K bullet, their plating was made stronger, but in the 1930s the tank had already become obsolete. The same fate awaited the French FT-17, although it was this model, which was already fitted with a rotating gun turret and 1.45-in (37-mm) cannon, which would mark the design of subsequent tanks.

During World War II, tanks were combined with formations of motorized infantry, engineers, artillery, and fighter-bombers, a strategic model in which the lightweight and fast German panzer proved to be highly effective. The British Mk IV, known as the Churchill, had an active role in the fighting, along with the Soviet T-34, considered the best tank in the war. These were armored with 1.8–2.95-in (45–75-mm) plates and were the genesis of the modern combat tank, developed from the 1960s. One of the best of the decade was the American M-60, which was in service until 1990 in the United States. It could reach 30 mph (48 km/h) and its initial versions carried a 4.13-in (105-mm) M68 gun and two machine guns, 0.5 and 0.3 in (12.7 and 7.62 mm).

When antitank missiles became commonly used in the 1970s, a generation of heavily armored vehicles emerged, like the American M1 Abrams (1980), whose M1A2 model included thermal viewers, position navigation equipment, and an armored mesh of depleted uranium. The Abrams, in their different and improved versions, are still used today.

Another of the world's most popular and advanced tanks is the German Leopard 2. Its most recent version, the A7+, is used today and incorporates third-generation composite armor, which includes tungsten and high-strength plastic and ceramic elements. Today, when the effectiveness of these heavily armored vehicles is being questioned, the arms industry is now focusing its efforts on developing small tanks and light armored vehicles for patrols and transporting troops, as well as combat vehicles for infantry and amphibious vehicles.

Leonardo's War Machines

The brilliant and multifaceted Leonardo da Vinci (1452–1519) designed a number of inventions for warfare, although most of his projects were too advanced for his time to be brought to fruition. His war machines included giant crossbows, siege towers, cluster bombs, a "machine gun," and even an armored car, considered to be the precursor to modern tanks.

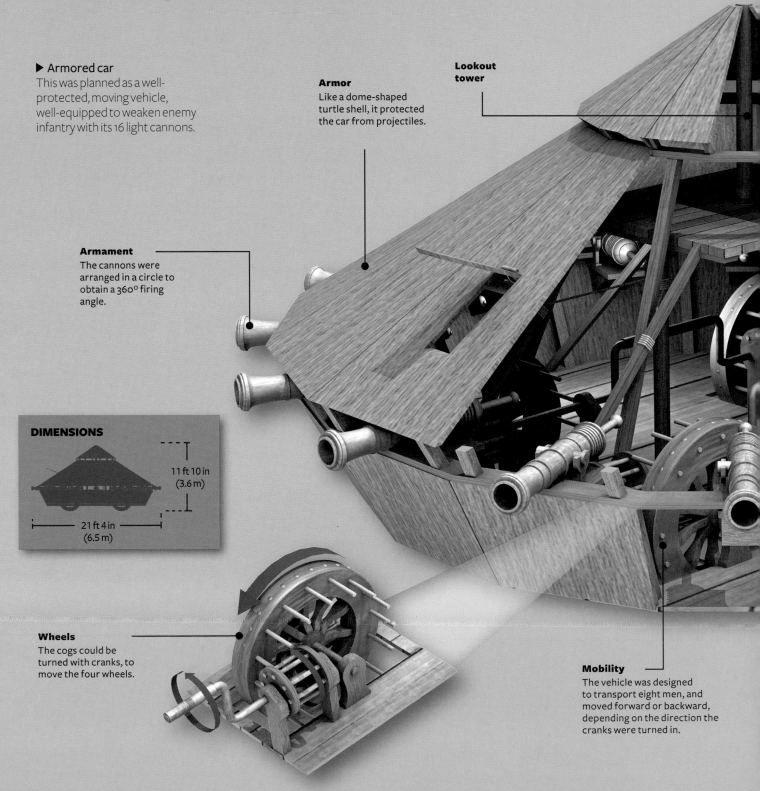

▶ Armored car
This was planned as a well-protected, moving vehicle, well-equipped to weaken enemy infantry with its 16 light cannons.

Armor
Like a dome-shaped turtle shell, it protected the car from projectiles.

Lookout tower

Armament
The cannons were arranged in a circle to obtain a 360° firing angle.

DIMENSIONS

11 ft 10 in
(3.6 m)

21 ft 4 in
(6.5 m)

Wheels
The cogs could be turned with cranks, to move the four wheels.

Mobility
The vehicle was designed to transport eight men, and moved forward or backward, depending on the direction the cranks were turned in.

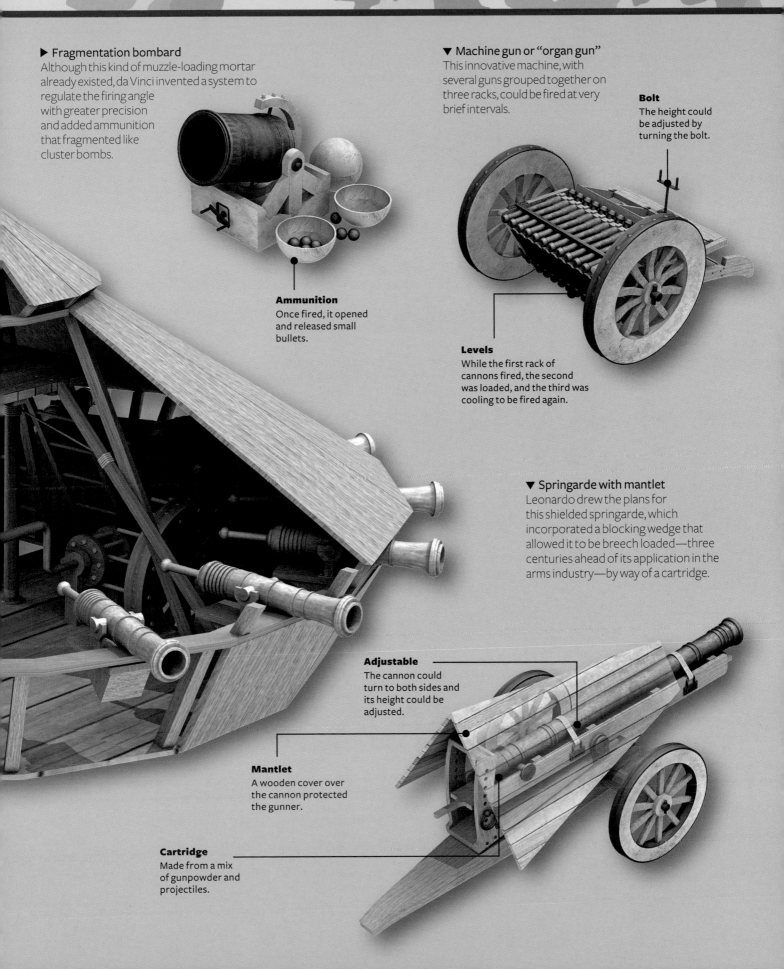

▶ **Fragmentation bombard**
Although this kind of muzzle-loading mortar already existed, da Vinci invented a system to regulate the firing angle with greater precision and added ammunition that fragmented like cluster bombs.

Ammunition
Once fired, it opened and released small bullets.

▼ **Machine gun or "organ gun"**
This innovative machine, with several guns grouped together on three racks, could be fired at very brief intervals.

Bolt
The height could be adjusted by turning the bolt.

Levels
While the first rack of cannons fired, the second was loaded, and the third was cooling to be fired again.

▼ **Springarde with mantlet**
Leonardo drew the plans for this shielded springarde, which incorporated a blocking wedge that allowed it to be breech loaded—three centuries ahead of its application in the arms industry—by way of a cartridge.

Adjustable
The cannon could turn to both sides and its height could be adjusted.

Mantlet
A wooden cover over the cannon protected the gunner.

Cartridge
Made from a mix of gunpowder and projectiles.

Mark I

On September 15, 1916, at the time of the Battle of the Somme, the German soldiers were witness to a terrifying new and powerful war machine: the tank. This was the Mark I, created to break the static nature of trench warfare by opening breaches in the enemy lines thanks to its armor and all-terrain capability.

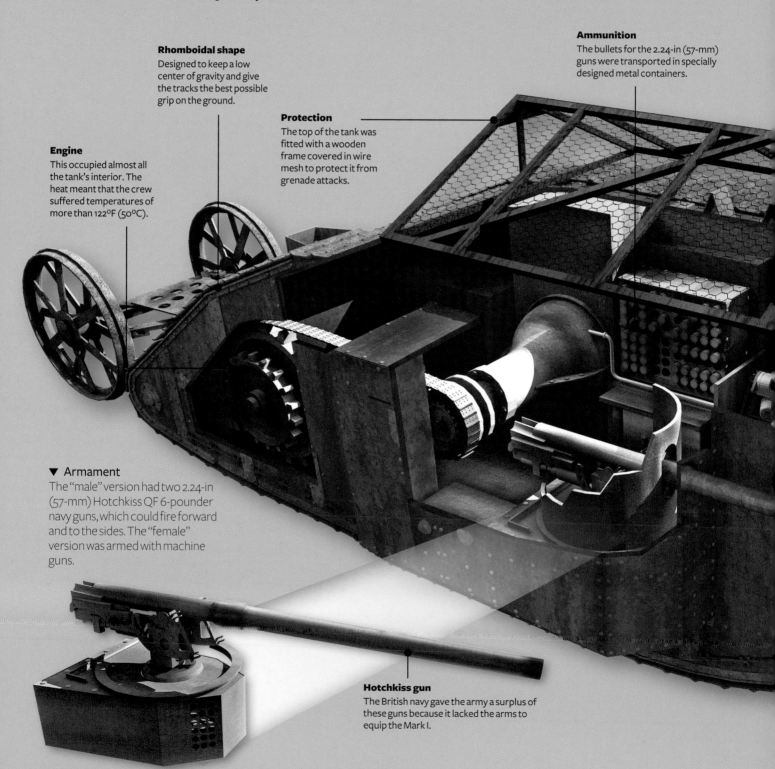

Rhomboidal shape
Designed to keep a low center of gravity and give the tracks the best possible grip on the ground.

Ammunition
The bullets for the 2.24-in (57-mm) guns were transported in specially designed metal containers.

Protection
The top of the tank was fitted with a wooden frame covered in wire mesh to protect it from grenade attacks.

Engine
This occupied almost all the tank's interior. The heat meant that the crew suffered temperatures of more than 122ºF (50ºC).

▼ **Armament**
The "male" version had two 2.24-in (57-mm) Hotchkiss QF 6-pounder navy guns, which could fire forward and to the sides. The "female" version was armed with machine guns.

Hotchkiss gun
The British navy gave the army a surplus of these guns because it lacked the arms to equip the Mark I.

Manufacturer ▸ William Foster & Co and Metropolitan Carriage from the design of William Tritton and Walter Gordon Wilson

Entry into service ▸ 1916

Units built ▸ 150

Crew ▸ 8

Empty weight ▸ 31 tons

Armor ▸ max 0.5 in (12 mm)

Armament ▸ 2 x 2.24-in (57-mm) Hotchkiss QF 6-pounder

Armament option ▸ 4 x 0.315-in (8-mm) Hotchkiss or Vickers machine guns

Engine ▸ 105 hp Foster-Daimler

Top speed ▸ 4 mph (6 km/h)

Range ▸ 24 miles (38 km)

Steering tail
Used to help steer the tank, the wheels were ineffective and easily damaged.

Entry
The tank was entered through the sponsons on the side of the vehicle where the guns were located.

Crew
It had eight crew members: two drivers (one handled the gears and the other the brakes); while at the rear, two managed the secondary engines, which directed the tracks, and the four remaining crew members handled the weapons.

H.M.L.S. "WE'RE ALL IN IT" A 13

Tracks
The speed of the tracks was varied to steer. Each track had a secondary engine for maneuvering purposes.

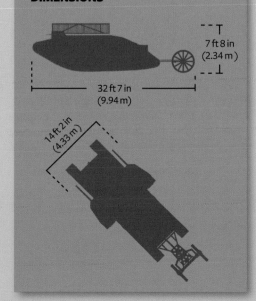

DIMENSIONS

7 ft 8 in (2.34 m)

32 ft 7 in (9.94 m)

14 ft 2 in (4.33 m)

German Armor

The famous series of German tanks, the *Panzerkampfwagen*, better known as panzers, played a key role in World War II and formed the backbone of the armored forces of the Third Reich. Combined with other lighter armored vehicles, the panzer dominated the first years of the war thanks to its mobility. Another of the great successes of the German arms industry was the Leopard 2 tank, a model that entered service in 1979 and remains active to this day.

THE PANZER Kpfw IN WORLD WAR II

▸ **Panzer I (A and B)**
Light tank. 1933–45

Designed as a training vehicle, it was unexpectedly effective against infantry at the beginning of the war.

▸ **Panzer II**
Light tank. 1936–45

Used often for reconnaissance, it formed part of Rommel's Afrika Korps and had a 0.787-in (20-mm) gun.

▸ **Panzer III**
Medium tank. 1939–45

This was the most numerous at the time of Operation Barbarossa, the invasion of the Soviet Union, in which it was outclassed by the Soviet T-34.

▸ **Panzer IV**
Medium tank. 1938–45

Noteworthy for its perfect combination of speed, armor and firepower, this was one of the best tanks of the war. It was fitted with a 75-mm (2.95-in) gun.

▸ **Panzer V "Panther"**
Medium tank. 1943–45

The German response to the Soviet T-34. The armor was improved from the Panzer III and included sloped frontal plating.

▸ **Panzer VI "Tiger I"**
Heavy tank. 1942–45

Twice as costly as the "Panther," it was designed for attack but was more effective in defensive actions because of its slow speed.

Production ▸ March 1944–April 1945
Gun ▸ 2.95 in (75 mm)
Weight ▸ 50–53 tons
Speed ▸ 29–34 mph (46–55 km/h)

Armor
Despite their well-deserved reputation, the panzers were inferior to the Soviet tanks, partly because of deficiencies in their armor, which had to be reinforced.

▶ Marder III
This light-medium armored vehicle was a tank destroyer, mounted with diverse configurations of armaments, such as a Soviet 3-in (76.2-mm) field gun or a German 2.95-in (75-mm) PaK 40/3.

Recycled Skodas
The obsolete chassis of the Czech panzer 38(t) was reused to produce the Marder III from 1941.

Innovations
One of the characteristics of the Panther Ausf.G is that the lateral plate was made of just one piece.

◀ Panther Ausf. G
The third and last series of Panthers. Among the improvements was an infrared night-vision system for battle.

MOST EXPORTED
This is one of the best tanks in production today. Its third-generation armor is extremely hard to pierce and it can even shoot down low-flying helicopters.

Leopard 2A5

The T-34 and Other Soviet Tanks

The former Soviet Union produced some of the light and heavy tanks most envied and copied in history. The most emblematic, the armored T-34, was crucial for halting the progress of Hitler's troops on the Eastern Front during World War II, tipping the balance of the war in favor of the Allies. In recent decades, the T-72, exported to various countries, stands as Russia's second most manufactured armored vehicle.

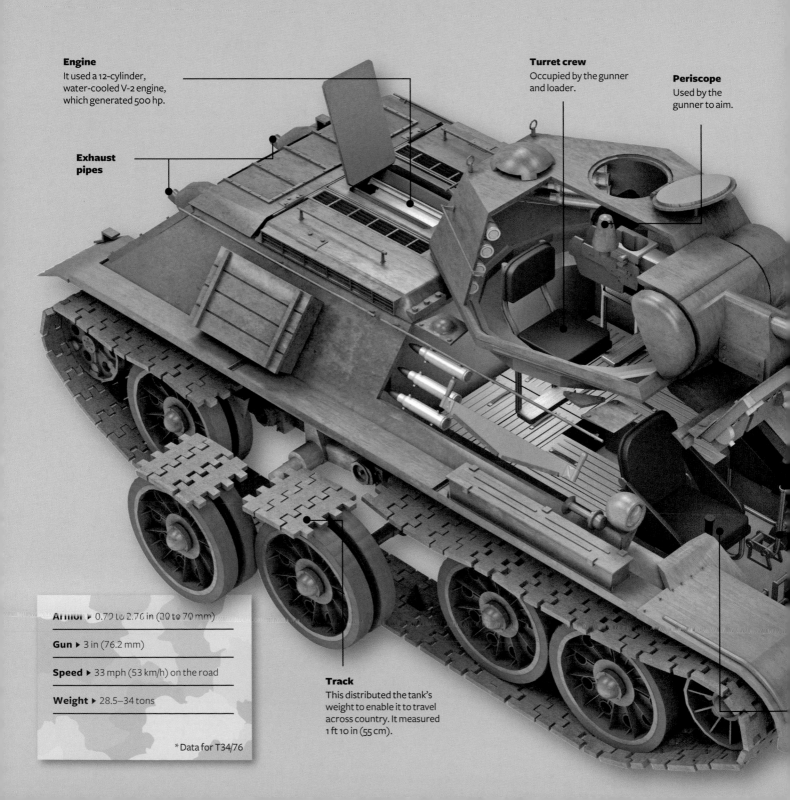

Engine
It used a 12-cylinder, water-cooled V-2 engine, which generated 500 hp.

Exhaust pipes

Turret crew
Occupied by the gunner and loader.

Periscope
Used by the gunner to aim.

Armor ▶ 0.79 to 2.76 in (20 to 70 mm)

Gun ▶ 3 in (76.2 mm)

Speed ▶ 33 mph (53 km/h) on the road

Weight ▶ 28.5–34 tons

*Data for T34/76

Track
This distributed the tank's weight to enable it to travel across country. It measured 1 ft 10 in (55 cm).

▼ T-34, the most effective
The success of this Soviet armored vehicle, of which almost 40,000 were produced between 1940 and 1944, is owed to its combination of speed and strength and the fact that it was easy to manufacture.

Gun
Initially a 3-in (76.2-mm) L11, in 1943 this was replaced by a 3.35-in (85-mm) ZiS-S-53 to compete with the improved Nazi tanks.

Machine gun
0.3 in (7.62 mm) with drum magazine.

Armor
Made from 1.8–3-in (45–75-mm) steel plating (depending on the part of the tank) in versions from 1940, 41 or 43, increased to 3.5 in (90 mm) in the 1944 version.

Radio antenna

Steering levers
Used to turn the tank.

Brake and acceleration pedals

Forward crew
Comprised the tank driver and machine gunner.

OTHER RED ARMY TANKS

T-18
Although it was considered a failure, the T-18 represented the Soviet Union's first steps in tank manufacturing. It was produced between 1928 and 1931.

Armor ▸ 0.63 in (16 mm)

Gun ▸ 1.46 in (37 mm)

Speed ▸ 11 mph (17 km/h)

Weight ▸ 6.5 tons

KV-1
This heavy tank's thick armor made it almost indestructible by the German tanks. It entered service in 1940.

Armor ▸ 3.54 in (90 mm)

Gun ▸ 3 in (76.2 mm)

Speed ▸ 22 mph (35 km/h)

Weight ▸ 47 tons

KV-2
Heavy tank, designed to attack fortifications. Produced between 1940 and 1942, it fired powerful shells.

Armor ▸ 4.33 in (110 mm)

Gun ▸ 5.98 in (152 mm)

Speed ▸ 22 mph (35 km/h)

Weight ▸ 64 tons

T-72A
One of the most popular Soviet armored vehicles today in Russia and other parts of the world. It entered service in 1971 and has been exported to countries like the former Yugoslavia or Iraq.

Armor ▸ 3.94 in (100 mm)

Gun ▸ 4.92 in (125 mm)

Speed ▸ 37 mph (60 km/h)

Weight ▸ 45 to 49 tons

Combined Attack

Tanks often coordinate their attacks with aircraft and motorized infantry troops. During World War II, Hitler applied this strategy very effectively in the so-called *blitzkrieg*, during the first years of the war. The German panzers, thanks to their speed and lightness, were the most effective in carrying out combined attacks with the famous Stuka planes.

The German tanks
A key piece in the army of the Third Reich, their use in street fighting was much more limited, leaving the Nazis without one of their main assets on the Eastern Front.

THE "LIGHTNING WAR"
The success of this tactic during the first years of World War II led the world to believe that Hitler would win the war. The Nazis were able to carry out surprise attacks with mobility and speed, the likes of which had never been seen before. They combined light and heavy armored vehicles, which opened the enemy lines, with infantry and close air support from bombers and dive bombers. The Nazi invasion of Poland in September 1939, and the subsequent fall of France in June 1940, were great triumphs of *blitzkrieg* tactics.

This illustration shows a combined attack by panzers, Stukas, and an SdKfz 222 armored car (in the foreground).

Air protection
The Stuka dive-bombed small targets, like artillery, to defend the Nazi tanks.

TANK EXPERT
One of the great architects of the "lightning war" was Heinz Guderian (1888–1954). As chief of the German Mobile Forces from 1938, he successfully applied his theories—expounded in *Achtung Panzer!* (1936)—in the invasion of a large part of Western Europe. He was in command of two panzer divisions on the Eastern Front and was appointed chief of the general staff of the German Army in 1941.

Other Classes of Armored Vehicles

As well as tanks, armies are equipped with an array of armored vehicles with very different functions. They are often divided into two major groups: infantry fighting (AIFV) and personnel carriers (APC). The main difference between the two is that the latter have armaments and armor solely for self-defense, while the former are also designed to support infantry and carry out attacks.

ARMORED INFANTRY FIGHTING VEHICLES (AIFV)
Armored and armed with an integral cannon of at least 0.787-in (20-mm) caliber, they can also carry an antitank missile launcher. They transport infantry troops to the front lines and give them protection during the offensive.

THE SOVIET BMP
This family of AIFVs has been around since the 1960s. The BMP-2 (pictured) and BMP-3 are still in service in many countries.

Armor ▸ 1.3 in (33 mm)

Cannon ▸ 1.18-in (30-mm) automatic 2A42

Speed ▸ 40 mph (65 km/h) on the road

Weight ▸ 15.5 tons

M2 BRADLEY
In operation since 1981, the American M2 has a crew of three to five people and can carry a squadron of six soldiers.

Armor ▸ approx 1.2 in (30 mm)

Cannon ▸ 0.98-in (25-mm) M242 Bushmaster

Speed ▸ 41 mph (66 km/h) on the road

Weight ▸ From 24 to 33 tons, depending on equipment

YPR-765
A Dutch variant of the North American AIFV series, this light vehicle has versions for multiple functions with different features for each.

Armor ▸ 0.5–1.5 in/12–38 mm (aluminum)

Cannon ▸ 0.98 in (25 mm)

Speed ▸ 40 mph (65 km/h) on the road

Weight ▸ 15 tons

Armored mission

The UN uses armored vehicles to transport troops on their humanitarian missions, such as those performed in the Yugoslav wars (1991–2001).

Security

Humanitarian aid convoys are often escorted by armored vehicles of the UN or other national protection forces.

ARMORED PERSONNEL CARRIERS OR APC

The number of different armored personnel carriers (APC) has grown much in recent years due to their maneuverability in urban settings and because they can be easily transported in cargo aircraft. The rifled armament of APCs should not exceed a caliber of 0.787 in (20 mm).

Prepared for self-defense

APCs are equipped with armaments to fend off attacks if necessary, like this French troop transporter, the VAB, with a Mephisto turret and HOT missiles.

Armored car escorts

Tankettes, like those used by the UN in the former Yugoslavia, can give protection and logistical support, perform reconnaissance tasks, or provide infantry support.

▲ The power of the U.S. Navy
The Nimitz aircraft carriers form the backbone of the U.S. Navy. In the photograph is the USS *Abraham Lincoln* (in the foreground) together with other U.S. ships.

CHAPTER 2
SEA

▲ Battle of Trafalgar
Fought in 1805 off the coast of Cadiz, this is one of the most famous naval battles in history, in which the British defeated the Franco-Spanish fleet.

INTRODUCTION

The Babylonians, Assyrians, Phoenicians, Egyptians, and Greeks, as well as many other peoples and cultures around the Mediterranean and along the shores of the Indian Ocean and Pacific Ocean, made use of seafaring vessels to conquer other lands. Their first weapons at sea were principally those carried by the soldiers who traveled aboard the ships. This was the case for many years, until they began to equip the vessels with the kinds of contraptions and war machines that had been successfully used on land: first, bows, arrows, and pikes; then rams, catapults, and crossbows; and later still, in Roman times, wooden structures that could be dismantled and used to board enemy ships or launch projectiles.

From that time onward, ships began to change. The Roman galleys, which were already equipped with fighting platforms, were followed by Byzantine dromonds, which were sailed up until around the thirteenth century, while in the Atlantic, the Viking drekars harried the coasts of northern Europe, and Muslim ships ruled the Mediterranean. However, warships, which were armed for boarding and attacking land targets, evolved very slowly. Rounded hulls were used in the Middle Ages and until the twelfth century, which made the boats sluggish, and the rudder (taken from the Arabs),

forecastle, and aftcastle were not incorporated into the structure of European ships until the thirteenth century. In the fourteenth century, the ships were armed with bombards and springalds and started incorporating openings on the bulwarks for cannons. From then on, the development of firearms and artillery brought a new direction to naval warfare, as vessels began to fight one another in the sea, as well as defend positions or launch attacks on land.

The Age of Discovery would also bring about rapid developments in the art of sailing. The rigging was higher and more complex and the hulls became sharper, allowing the boats to travel faster. The caravels of the fifteenth century developed into the large galleys of the sixteenth and seventeenth centuries, like the 1637 *Sovereign of the Seas*, with its 3 decks and 102 guns, which, in turn, made way for smaller vessels, though no less suited to warfare, like the brigantines and frigates, in the seventeenth and eighteenth centuries. The latter survived for several years after the arrival of steam boilers and steel, although the Industrial Revolution would once again change warships forever and, in so doing, would also change naval strategy. Ships, like the new dreadnoughts, were armored, used enormous boilers, new engines, and large propellers and had heavy artillery and torpedoes incorporated into their weaponry.

The turn of the twentieth century saw high-speed technological developments and the discovery of new energy sources, bringing improvements every few years to the accuracy and efficiency of naval weapons. As a consequence, world powers invested huge sums of money in their continual renovation. In the first decades of the last century, the oceans were patrolled by large numbers of submarines, while on the water's surface the different navies expanded their fleets, which eventually became the ultimate symbol of military power. After World War II, destroyer escorts, frigates, and destroyers were armed with 3-in and 5.25-in (76-mm and 133-mm) guns, fire-control radar, and SAM antiaircraft missile launchers, successors of the German V–2 rockets. They also had torpedo tubes and short-range antisubmarine weapons, but by 1965, with the development of antiaircraft guided missile systems and the increase in helicopter carriers, naval artillery was reduced to just one or two guns per ship. Between 1950 and 1970, there were notable improvements in sonar

systems and detection equipment, as well as in missiles and torpedoes, such as the United States' ASROC or the Australian Ikara, equipped with SM3 missile systems and an air defense network together with sophisticated radar systems. After twenty years developing engines and nuclear weapons during the Cold War years, ships came to be armed exclusively with missiles, like the French Exocet or British Sea Wolf. Some ships incorporated just one 1.6-in (40-mm) gun and an antiaircraft or missile defense weapon.

Developments in pinpoint accurate fire-control and detection systems and research into computer-operated weapons, which began in the 1980s, have yet again changed the way warships are used. Now boats are armed with long-range rockets and nuclear warheads, use intelligent guidance systems and incorporate electronic countermeasures. Furthermore, the advance of antiaircraft weapons has led to destroyers and frigates now having Vertical Launching Systems (VLS),

containing dozens of cells and with ranges of up to 60 miles (100 km). The longest-range missile is the Mk–41, developed by the U.S. Navy, which has great versatility thanks to cells that can each house different missile types, and is used today on more than 200 ships in 11 different navies around the world. Today, destroyers and frigates sail alongside littoral combat ships (LCS), which measure around 330 ft (100 m) in length and are similarly equipped in weapons and detection systems. These escort enormous aircraft carriers, which offer air supremacy and have brought major changes to naval war tactics in the last 50 years.

In the first decades of the twenty-first century, a period in which the world's main naval fleets have incorporated new submarines armed with intercontinental missiles, many of which are propelled by nuclear power (although continually updated diesel-electric submarines, with very high levels of sound-reducing insulation, are still manufactured), new developments in arms and defense systems come at a dizzying pace. The new generations of warships will very possibly be entirely invisible to radar and powered by IPS (Ion Propulsion System). They will be equipped with cutting-edge artillery like EMRG guns mounted on electromagnetic rails, with a range of 200 nautical miles, which integrate a GPS/inertial navigation system and whose missiles reach a speed of Mach 5. These new artillery systems also have the possibility of direct fire with antimissile capacity, are immune to electronic countermeasures, and can be used against aircraft and surface targets. In recent years, navies have also been gradually equipping their ships with different unmanned systems. In theory, these are for exploration and supply purposes, but equipped with protection and radar and satellite guidance systems, and with remarkable ranges, they carry weapons that can be detonated remotely and with pinpoint accuracy.

▲ Sinking of the HMS *Victoria*
This British battleship, one of the most modern ships of its time, was sunk in 1893 near Tripoli after colliding with another British battleship.

Chronology

The seas have been the main stage for wars waged throughout history. Over the last 4,000 years, from the appearance of the first armed ships to the nuclear-missile-carrying submarines and transoceanic aircraft carriers of the twenty-first century, military genius has developed increasingly sophisticated ships and weaponry, turning navies into key strategic pieces in the operational structure of the world's major armies.

circa 1800 BCE
Bronzework is introduced into Central Europe from Greece.

480 BCE
The Athenians defeat the Persian fleet in the Battle of Salamis.

1522
Magellan sails around the world.

circa 1200 BCE
The Phoenicians, now independent from Egypt, begin their maritime supremacy. Iron metallurgy begins in the Middle East.

260 BCE
The Roman fleet, led by Gaius Duilius, defeats the Carthaginians in Mylae.

330 CE
Constantinople, named capital of the Eastern Roman or Byzantine Empire.

1405
Zheng He's first fleet, which includes some of the biggest ships in the world, leaves Nanjing.

1571
John of Austria, aided by Venice and the papacy, defeats the Ottomans at the Battle of Lepanto.

circa 750 BCE
Greece begins to expand across the Mediterranean.

1081
Battle of Dyrrhachium (Albania), between the Normans and Byzantines. Ships without oars are used.

circa 510 BCE
Rome recognizes Carthage's maritime monopoly.

circa 790 CE
Viking raids on the British Isles.

1340
At the outbreak of the Hundred Years' War, the English fleet defeats the French at Sluys (Sluis), giving England control over the English Channel.

1492
Christopher Columbus sets foot in America and discovers the islands of San Salvador (Guanahani), Cuba (Juana), and Santo Domingo (Hispaniola).

1176 BCE
Egyptian victory over the Sea Peoples in the Battle of the Delta.

31 BCE
In the Battle of Actium, hundreds of Octavian's (Augustus's) ships confront the combined fleets of Antony and Cleopatra.

985 CE
Eric the Red's second expedition to Greenland, where he takes Icelandic colonists. The Vikings sight America for the first time.

circa 500 BCE
Iron casting in China.

1588
Defeat of the Spanish Armada by the English fleet.

2000 BCE . . . .

"To arm the dromons [...] we command that pots full of prepared fire, according to the prescribed method of their preparation, should be hurled; on shattering they easily burn up the ships of the enemy. Make use also of the other method, that is, of the small siphons thrown by hand from behind the iron shields held by the soldiers."

Leo VI the Wise, Byzantine Emperor. *Taktikon Uspensky*, **1, 19 (tenth century)**

1719–20
After the Northern War on the Aland Islands, Russia becomes the dominant power of the Baltic.

1805
The British Navy is pitted against the Franco-Spanish fleet at the Battle of Trafalgar, which claims the life of Admiral Nelson.

1769
The steam engine is patented.

1775
The United States Marine Corps is created during the American War of Independence.

1827
Battle of Navarino (Greek War of Independence). The combined British, French, and Russian fleet defeats the Ottoman-Egyptian armada.

1798
The British claim victory over the French at the Battle of the Nile (also known as the Battle of Aboukir Bay).

1905
At the Battle of Tsushima, the Japanese attack a Russian expeditionary fleet, with the loss of 21 Russian ships.

1906
Launching of the battleship HMS *Dreadnought* of the British Royal Navy.

1912
Britain moves its fleet from the Mediterranean to the North Sea.

1916
Battle of Jutland, in the North Sea, between the Kaiser's fleet and the British Navy, which involves more than 250 ships .

1917
The Canadian physicist Robert Boyle builds a prototype sonar system.

1942
Battle of Midway in the north Pacific, where U.S. carrier-borne aircraft win a victory over a Japanese naval force, with the loss of three Japanese carriers.

1944
Normandy landings.

Decisive Allied victory over the Japanese fleet at the Battle of Leyte Gulf (the Philippines) in the Pacific War.

1954
Launch of the first nuclear-powered submarine, the USS *Nautilus*.

1960
Launch of the first nuclear-powered aircraft carrier, the USS *Enterprise* (CVN–65).

1982
Falklands War between Argentina and the United Kingdom.

1990
Gulf War in Iraq.

1991
Breakup of the Soviet Union.

2003
Iraq War. The United States, United Kingdom, and Canada deploy their fleets in the Persian Gulf.

2011
International intervention in Libya. In the first coalition-led attack, British and North American ships and submarines launch more than 100 Tomahawk cruise missiles.

2012
The first aircraft carrier of the Chinese Navy, the *Liaoning*, enters service.

Great Admirals

They wrote some of the most glorious chapters of naval warfare. Admired by their crews and feared by their enemies, they commanded ships, squadrons, and, in some cases, entire navies. In their capacity as experienced seafarers, they combined leadership qualities with great strategic skill to become pioneers in the art of warfare on the seas.

1371–1433
Zheng He
Chinese soldier and mariner. Between 1405 and 1433 he commanded seven major expeditionary voyages into the Indian Ocean, which reached as far as the shores of Mozambique and included one of the largest ships ever built until then.

1526–1588
Álvaro de Bazán y Guzmán
Captain General of the Spanish Armada at the age of 28 and a key figure in the victory of the Battle of Lepanto against the Turks, he was the first to use marine infantry for amphibious operations. In 1585, he was appointed Captain General of the Sea.

1545–1598
Yi Sun-sin
Korean admiral, famous for building turtle ships in 1592 from old design plans. He led a small fleet to defend against Japan's repeated attempts to conquer Korea, and was eventually shot dead fighting the Japanese.

1607–1676
Michiel Adriaenszoon de Ruyter
Dutch admiral, known for his expertise in line-ahead, line-abreast, and boarding maneuvers. He is considered to be one of the best naval tacticians in history. In 1667, he launched a raid on the River Thames, which led England to signing the Treaty of Breda. He died in the Franco-Dutch War.

Zheng He

Álvaro de Bazán y Guzmán

Yi Sun-sin

Michiel Adriaenszoon de Ruyter

"There's the ideal ship! And if it's true that the engineer has more confidence in a craft than the builder, and the builder more than the captain himself, you can understand the utter abandon with which I place my trust in this Nautilus, since I'm its captain, builder and engineer all in one!"

Jules Verne, *Twenty Thousand Leagues Under the Sea* (1869)

1758–1805

Horatio Nelson

One of history's most famous admirals. He was defeated on just one occasion, in 1797, when he lost half of his left arm in battle. He was the tragic hero of the decisive Battle of Trafalgar, where he was killed in combat. The Royal Navy, which he had commanded, then went on to defeat the Franco-Spanish fleet.

1841–1920

John Arbuthnot "Jacky" Fisher

First Sea Lord of the British Royal Navy, which he completely modernized. He is considered to be the creator of the battle-cruiser concept, and a key figure in the development of the destroyer and torpedoes. He is also credited with the design of HMS *Dreadnought*.

1848–1934

Tōgō Heihachirō

He was instrumental in the creation and structure of the Imperial Japanese Navy. Known as the "Nelson of the East," Admiral Tōgō destroyed the Russian fleet in Port Arthur in 1904 and astonished the world with his strategy at the Battle of Tsushima (1905) against the Russian Baltic Fleet.

1885–1966

Chester William Nimitz

Commander-in-Chief of the United States Navy during World War II. An entire generation of ten nuclear-powered aircraft carriers were named after him, the USS *Nimitz* (CVN–68 to 77), built between 1975 and 2009.

Horatio Nelson | John Arbuthnot "Jacky" Fisher | Tōgō Heihachirō | Chester William Nimitz

▲ Battle of the Aegadian Isles
Depiction of the battle that took place in 241 BCE off the coast of
Sicily between the Carthaginian and Roman fleets, during the
First Punic War.

THE FIRST SHIPS

The first ships capable of waging war on the seas were built between the fourth and third millennium before Christ around the Eastern Mediterranean, the Indus Valley, and China, where complex and ancient societies were flourishing. There is evidence of Chinese naval constructions dating back around 4,000 years, but for historians the knife handle of Gebel el-Arak (3300–3200 BCE, The Louvre), featuring a carving of Egyptian and Sumerian vessels in battle, is the oldest representation of naval warfare.

In the early years of the New Kingdom of Egypt (between 1570 and 1070 BCE), the Siege of Avaris, the capital of the Hyksos, by the troops of Pharaoh Ahmose I, provides us with information on history's first known naval blockades. However, the reliefs found in Medinet Habu, the Temple of Ramesses III, are where the first official warships are clearly depicted. They tell the story of the Battle of the Delta (around 1176 BCE), which the pharaoh waged against the Sea Peoples. This great seafaring confederation of tribes and peoples threatened the north of the kingdom after conquering the Levant's most important port, Ugarit (in modern-day Syria, close to the current border with Turkey), which was a vital outpost for Egyptian trade and logistics. Thanks to good strategy, victory went to the pharaoh's fleet, whose ships had solid hulls, no ropes, and were propelled by rowers protected by a raised bulwark. The vessels were equipped with small towers fore and aft, a mast, and an easily managed loose sail.

Experts still debate the influence of the Mycenaean shipbuilders on Egypt or vice versa, although they all agree that it was the "Great Green"—as the Mediterranean was known to the Egyptians 3,500 years ago—where sea vessels designed for war evolved at the greatest speed. It was just 300 years later that the first triremes, of Corinthian origin, sailed its seas. These swift vessels, which some believe were copied from the Egyptians by the Persians and then imitated by the Greeks, were the rulers of the high seas for centuries, until they were surpassed, first by the large galleys from the Hellenistic Age, and then by the ships of ancient Rome. The empire that came to completely dominate the waters, known as Mare Nostrum, possessed boats like the liburnians, weighing around 16.5 tons, with 50 oars and a 70-man crew, which already incorporated battle decks, ballistas, catapults, an above-water ram, and wooden towers that could be easily dismantled. These were followed by the Byzantine dromonds, which had as many as three masts equipped with lateen sails and two banks of rowers. They navigated the seas from the sixth century, and inflicted on their foe the so-called "Greek fire." This was a flammable substance that continued to burn in the water and was launched at the enemy through bronze siphons, which were sometimes portable, allowing the weapon to be used from the ships' sides.

Egyptian Warships

Although it is likely that the ancient Egyptians had been using ships for military purposes right from the early days of the empire, the exact time they actually assembled a war fleet is unknown. There would certainly have been earlier squadrons, but the first evidence can be found during the reign of Ramesses III (1184–53 BCE). They were ships with low hulls, designed for ship-to-ship combat.

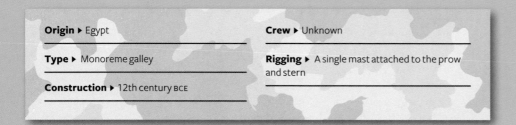

Origin ▶ Egypt

Type ▶ Monoreme galley

Construction ▶ 12th century BCE

Crew ▶ Unknown

Rigging ▶ A single mast attached to the prow and stern

Mast and sail
It had a single mast attached fore and aft and a square sail, which actually rested on the lower yard, the upper yard being mobile. The sail itself was wider than it was long.

Forecastle
It had raised castles fore and aft, where most of the soldiers, mainly archers, were positioned, to fire at enemy ships.

Ram
Made from wood reinforced with bronze and shaped as a lion's head.

EARLIER SHIPS
The Egyptians had previously copied ships used by other peoples, like the Greeks, Phoenicians, or Romans.

Trihemiolia (3rd century BCE)

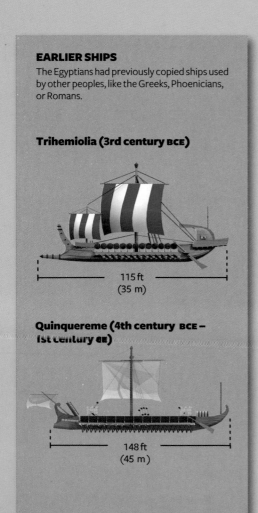

115 ft
(35 m)

Quinquereme (4th century BCE – 1st century CE)

148 ft
(45 m)

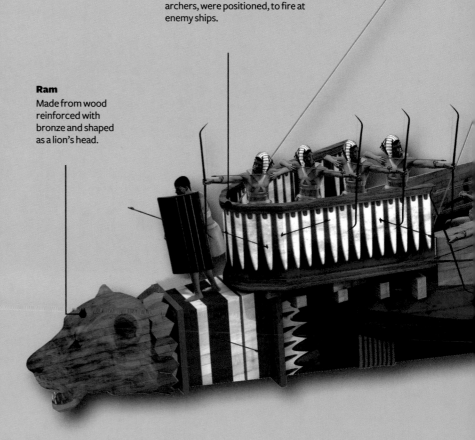

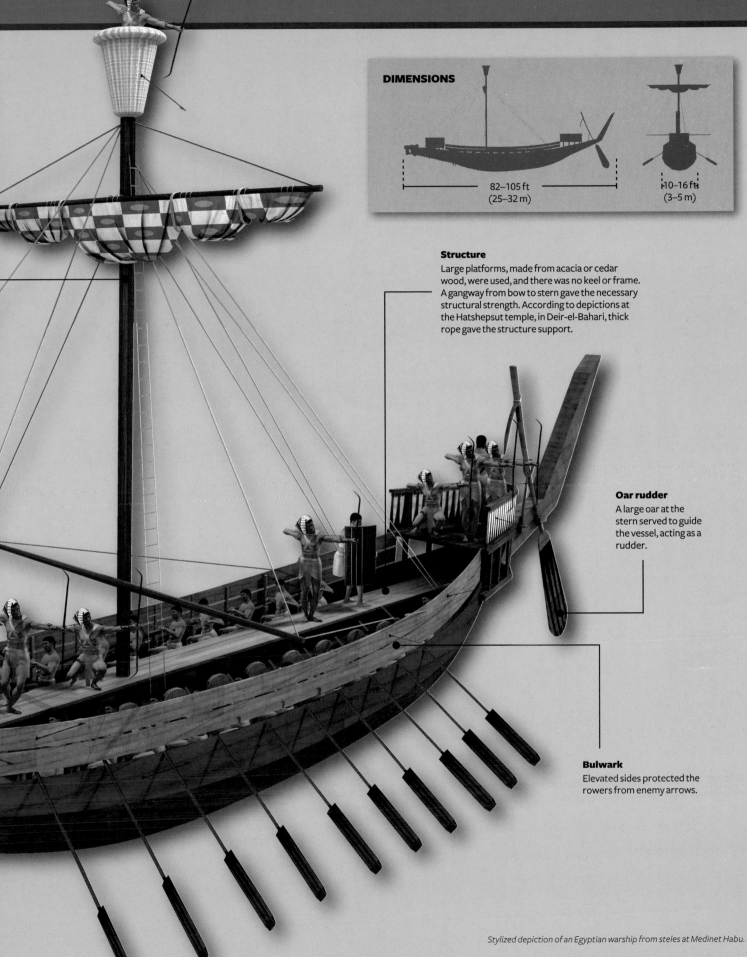

DIMENSIONS

82–105 ft
(25–32 m)

10–16 ft
(3–5 m)

Structure
Large platforms, made from acacia or cedar wood, were used, and there was no keel or frame. A gangway from bow to stern gave the necessary structural strength. According to depictions at the Hatshepsut temple, in Deir-el-Bahari, thick rope gave the structure support.

Oar rudder
A large oar at the stern served to guide the vessel, acting as a rudder.

Bulwark
Elevated sides protected the rowers from enemy arrows.

Stylized depiction of an Egyptian warship from steles at Medinet Habu.

The First Naval Battle in History

Under the reign of Ramesses III, Egypt fought against the Sea Peoples, a confederation of peoples of different origins, who were harrying the Egyptian coastline. Although the Sea Peoples had a large fleet and experienced seafarers, Ramesses III was able to defeat them, circa 1176 BCE. His tactic consisted in ambushing the enemy ships at the mouth of the Nile, where his army claimed victory thanks to the coordination of the navy and infantry.

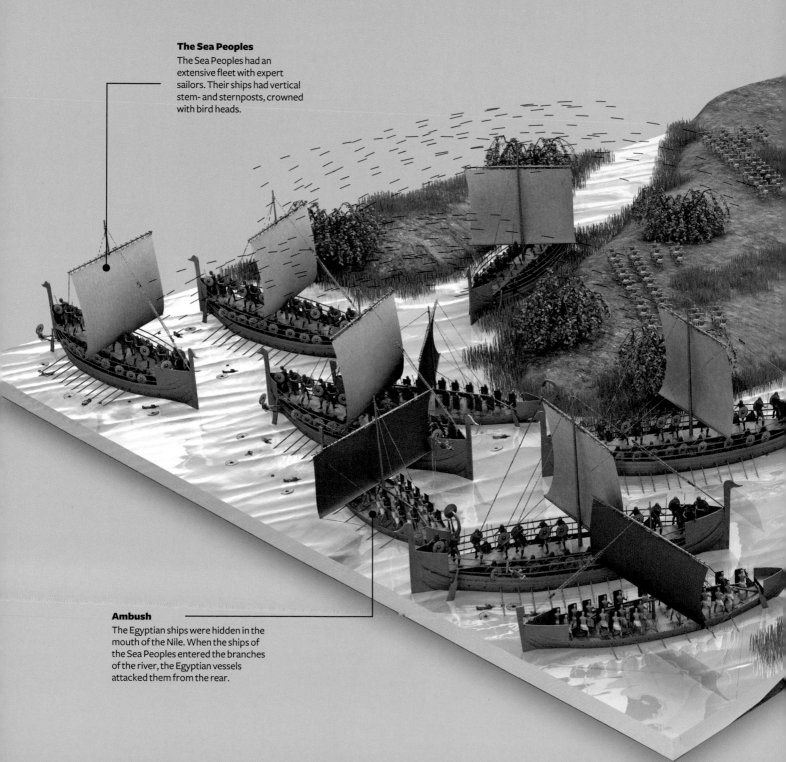

The Sea Peoples
The Sea Peoples had an extensive fleet with expert sailors. Their ships had vertical stem- and sternposts, crowned with bird heads.

Ambush
The Egyptian ships were hidden in the mouth of the Nile. When the ships of the Sea Peoples entered the branches of the river, the Egyptian vessels attacked them from the rear.

Channels
On entering the branches of the Nile, the enemy ships lost the ability to maneuver, which made them more vulnerable.

Close combat
The enemy soldiers that reached the banks were captured by the infantry.

Egyptian ships
The Egyptian ships were inferior to those of the Sea Peoples, but more suitable for sailing in the delta. Ramesses III used this situation to his advantage.

Attack from land
The vanguard of the enemy fleet was attacked by the Egyptian infantry, who launched a volley of spears, javelins, and arrows at the enemy ships.

▶ Record of the battle
The Battle of the Delta is the first naval battle to be recorded. It is mentioned in texts from the era and was depicted in the great stele of Medinet Habu, the funerary temple of Ramesses III (pictured).

The Greek Trireme

Equipped with three lines of oars, the triremes gave the Greek fleets four centuries of rule over the Mediterranean. Long, narrow, and with a shallow draft, these ships were fast and had great maneuverability. In combat, thanks to the propulsion of the 170 rowers, the trireme reached very high speeds and ploughed into enemy ships, destroying their hulls with the ram.

Origin ▶ Corinthian

Type ▶ Trireme Galley

Construction ▶ 7th–2nd century BCE

Crew ▶ 200 men, including 170 rowers and 14 soldiers

Weight ▶ 40–50 tons

Displacement ▶ 55 tons

Rigging ▶ 2 masts, square sails

Average speed ▶ 5 knots

Maximum speed ▶ 9–14 knots

Rudder
At the stern, two oars performed the function of a rudder.

Apostis
The Greeks fitted the hulls with a frame that protruded from the side to make rowing easier.

Oars
These measured 14 ft 9 in (4.5 m) in length. Great expertise and skill were needed to maneuver these ships, so the rowers were not slaves, but rather free men.

DIMENSIONS

105–121 ft
(32–37 m)

11.5–20 ft
(3.5–6 m)

Sails
They had a large square sail and another smaller one, which, in combat, were either lowered or left on land so as not to interfere in the maneuvers.

Ram
The keel ended in a bronze-reinforced ram positioned at water level. This was the trireme's main weapon, which it used to plow into enemy ships and rip holes in their hulls.

Depiction of a possible version of a Greek trireme.

The Roman Galley

The galleys gave the Roman navy complete control over the Mediterranean from the third century BCE. The Romans built triremes, quadriremes, and quinqueremes and incorporated fighting towers and ramps for boarding (*corvus*). After the first century BCE, the Roman navy included other faster and lighter galleys known as liburnians, used to patrol coastlines and rivers, but also very effective in combat.

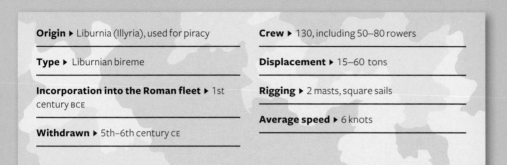

Origin ▶ Liburnia (Illyria), used for piracy

Type ▶ Liburnian bireme

Incorporation into the Roman fleet ▶ 1st century BCE

Withdrawn ▶ 5th–6th century CE

Crew ▶ 130, including 50–80 rowers

Displacement ▶ 15–60 tons

Rigging ▶ 2 masts, square sails

Average speed ▶ 6 knots

Tower
Added by the Romans to the galleys, these were fortified towers from where projectiles were launched.

Spritsail
A headsail typical of Roman galleys.

Hull
Built from cedar, pine, and fir wood.

▲ Corvus
The *corvus* (crow) was a gangplank with a metal spike at one end. At close quarters it would be dropped onto the enemy boat where the spike would grip the deck, allowing the ship to be boarded.

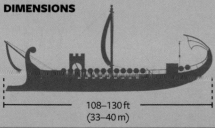

DIMENSIONS

108–130 ft
(33–40 m)

16–26 ft
(5–8 m)

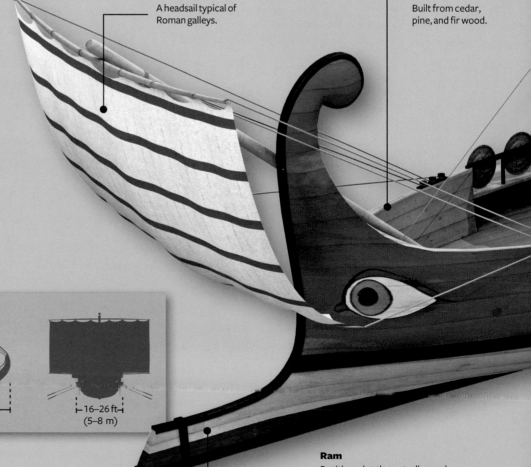

Ram
Positioned at the waterline and reinforced with metal, it was used to charge enemy ships.

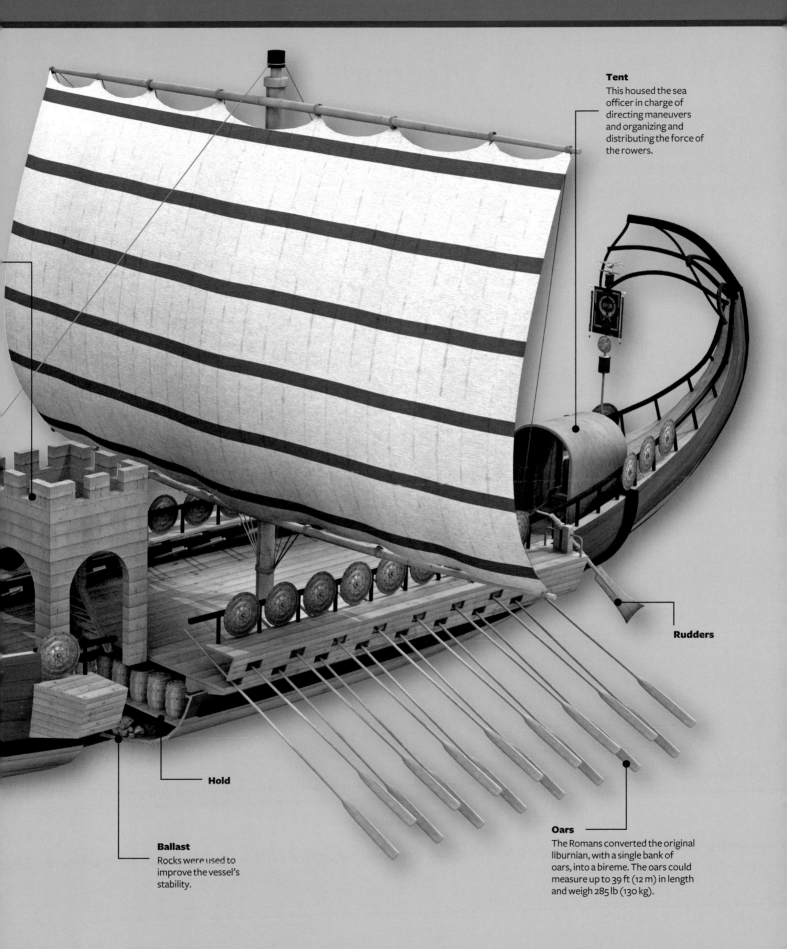

Tent
This housed the sea officer in charge of directing maneuvers and organizing and distributing the force of the rowers.

Rudders

Hold

Ballast
Rocks were used to improve the vessel's stability.

Oars
The Romans converted the original liburnian, with a single bank of oars, into a bireme. The oars could measure up to 39 ft (12 m) in length and weigh 285 lb (130 kg).

The Byzantine Dromond

The dromond was the Byzantine navy's prototype warship between the sixth and thirteenth centuries. Over time, these ships, which were designed for speed, increased in size and perfected their rigging. The dromonds were armed with rams, platforms for archers, ballistas, catapults, and bronze siphons, like flamethrowers, which spat out the devastating "Greek fire."

Origin ▶ Byzantine Empire	
Type ▶ Bireme galley	
Construction ▶ circa 6th–13th century	
Crew ▶ around 300 (rowers, marines, and soldiers)	
Rigging ▶ 2 or 3 masts with square or lateen sails, or a combination of both	
Average speed ▶ 4 knots	

Sails
The sails could be square or lateen, or a combination of both.

Midcastle
Located around the central mast, this was probably used as a platform for archers.

▲ **"Greek fire"**
This was a flammable mix, possibly comprising naphtha, quicklime, sulfur, and tar, which continued to burn in the water. It was launched using a siphon mechanism, similar to a modern flamethrower.

Ram
This was a kind of wooden spur in the bow, which was used to smash the oars and flanks of enemy ships.

Masts
It is believed that the larger dromonds must have had two or three masts.

Rudder
Consisting of two large blades.

Ballistas
For firing projectiles.

Oars
There were between 21 and 50 oars each side, each operated by two men. There is evidence that there were also dromonds with three banks of oars.

DIMENSIONS

100–165 ft
(30–50 m)

16 ft
(5 m)

Reconstruction of a late model of a large war dromond

▲ Battle of the Nile or Aboukir Bay
In 1798, during the French Revolutionary Wars, the British fleet, captained by Admiral Nelson, defeated the French at Aboukir Bay.

ARMED SHIPS

Although it was not until the fourteenth century that naval artillery began to develop properly, when China discovered gunpowder in the ninth century warships incorporated the technology into their weaponry. As well as various new types of crossbows and lightweight catapults, incendiary arms, explosives, and gunpowder-launched projectiles (lead balls or volleys of arrows) were fired at the enemy through bamboo tubes. That was how the warships of one of the most astounding fleets in history were equipped: between 1405 and 1433, Admiral Zheng led seven expeditions to the "Western Ocean" from Nanjing, southeast China's economic and political capital for a thousand years. On his first voyage alone, 317 ships departed, including some of the largest vessels ever built, with up to nine masts, over 330 ft (100 m) long with a beam of 165 ft (50 m), although those destined for battle, the *fuchuan*, had "just" five masts and an overall length of 165 ft (50 m). They traveled the coasts of Southeast Asia, Indonesia, Ceylon, India, the Persian Gulf, and East Africa up to the Mozambique Channel.

In that time, while the first "turtle ships" had already been developed in Korea, with roofs clad in wooden armor and artillery fore and aft and on both sides, in Europe sailors looked to the Atlantic from the raised decks of the galleys (some 130 ft/40 m long, with a beam of 20 ft/6 m) and at the new lands they discovered aboard the oarless caravels used to reach America, propelled by sails and rigs.

At the end of the fifteenth and during the sixteenth centuries, the need for large boats capable of crossing the oceans paved the way for powerful galleons like the three-masted *Nuestra Señora de Atocha* (112 ft/ 34 m long, with a beam of 33 ft/10 m, and carrier of a vast treasure), which were armed with a large number of bombards and cannons and had great firepower. These marked the beginning of a golden age for sailing and a new era in naval warfare. The first large-scale battles on the high seas were waged in this time, making the royal fleets and their sailors crucial to the balance of power in Europe.

From the seventeenth century, the evolution of naval artillery and new naval formations of combat squadrons led to the appearance of the "ship of the line," which carried no less than a hundred cannons across three decks. Developed in England and designed to form lines of battle, it displaced between 1,000 and 3,500 tons and was a highly powerful ship, although slow, requiring the assistance of smaller and much faster vessels, like the brigantine, schooner, frigate, which had two gun decks, or the corvette, which had just one. This type of ship dominated until the nineteenth century, when the steam engine would replace sails, and iron and steel would take the place of wood. A dry dock in Portsmouth Harbour, in the south of England, preserves the only ship of the line to have survived until today in its original condition. Now serving as a museum, the legendary HMS *Victory*, armed with 104 cannons, was Admiral Horatio Nelson's flagship in the Battle of Trafalgar.

The Fleet of Zheng He

Zheng He, admiral of the Chinese navy during the Ming dynasty, captained the largest fleet that had ever been seen. He made seven voyages with around 300 ships and 30,000 men, aimed at exploring, trading, and establishing diplomatic relations with coastal peoples. The fleet had various vessel types, but the most impressive of all were the treasure ships, which, according to descriptions from the era, had an overall length of over 330 ft (100 m).

Origin ▶ China

Type ▶ Chinese junk. Treasure ship

Construction ▶ Around 1404

Withdrawn ▶ 1433

Crew ▶ Between 500 and 1,000

Displacement ▶ 3,350 tons

Rigging ▶ 9 masts, 12 square sails

Cranes
Used for loading and unloading cargo.

Sails
It is thought to have been powered by 12 square sails, made from natural fibers and reinforced with bamboo canes.

Bow
It had a short bow and no keel. Two large anchors, measuring over 6 ft 6 in (2 m), hung from the bow.

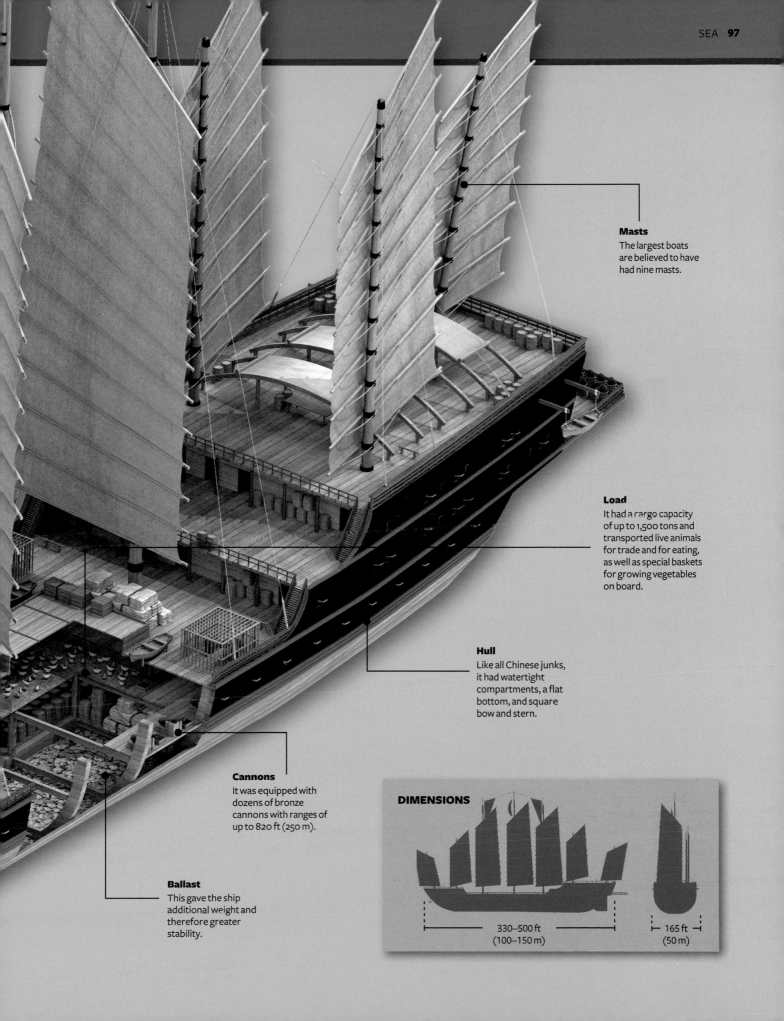

Masts
The largest boats are believed to have had nine masts.

Load
It had a cargo capacity of up to 1,500 tons and transported live animals for trade and for eating, as well as special baskets for growing vegetables on board.

Hull
Like all Chinese junks, it had watertight compartments, a flat bottom, and square bow and stern.

Cannons
It was equipped with dozens of bronze cannons with ranges of up to 820 ft (250 m).

Ballast
This gave the ship additional weight and therefore greater stability.

DIMENSIONS

330–500 ft
(100–150 m)

165 ft
(50 m)

Korean Turtle Ships

The turtle ships or Geobukseon date back to the early fifteenth century, but the ultimate design is attributed to Admiral Yi Sun-sin, who ordered their construction to defend against the Japanese invasion of Korea in 1592–98. The Geobukseon were strong and stable vessels, but also light, fast, and highly maneuverable. They were equipped with powerful artillery and clad in a shell of plates and metal spikes.

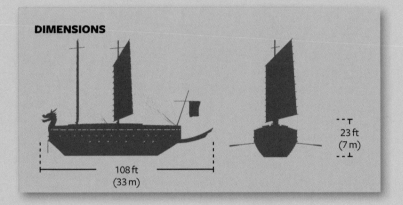

DIMENSIONS

108 ft
(33 m)

23 ft
(7 m)

Sails

The two sails were reinforced with a series of rods, which lent them great strength. In battle, the masts and sails could be taken down.

Shell

Made of hexagonal plates, it protected the main deck and was covered in iron spikes to defend against boarding. It is unclear whether the shell was made of iron or wood.

Dragon's head

According to 18th-century drawings—the only graphic evidence of these ships—this was incorporated like a figurehead (similar to the Chinese dragon ships). However, recent research shows that the dragon's head was probably located at the waterline and served as a ram.

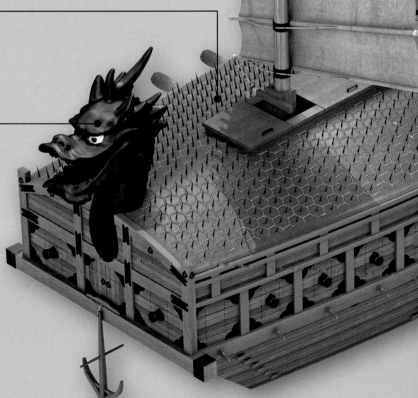

Origin ▶ Korea	
Type ▶ Panokseon	
Construction ▶ Circa 1591	
Crew ▶ 130 (70–80 rowers and 50–60 soldiers)	
Rigging ▶ 2 folding masts, square sails	

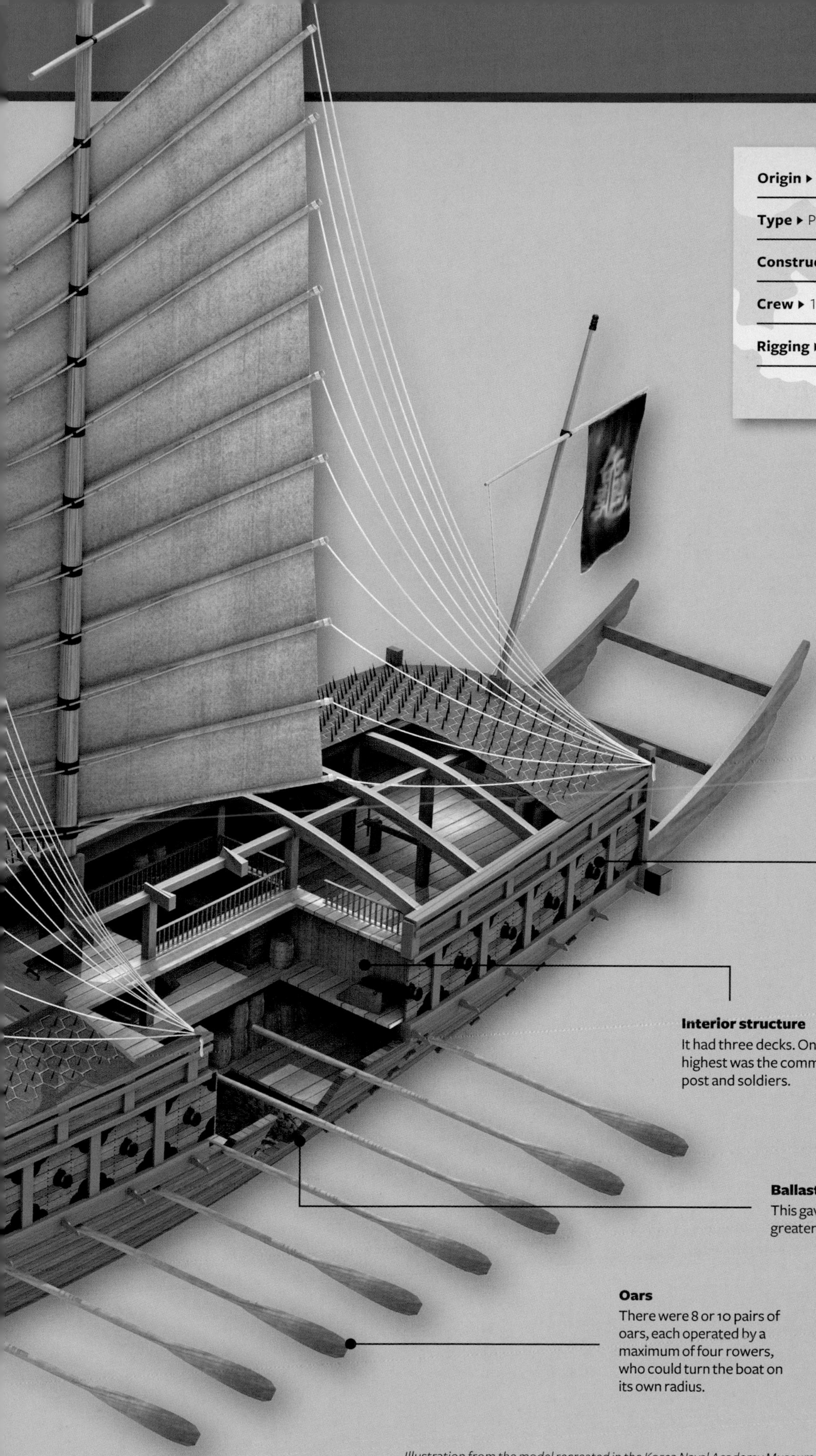

Cannons

It was equipped with more than 20 cannons of different types, located port and starboard, fore and aft, with ranges of between 650 and 1,970 ft (200 and 600 m). This allowed the ship to fire in all directions.

Interior structure

It had three decks. On the highest was the command post and soldiers.

Ballast

This gave the ship greater stability.

Oars

There were 8 or 10 pairs of oars, each operated by a maximum of four rowers, who could turn the boat on its own radius.

Illustration from the model recreated in the Korea Naval Academy Museum, in Jinhae-gu, based on drawings from the 18th century.

The Galley *Real*

In the fifteenth and sixteenth centuries, the galleys—large, fast, and maneuverable ships with a shallow draft—were the most powerful warships in the Mediterranean. In combat, galleys weakened enemy ships with fire from the bows, rammed them, and then boarded. The *Real*, built in 1568, was the largest galley of its time. Commanded by Don John of Austria, it was the flagship of the Spanish fleet at the Battle of Lepanto, in which the ships of the Holy League defeated the Ottoman squadron of Ali Pasha.

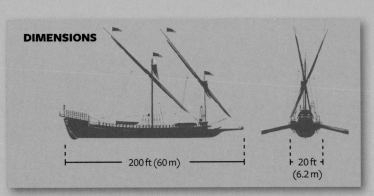

DIMENSIONS

200 ft (60 m)

20 ft
(6.2 m)

Yard

Ratchet shaft

Rigging
It had two masts that rose to heights of 72 and 50 ft (22 and 15 m), with lateen sails measuring 7,430 ft² (690 m²).

▲ **Stern**
As it accommodated a member of the royal family, the ship was lavishly decorated with religious and mythological bas-reliefs, sculptures, and paintings.

Bow armaments
It had five cannons. The central gun was the largest at 32 lb (14.5 kg) and used 30-lb (13.6-kg) ammunition.

Ram
Made from oak and pine, it carried a detachable figurehead of Neptune holding a trident and riding a dolphin.

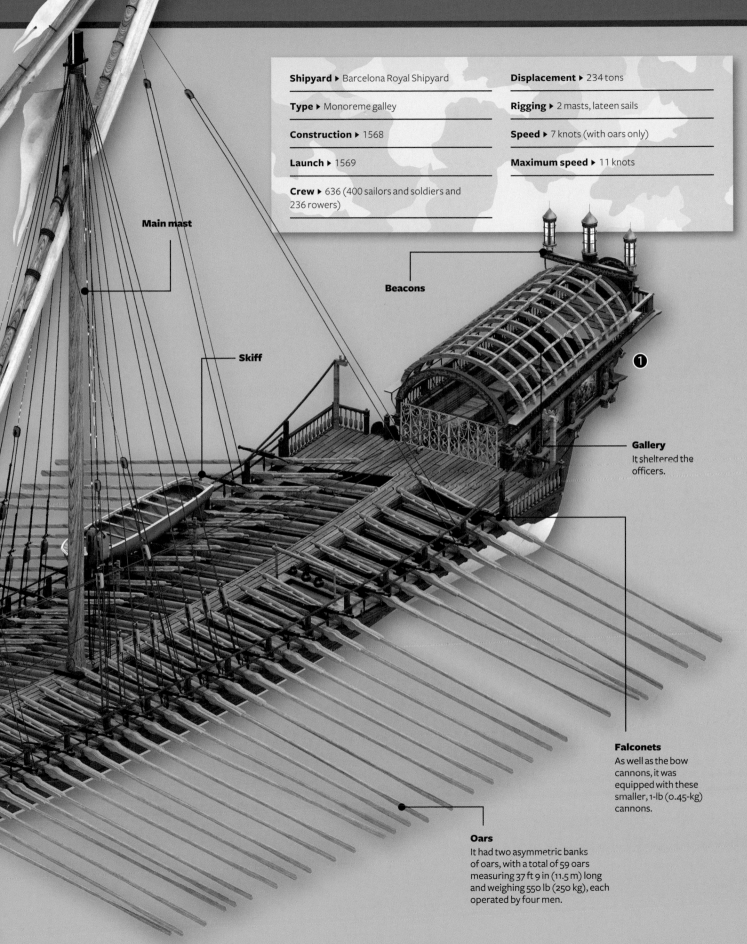

Shipyard ▶ Barcelona Royal Shipyard

Type ▶ Monoreme galley

Construction ▶ 1568

Launch ▶ 1569

Crew ▶ 636 (400 sailors and soldiers and 236 rowers)

Displacement ▶ 234 tons

Rigging ▶ 2 masts, lateen sails

Speed ▶ 7 knots (with oars only)

Maximum speed ▶ 11 knots

Main mast

Beacons

Skiff

①

Gallery
It sheltered the officers.

Falconets
As well as the bow cannons, it was equipped with these smaller, 1-lb (0.45-kg) cannons.

Oars
It had two asymmetric banks of oars, with a total of 59 oars measuring 37 ft 9 in (11.5 m) long and weighing 550 lb (250 kg), each operated by four men.

The Galleons

Galleons were powerful ships with a high cargo capacity and well equipped for combat and transoceanic voyages. They formed the bulk of the European fleets of the sixteenth and seventeenth centuries, although it was Spain that made widespread use of them, especially in fleet systems aimed at protecting trade routes to America. One of these galleons was *Nuestra Señora de Atocha*, which was shipwrecked during a hurricane in Florida in 1622 while carrying a valuable cargo.

Foremast

DIMENSIONS

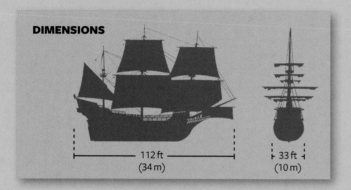

112 ft
(34 m)

33 ft
(10 m)

◀ Cannons
Galleons had 20 or 30 cannons. Depending on the caliber of the ammunition, they were divided into cannons, demicannons and quarter cannons.

Prow
It had fore- and aftcastles, while the ram lost its attacking function.

Culverins
Located on the castles, these were cannons forged from a single piece. They usually measured between 3 ft and 10 ft (1–3 m) in length and fired light-caliber balls.

Hull
Galleons were shorter and wider than galleys, and longer and narrower than a carrack.

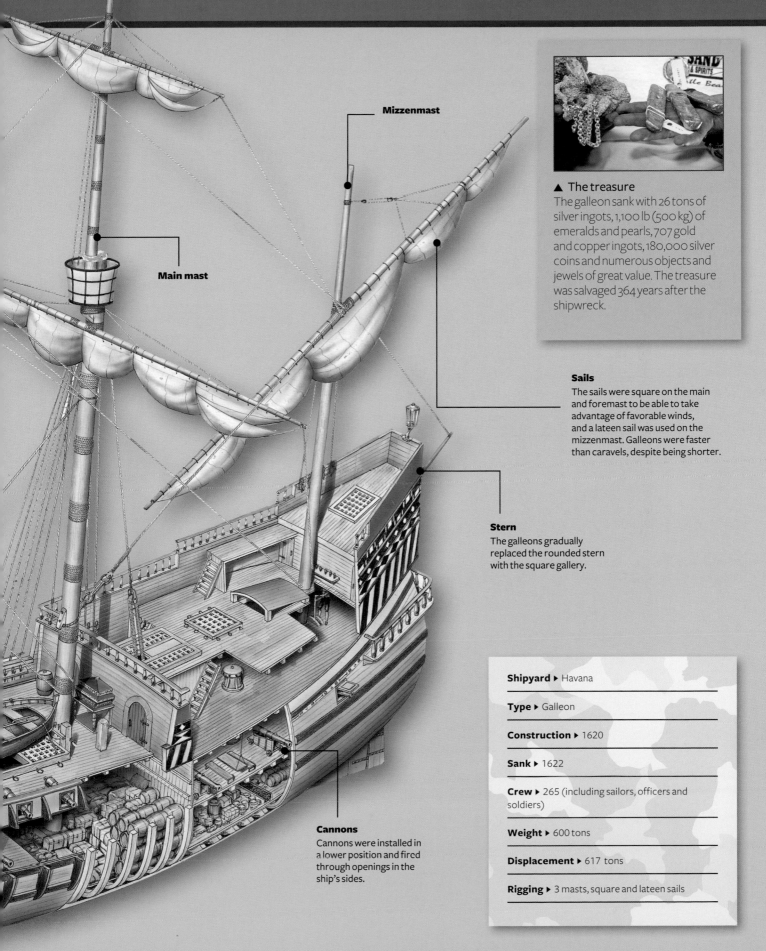

Mizzenmast

Main mast

▲ The treasure
The galleon sank with 26 tons of silver ingots, 1,100 lb (500 kg) of emeralds and pearls, 707 gold and copper ingots, 180,000 silver coins and numerous objects and jewels of great value. The treasure was salvaged 364 years after the shipwreck.

Sails
The sails were square on the main and foremast to be able to take advantage of favorable winds, and a lateen sail was used on the mizzenmast. Galleons were faster than caravels, despite being shorter.

Stern
The galleons gradually replaced the rounded stern with the square gallery.

Cannons
Cannons were installed in a lower position and fired through openings in the ship's sides.

Shipyard ▸	Havana
Type ▸	Galleon
Construction ▸	1620
Sank ▸	1622
Crew ▸	265 (including sailors, officers and soldiers)
Weight ▸	600 tons
Displacement ▸	617 tons
Rigging ▸	3 masts, square and lateen sails

Queen Anne's Revenge

Flagship of the feared pirate Edward Teach, also known as "Blackbeard," *Queen Anne's Revenge* was an English frigate, a fast, eighteenth-century warship with three masts and two decks equipped with easily maneuverable guns, ideal for fast, improvised attacks. Captured first by the French and then by pirates, it passed into legend during the three years it was captained by Blackbeard from 1715 to 1718, as it raided the coasts of Africa and the Caribbean.

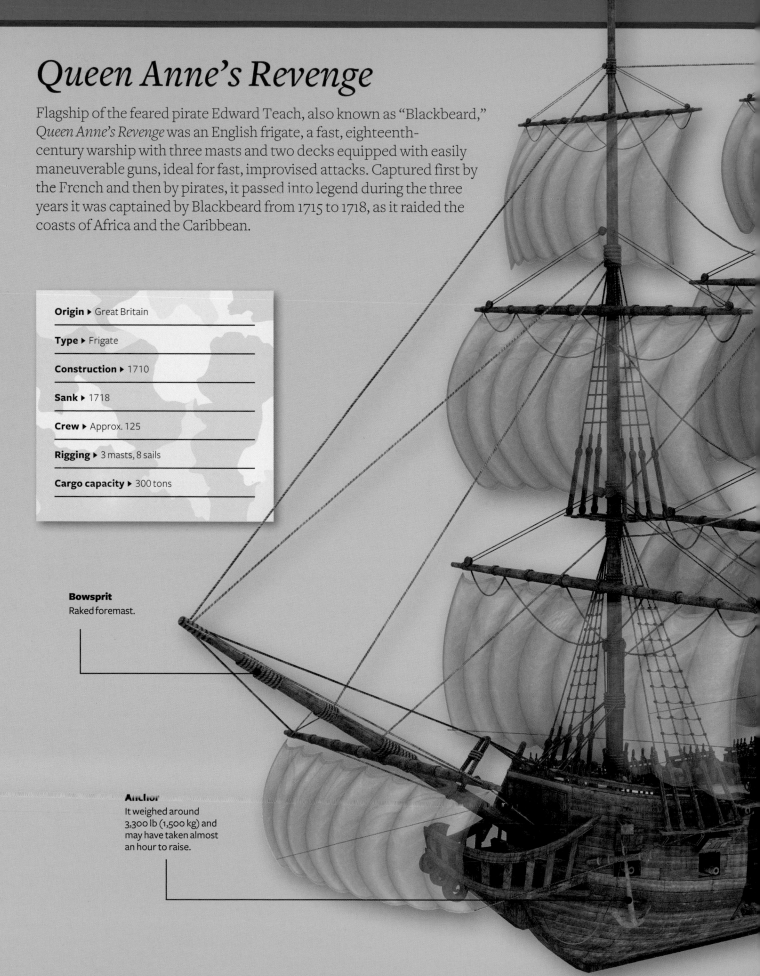

Origin ▸ Great Britain

Type ▸ Frigate

Construction ▸ 1710

Sank ▸ 1718

Crew ▸ Approx. 125

Rigging ▸ 3 masts, 8 sails

Cargo capacity ▸ 300 tons

Bowsprit
Raked foremast.

Anchor
It weighed around
3,300 lb (1,500 kg) and
may have taken almost
an hour to raise.

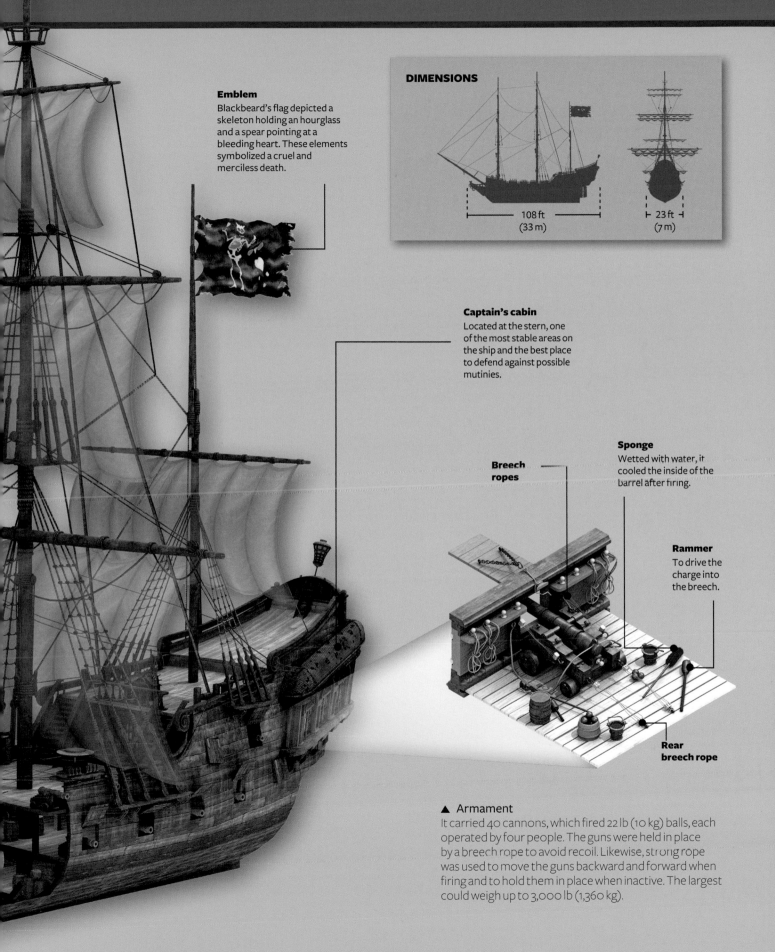

Emblem
Blackbeard's flag depicted a skeleton holding an hourglass and a spear pointing at a bleeding heart. These elements symbolized a cruel and merciless death.

DIMENSIONS

108 ft
(33 m)

23 ft
(7 m)

Captain's cabin
Located at the stern, one of the most stable areas on the ship and the best place to defend against possible mutinies.

Sponge
Wetted with water, it cooled the inside of the barrel after firing.

Breech ropes

Rammer
To drive the charge into the breech.

Rear breech rope

▲ Armament
It carried 40 cannons, which fired 22 lb (10 kg) balls, each operated by four people. The guns were held in place by a breech rope to avoid recoil. Likewise, strong rope was used to move the guns backward and forward when firing and to hold them in place when inactive. The largest could weigh up to 3,000 lb (1,360 kg).

A Change in Warfare: the Line of Battle

Europe's maritime expansion in the sixteenth century prompted spectacular growth in national fleets and more professional navies. The need to protect trade routes, and rivalry between the major European powers, led to the development of powerful warships, whose artillery played a key role. These ships, known as "ships of the line," led to some of the biggest naval battles in history between the seventeenth and mid-nineteenth centuries.

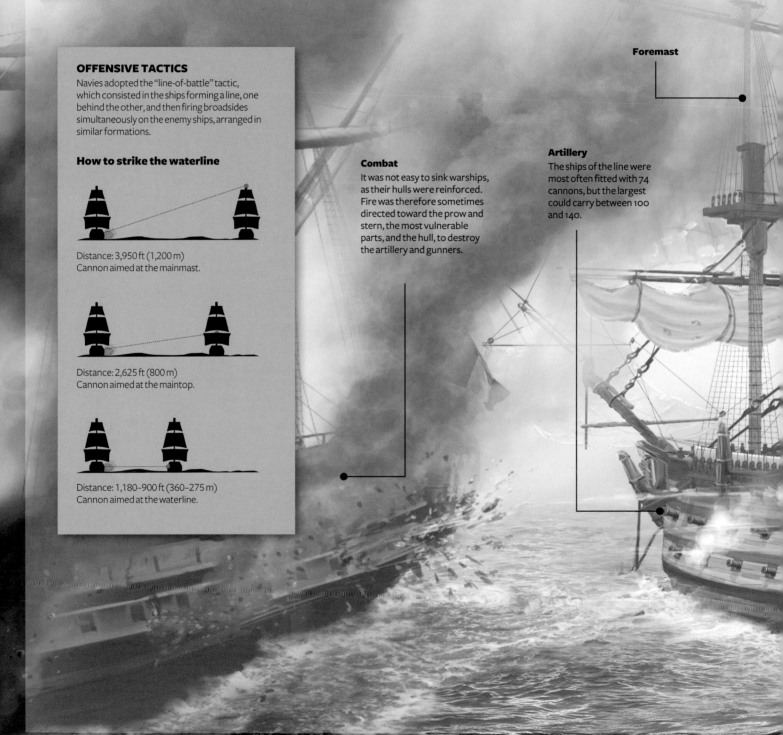

OFFENSIVE TACTICS

Navies adopted the "line-of-battle" tactic, which consisted in the ships forming a line, one behind the other, and then firing broadsides simultaneously on the enemy ships, arranged in similar formations.

How to strike the waterline

Distance: 3,950 ft (1,200 m)
Cannon aimed at the mainmast.

Distance: 2,625 ft (800 m)
Cannon aimed at the maintop.

Distance: 1,180–900 ft (360–275 m)
Cannon aimed at the waterline.

Foremast

Combat
It was not easy to sink warships, as their hulls were reinforced. Fire was therefore sometimes directed toward the prow and stern, the most vulnerable parts, and the hull, to destroy the artillery and gunners.

Artillery
The ships of the line were most often fitted with 74 cannons, but the largest could carry between 100 and 140.

Main mast

Mizzenmast

Masts
The three masts were kept stable using iron rings and platforms.

Batteries
The cannons were spread across two, three, or even four decks. The lower deck, just above the waterline, was used to store gunpowder and housed the heavier guns.

RETREAT

The retreating ship would protect itself by making a half turn, firing a volley of shots, followed by another, and then setting its course to retreat.

Holding an advantageous position with respect to the enemy ship was just as important as a ship's artillery. The windward ship (positioned with the enemy, or other squadrons and ships, downwind and so able to bear down on them) could fire at its adversary's waterline, while the latter could only aim at the mast.

HMS *Victory*

Flagship of Admiral Horatio Nelson in the Battle of Trafalgar (1805), she was celebrated in history after the British victory over the Franco-Spanish fleet. She was one of the largest ships of the line of her time, with 6 levels, 37 sails, and a mast that rose to 205 ft (62.5 m) above the waterline—6,000 oaks, elms, and holm oaks were used for her construction.

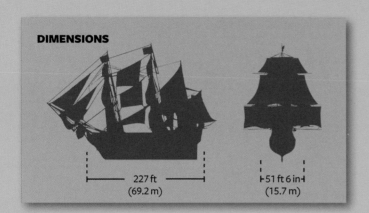

DIMENSIONS

227 ft
(69.2 m)

51 ft 6 in
(15.7 m)

Masts
The masts and bowsprit were divided into sections and made from pine or fir wood to make them lighter.

Galleries
At the stern were the recreational and rest areas for the captain and officers.

Cannons
In the Battle of Trafalgar, HMS *Victory* carried 104 cannons spread across three decks. At a decisive moment in the battle, a gun operated by 12 men was able to fire a shot per minute.

Orlop
This deck, located below the waterline, was used as storage, a mess, and an operating theater during combat.

Hold
Provisions could be kept here for six months. It also contained ballast.

Hull
The hull was clad in 4,000 copper plates to prevent woodworm.

▲ **Armament**
HMS *Victory* had three gun decks. On the first (above the waterline) were thirty 32-lb (14.5-kg) cannons; the second deck carried twenty-eight 24-lb (10.9-kg) cannons; and the third thirty 12-lb (5.4 kg) cannons. There were another twelve 12-lb cannons on the quarterdeck and two more in the forecastle, which also housed two carronades (short-range guns).

Dockyard ▶	Chatham, Kent (United Kingdom)
Type ▶	Ship of the line
Laid down ▶	July 23, 1759
Launched ▶	May 7, 1765
Commissioned ▶	February 1, 1778
Crew ▶	850 (in 1805)
Rigging ▶	3 masts
Displacement ▶	3,900 tons
Speed ▶	8–9 knots
Cost ▶	£ 63,176

Bowsprit

Figurehead
The 1803 restoration included two cupids, one with a blue sash (symbolizing the love of God) and the other with a red sash (symbol of wisdom).

▲ **HMS** *Rodney*
Royal Navy battleship in action during World War II
(1943), firing its 16-in (406-mm) guns.

BATTLESHIPS

Constant technological innovation from the nineteenth century on led to major changes in warships in a relatively short period of time. Sails and masts made way for steam engines, and wooden hulls were replaced with almost indestructible metal structures. The eighteenth-century iron and bronze cannons mounted on gun carriages became breech-loading guns, which no longer fired heavy metal balls, but rather explosive shells. Warships, therefore, had to be capable of not only inflicting serious damage on enemy ships, but also of protecting themselves from similar attacks. All the world powers began to incorporate new and remarkable ships into their fleets, which became floating fortresses where the artillery, with its increasing range and precision, was located above deck, and not below.

The first ironclad battleship was built by the French: *Gloire*, launched in 1859, carried a steam engine, six boilers, and a six-blade propeller, and her hull was protected with 4.7-in (120-mm) and 2.95 in (75-mm) iron plates in her center and at either end, respectively. She displaced 6,230 tons and had a complement of 570 men, but in just 20 years was rendered obsolete. Something similar was the case for the 1860 English battleship HMS *Warrior*, an armored frigate with an iron hull, which has been moored in Portsmouth, England, as a naval museum since 1987. Sharing the same fate in the Japanese port of Yokosuka is a warship considered to be the best in history at maritime warfare, the battleship *Mikasa*, built in England to Japanese specifications. Launched in 1900, she had a crew of 860 men and was propelled by triple-expansion steam engines, which displaced more than 15,300 tons. Armed with multiple guns: two twin 12-in (305-mm) caliber, fourteen 6-in (152-mm), twenty 3-in (76-mm), twelve 1.9-in (47-mm); plus four 18-in (457-mm) torpedo tubes, she was highly effective in the 1904–05 Russo-Japanese War.

The *Mikasa*'s guns were still smoking when a battleship was launched in England that would once again completely change the rules of naval warfare. HMS *Dreadnought* of the British Royal Navy astounded the world when she entered service in 1906 with two fundamental innovations: heavy guns of a uniform caliber (ten 12-in/305-mm guns on five turrets) and a steam-turbine propulsion system. This ship began an arms race that would continue for decades and in which the United States, Russia, England, France, Holland, Italy, and Germany would all take part. Navies all over the world competed in battleship construction. Just 30 years later saw the launch (and sinking eight months later) of the *Bismarck*, the largest warship ever built by Germany, which in the Battle of the Denmark Strait (1941) sank the British battlecruiser HMS *Hood* and seriously damaged the battleship HMS *Prince of Wales*. After World War II, despite the superiority of aircraft and the development of aircraft carriers, which put an end to naval combat based on dueling artillery, the days of the battleships, battlecruisers, destroyers, and torpedo ships weren't yet finished.

The Battleship *Mikasa*

In 1896, Japan launched a naval expansion program that was to last ten years. It turned to Great Britain, France, and Italy, for the construction of its fleet, which consisted primarily of large armored warships known as battleships. The *Mikasa* was the sixth to be built in England and one of the best warships of her time. As flagship of Admiral Tōgō, she was decisive in the naval battles at Port Arthur and Tsushima, contributing to Japan's victory in the Russo-Japanese War of 1904–05.

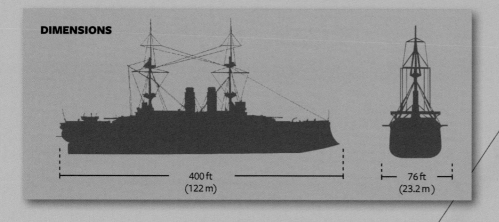

DIMENSIONS

400 ft
(122 m)

76 ft
(23.2 m)

Bridge
The nerve center of the battleship, this was where the officers met to take decisions.

Main guns
Fitted with two steel twin guns, one at the bow and the other at the stern. Capable of firing three 12-in/305-mm (40 caliber) shells every two minutes, with a range of 6 miles (10 km). The forward turret was operated by 40 men and protected with 13.8-in (35-cm) armor.

Emblem
The Imperial Seal of Japan, the golden chrysanthemum, was displayed on the prow of the ship.

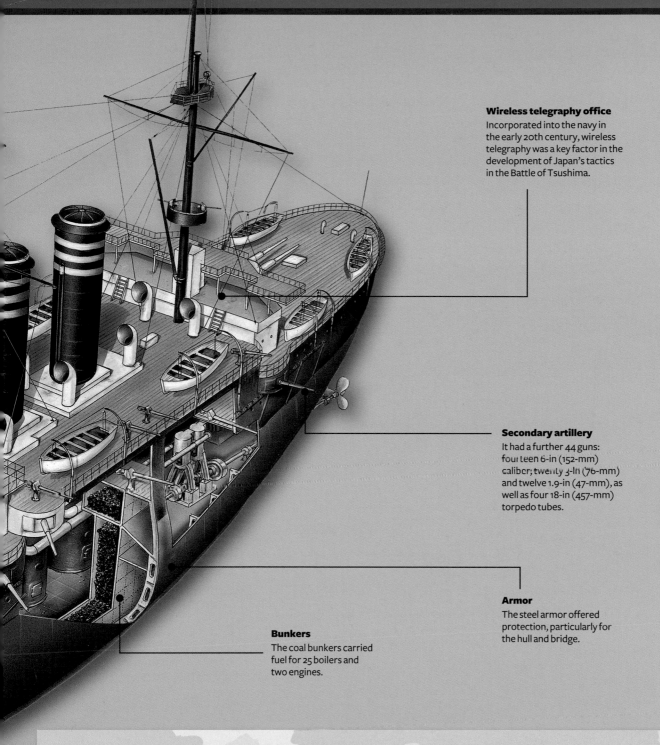

Wireless telegraphy office
Incorporated into the navy in the early 20th century, wireless telegraphy was a key factor in the development of Japan's tactics in the Battle of Tsushima.

Secondary artillery
It had a further 44 guns: fourteen 6-in (152-mm) caliber; twenty 3-in (76-mm) and twelve 1.9-in (47-mm), as well as four 18-in (457-mm) torpedo tubes.

Armor
The steel armor offered protection, particularly for the hull and bridge.

Bunkers
The coal bunkers carried fuel for 25 boilers and two engines.

Shipyard ▸ Vickers, Barrow-in-Furness (England)	**Struck ▸** 1923. Preserved as a museum ship in 1926	**Propulsion ▸** 2 propellers; 25 Belleville boilers; 2 triple-expansion engines
Type ▸ Battleship class Mikasa	**Crew ▸** Up to 860	**Armor ▸** 9 in (230 mm)
Laid down ▸ January 24, 1899	**Normal displacement ▸** 16,950 tons	**Fuel capacity ▸** 780 tons of coal (1,750 max.)
Launched ▸ November 8, 1900	**Speed ▸** 18 knots	
Commissioned ▸ March 1, 1902	**Power ▸** 15,000 shp	

Dreadnought Battleships

In 1906, the British Navy revolutionized military naval technology with the construction of a new kind of battleship: HMS *Dreadnought*. She was the first to have a system of steam turbines, making her the fastest boat of her time. She was also the first to have a main battery of large-caliber uniform guns, giving her heavy, long-range firepower. From this moment onward, ships of this type came to be known by the generic name "dreadnought."

Shipyard ▸ Portsmouth (England)	**Decommissioned** ▸ March 31, 1920	**Propulsion** ▸ 18 Babcock & Wilcox boilers; 4 Parsons steam turbines; 4 propellers
Type ▸ Dreadnought-class battleship	**Crew** ▸ Up to 773	**Power** ▸ Up to 23,000 shp
Laid down ▸ October 2, 1905	**Weight** ▸ 23,200 tons	**Range** ▸ 6,620 nautical miles (12,260 km) at 10 knots
Launched ▸ February 10, 1906	**Displacement** ▸ 19,960 tons	
Commissioned ▸ December 2, 1906	**Maximum speed** ▸ 21 knots	

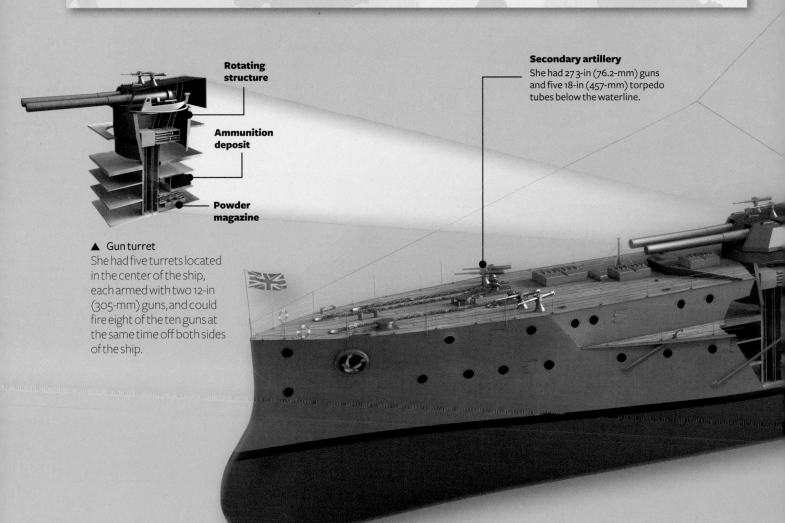

Rotating structure

Ammunition deposit

Powder magazine

Secondary artillery
She had 27 3-in (76.2-mm) guns and five 18-in (457-mm) torpedo tubes below the waterline.

▲ Gun turret
She had five turrets located in the center of the ship, each armed with two 12-in (305-mm) guns, and could fire eight of the ten guns at the same time off both sides of the ship.

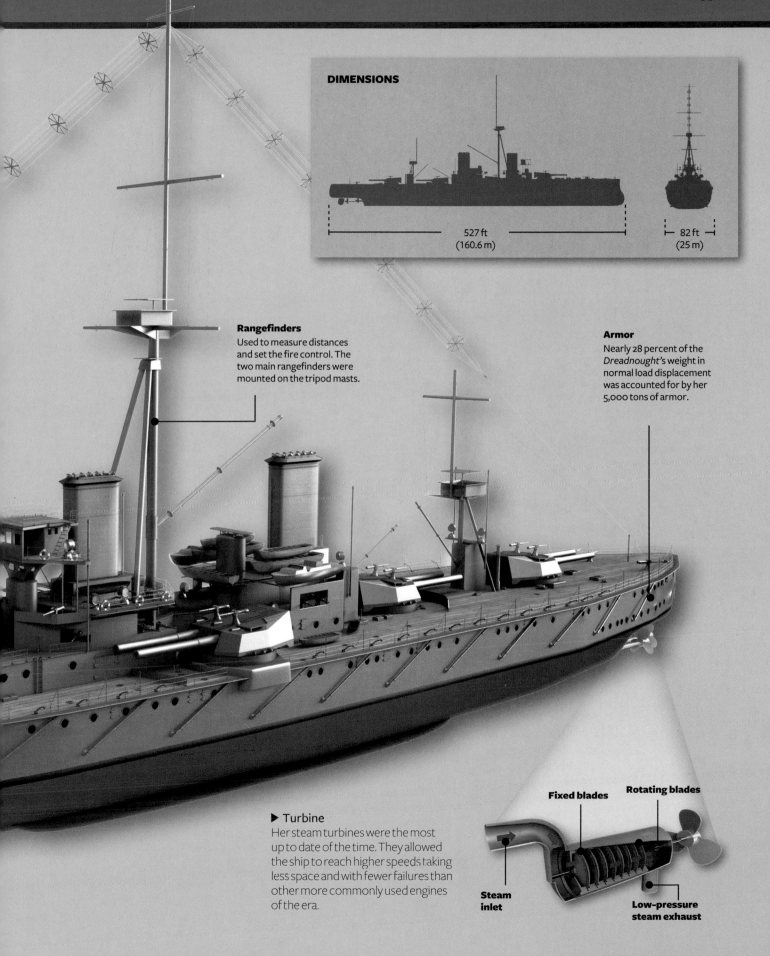

DIMENSIONS

527 ft
(160.6 m)

82 ft
(25 m)

Rangefinders
Used to measure distances and set the fire control. The two main rangefinders were mounted on the tripod masts.

Armor
Nearly 28 percent of the *Dreadnought*'s weight in normal load displacement was accounted for by her 5,000 tons of armor.

▶ Turbine
Her steam turbines were the most up to date of the time. They allowed the ship to reach higher speeds taking less space and with fewer failures than other more commonly used engines of the era.

Fixed blades

Rotating blades

Steam inlet

Low-pressure steam exhaust

Battleship *Bismarck*

The *Bismarck* was the largest ship of the Kriegsmarine, the navy of the Third Reich. Her armor and armament made her the most powerful battleship of her time. Her life, however, was short. She took part in just one operation, the *Rheinübung* (May 1941) with the mission of destroying the Allied convoys that were traveling between North America and the United Kingdom. She sank the British battlecruiser HMS *Hood* and caused damage to HMS *Prince of Wales*. Soon after, however, after a three-day pursuit by the British navy, she was sunk.

DIMENSIONS

823 ft 6 in
(251 m)

118 ft
(36 m)

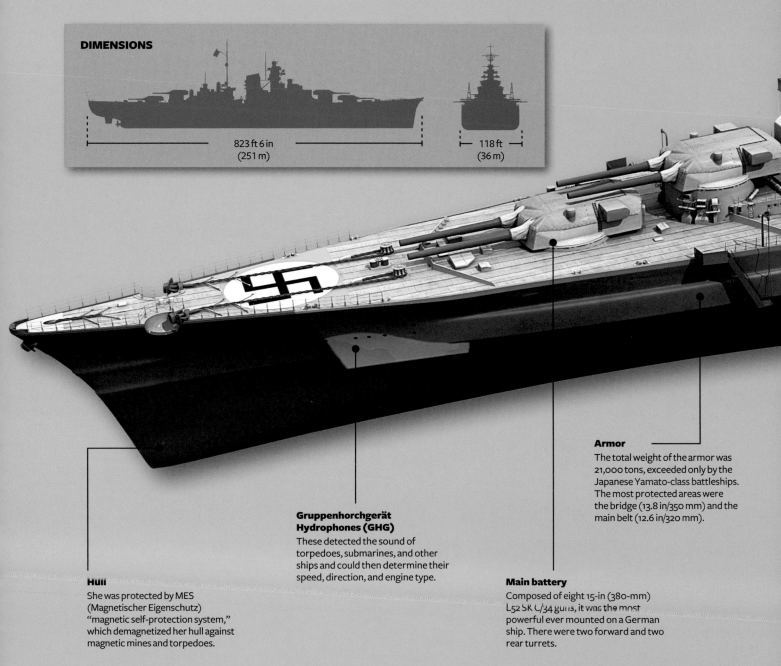

Armor
The total weight of the armor was 21,000 tons, exceeded only by the Japanese Yamato-class battleships. The most protected areas were the bridge (13.8 in/350 mm) and the main belt (12.6 in/320 mm).

Gruppenhorchgerät Hydrophones (GHG)
These detected the sound of torpedoes, submarines, and other ships and could then determine their speed, direction, and engine type.

Hull
She was protected by MES (Magnetischer Eigenschutz) "magnetic self-protection system," which demagnetized her hull against magnetic mines and torpedoes.

Main battery
Composed of eight 15-in (380-mm) L52 SK C/34 guns, it was the most powerful ever mounted on a German ship. There were two forward and two rear turrets.

Bridge (command posts)
Located forward, aft, and on the maintop, they commanded the main and secondary artillery fire. They had an optical rangefinder and radar.

Antiaircraft battery
Comprising: sixteen 4.1-in (105-mm) guns, sixteen 1.5-in (37-mm) guns, and twelve 0.8-in (20-mm) guns.

Secondary battery
The secondary armament was formed by twelve 5.9-in (150-mm) L55 SK C/28 guns (arranged in six twin-gun turrets).

▲ **Arado Ar 196 A3 floatplanes**
She carried four reconnaissance floatplanes, which were launched using a 105-ft (32-m) long twin catapult system, which could be telescopically extended to 157 ft 6 in (48 m).

Shipyard ▶ Blohm & Voss (Hamburg)	**Sunk** ▶ May 27, 1941	**Standard displacement** ▶ 46,000 tons
Type ▶ Bismarck-class battleship	**Crew** ▶ 2,065 (more than 2,200 during Operation Rheinübung)	**Maximum speed** ▶ 30.5 knots
Laid down ▶ July 1, 1936		**Propulsion** ▶ 12 Wagner boilers, 3 Blohm & Voss steam turbines, 3 three-blade propellers
Launched ▶ February 14, 1939	**Weight** ▶ 56,000 tons	
Commissioned ▶ August 24, 1940	**Fuel capacity** ▶ 8,700 tons	
	Draft ▶ 30 ft 6 in (9.3 m)	

▲ **USS** *Nautilus*
The first nuclear-powered submarine (launched in 1954) photographed off the coast of New York.

SUBMARINES AND AIRCRAFT CARRIERS

The incorporation of the torpedo into naval artillery in the nineteenth century was a key factor in the development of submarines, which evolved parallel to aircraft and aircraft carriers. These lethal "ship hunters" once again changed the rules of maritime warfare and contributed to the emergence of state-of-the-art weapons and detection systems. The first to be used by the military, designed by Frenchman Brutus Amédée Villeroi, was the USS *Alligator*, which fought in the American Civil War and disappeared in 1863, seven years before Jules Verne wrote his novel *20,000 Leagues Under the Sea*. A quarter of a century later, the Irish engineer John Philip Holland designed one that was purchased by the United States, Russia, the United Kingdom, and Japan. It had two engines—an internal combustion engine for surface navigation and an electric, battery-powered engine for submerged operations. A decade later, the French submarine *Aigrette* was already using a diesel engine for the surface and, after this model, 74 had been built before 1914. Between 1939 and 1945, the German navy lost 785 submarines, including the *U-47*, which had sunk thirty enemy ships in just two years and disappeared in 1941 in a joint attack by two English corvettes.

In 1942, with the construction in the United States of the first nuclear reactor (the Manhattan Project), military engineering turned its sights toward this form of energy, and in 1954 the first nuclear-powered submarine was launched, USS *Nautilus*, in service until 1980. In 1957, it was the first to reach 60,000 submerged nautical miles (Jules Verne's 20,000 leagues) and to navigate under the Arctic ice cap in 1958. Today, it is a museum-boat in Groton (Connecticut), where, during World War II, a submarine was built every two weeks.

Just seven years after the invention of the airplane came the first experimental takeoff from the deck of a ship. It was in 1910 on the North American battlecruiser USS *Birmingham* (CL-2), and marked the beginning of a new era in naval warfare—that of the aircraft carriers. The most powerful weapon of any army, their initial development was led by the United States, Great Britain, and Japan. The first were designed using the structures of battlecruisers or battleships, although the Japanese carrier *Hōshō*, launched in 1921, would soon become the standard model to follow. These enormous war machines, which evolved at the same speed as the aircraft they carried, played a crucial role in World War II and have always been equipped with the most cutting-edge technology of their time, making them the most powerful command ships. In 1960, the first nuclear-powered aircraft carrier was launched, the USS *Enterprise* (CVN-65), and in 1976 the first Nimitz class entered into service: the USS *Nimitz* (CVN-68), one of the largest in the world, and still active. Propelled by two Westinghouse A4W nuclear reactors, it has the most up-to-date radars and guidance systems, countermeasure and antitorpedo electronic warfare equipment, and a practically unlimited range. It is the flagship of a battle group that also includes four destroyers, and carries ninety planes and a helicopter squadron. The United States has ten Nimitz aircraft carriers, which will gradually be replaced after 2015 by those of a new class.

Submarine *U-47*

German World War II submarines, known as "U-boats," were a formidable enemy for the Allied fleets between 1939 and 1943. Despite their relatively low speed, armed with torpedo launchers and mines, their tactic of attacking in groups was deadly. The most famous is the *U-47*. Before being sunk in 1941, this submarine, commanded by Günther Prien, sank around 30 Allied ships (almost 165,000 tons), including in 1939, the battleship HMS *Royal Oak* , anchored in the British navy base at Scapa Flow.

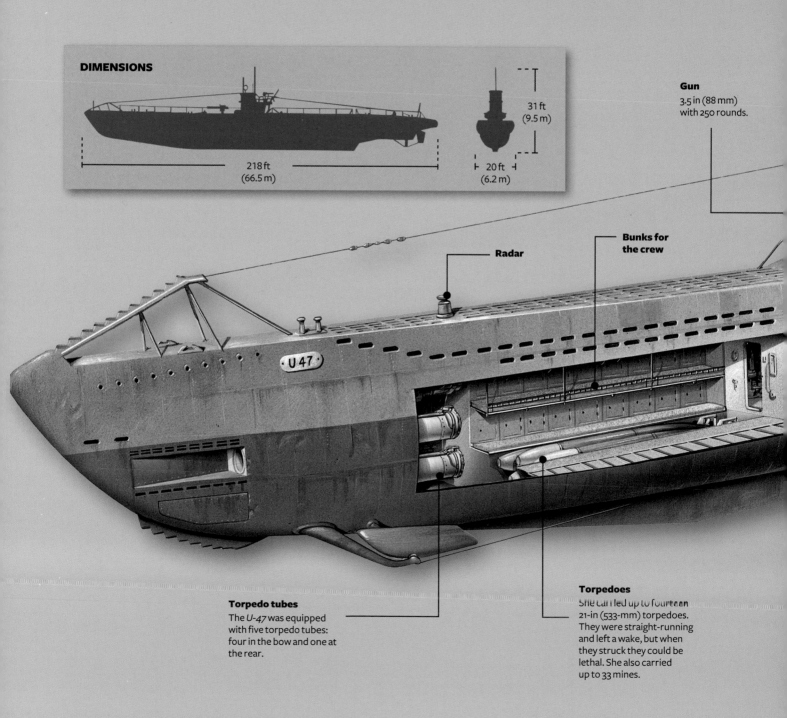

DIMENSIONS

218 ft
(66.5 m)

31 ft
(9.5 m)

20 ft
(6.2 m)

Gun
3.5 in (88 mm)
with 250 rounds.

Radar

**Bunks for
the crew**

U 47

Torpedo tubes
The *U-47* was equipped
with five torpedo tubes:
four in the bow and one at
the rear.

Torpedoes
She carried up to fourteen
21-in (533-mm) torpedoes.
They were straight-running
and left a wake, but when
they struck they could be
lethal. She also carried
up to 33 mines.

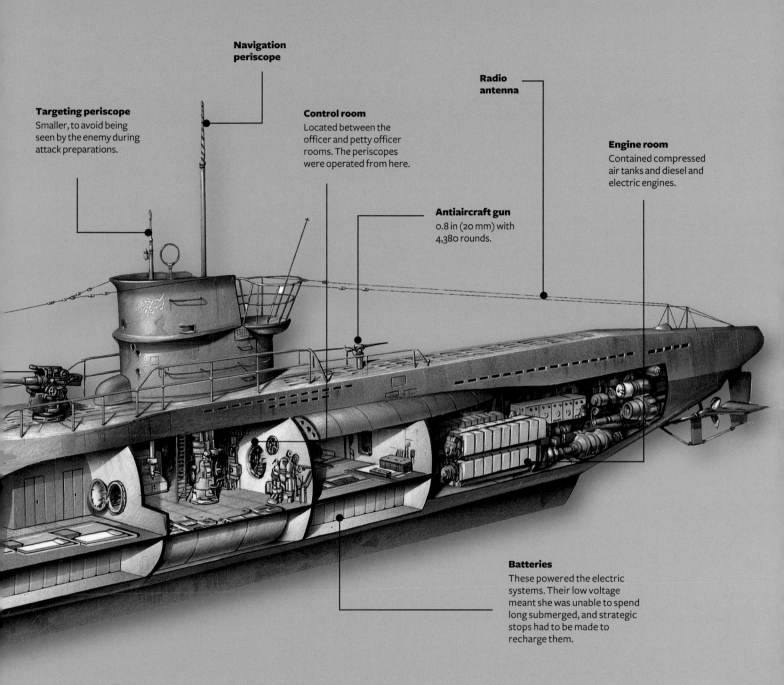

Navigation periscope

Targeting periscope
Smaller, to avoid being seen by the enemy during attack preparations.

Control room
Located between the officer and petty officer rooms. The periscopes were operated from here.

Radio antenna

Engine room
Contained compressed air tanks and diesel and electric engines.

Antiaircraft gun
0.8 in (20 mm) with 4,380 rounds.

Batteries
These powered the electric systems. Their low voltage meant she was unable to spend long submerged, and strategic stops had to be made to recharge them.

Shipyard ▸ F Krupp Germaniawerft AG (Kiel)	**Crew** ▸ 4 officers and 35–40 sailors (in 1939)	**Propulsion** ▸ 2 MAN M6V diesel engines; 2 AEG electric engines; 2 three-blade propellers
Type ▸ Type VII B Oceangoing submarine	**Standard displacement** ▸ 830 tons; 944 tons submerged	**Power** ▸ 2 x 1,160 shp
Laid down ▸ February 27, 1937	**Speed** ▸ 17.2 knots (surfaced), 8 knots (submerged)	**Operating depth** ▸ 330 ft/100 m (650 ft/200 m max.)
Launched ▸ October 29, 1938	**Fuel capacity** ▸ 119 tons	**Dive time** ▸ 30–50 seconds
Commissioned ▸ December 17, 1938		
Sunk ▸ Thought to be March 7, 1941		

USS *Nimitz* Aircraft Carrier

The USS *Nimitz* (CVN–68) is the flagship of Strike Group Eleven of the United States Navy. Laid down in 1975, it was the first of ten Nimitz-class aircraft carriers, which form the backbone of the U.S. Navy. Powered by nuclear reactors, they are the largest in the world and the only ships of their kind. They were designed to transport an unusually high number and wide variety of aircraft and are able to remain at sea for long periods of time, supplied by their own planes.

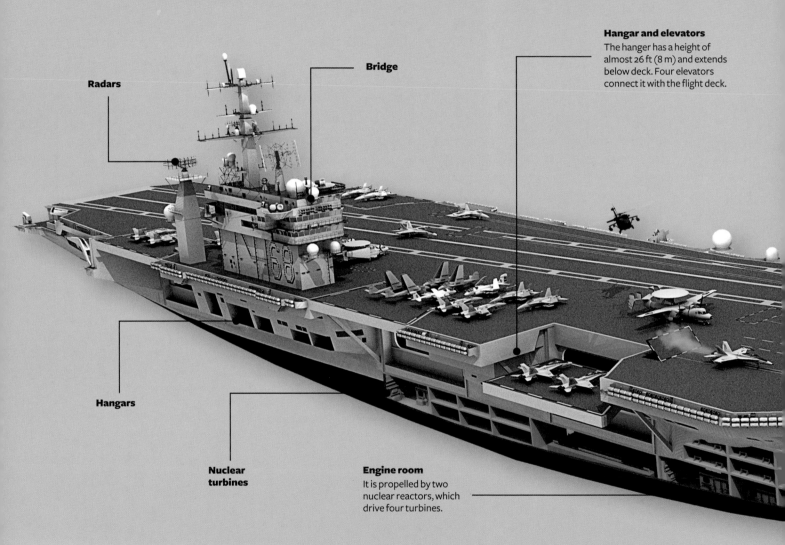

Radars

Bridge

Hangar and elevators
The hanger has a height of almost 26 ft (8 m) and extends below deck. Four elevators connect it with the flight deck.

Hangars

Nuclear turbines

Engine room
It is propelled by two nuclear reactors, which drive four turbines.

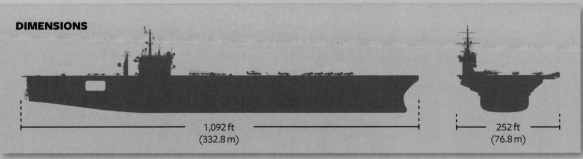

DIMENSIONS

1,092 ft
(332.8 m)

252 ft
(76.8 m)

Shipyard ▸ Newport News Shipbuilding	Commissioned ▸ May 3, 1975	Cruising speed ▸ 31.5 knots
Type ▸ Nimitz-class aircraft carrier	Units built ▸ 10	Propulsion ▸ 2 Westinghouse A4W nuclear reactors; 4 steam turbines; 4 propellers
Laid down ▸ June 22, 1968	Crew ▸ 3,200 plus 2,480 (air wing)	Planes carried ▸ 90
Launched ▸ May 13, 1972	Displacement ▸ 110,250 tons	Power ▸ 260,000 shp (194 MW)

AIRCRAFT CARRIED

McDonnell Douglas F/A-18 Hornet

Sikorsky SH-60 Seahawk

Northrop Grumman E-2 Hawkeye

Northrop Grumman EA-6B Prowler

Grumman C-2 Greyhound

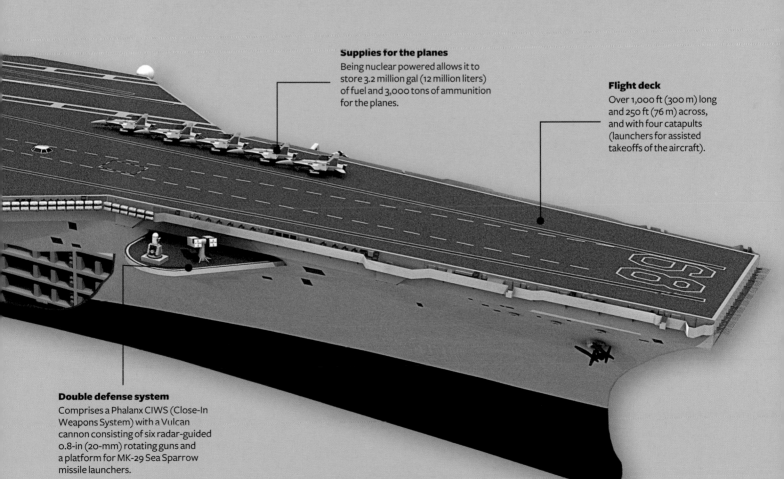

Supplies for the planes
Being nuclear powered allows it to store 3.2 million gal (12 million liters) of fuel and 3,000 tons of ammunition for the planes.

Flight deck
Over 1,000 ft (300 m) long and 250 ft (76 m) across, and with four catapults (launchers for assisted takeoffs of the aircraft).

Double defense system
Comprises a Phalanx CIWS (Close-In Weapons System) with a Vulcan cannon consisting of six radar-guided 0.8-in (20-mm) rotating guns and a platform for MK-29 Sea Sparrow missile launchers.

The Nuclear Submarine

The first nuclear submarines appeared in the 1950s and quickly became a key element in the world's major navies. Nuclear power allowed these modern submarines, armed with medium- and long-range missiles and torpedoes, to have an almost unlimited range, able to submerge to depths of over 820 ft (250 m) for months at a time and maintain a speed of between 25 and 40 knots. There are few countries, however, that can afford to manufacture them.

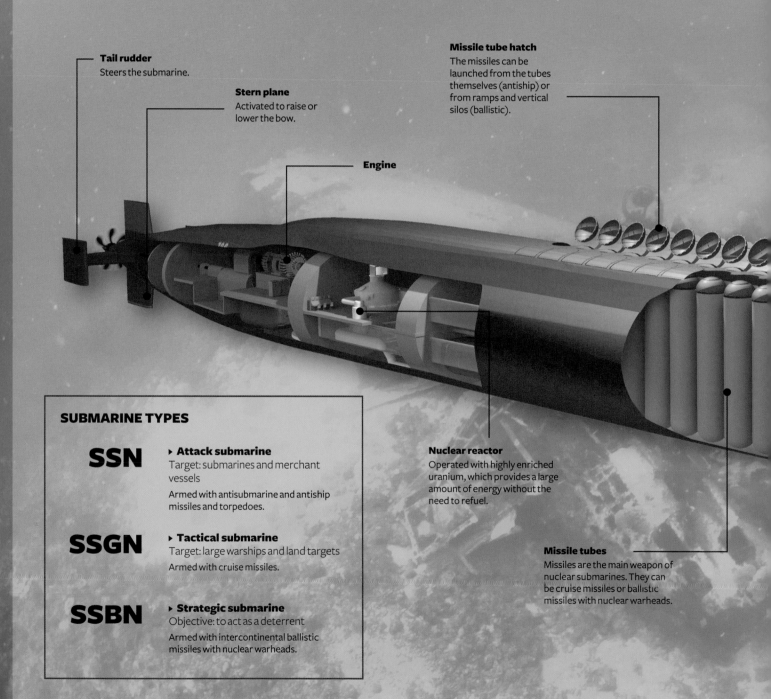

Tail rudder
Steers the submarine.

Stern plane
Activated to raise or lower the bow.

Engine

Missile tube hatch
The missiles can be launched from the tubes themselves (antiship) or from ramps and vertical silos (ballistic).

Nuclear reactor
Operated with highly enriched uranium, which provides a large amount of energy without the need to refuel.

Missile tubes
Missiles are the main weapon of nuclear submarines. They can be cruise missiles or ballistic missiles with nuclear warheads.

SUBMARINE TYPES

SSN
▸ **Attack submarine**
Target: submarines and merchant vessels
Armed with antisubmarine and antiship missiles and torpedoes.

SSGN
▸ **Tactical submarine**
Target: large warships and land targets
Armed with cruise missiles.

SSBN
▸ **Strategic submarine**
Objective: to act as a deterrent
Armed with intercontinental ballistic missiles with nuclear warheads.

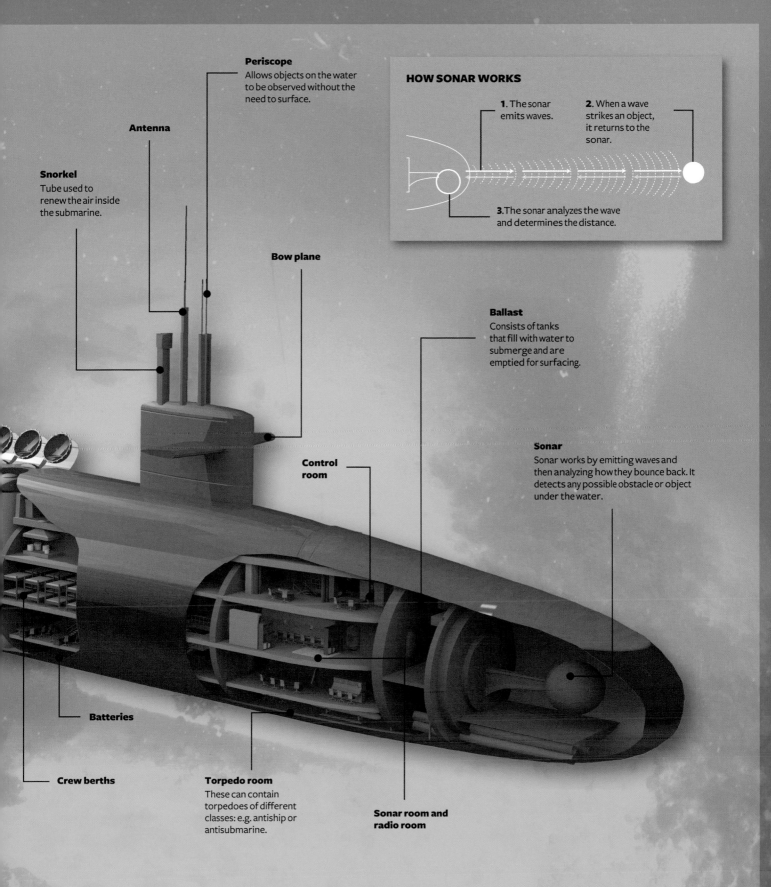

Periscope
Allows objects on the water to be observed without the need to surface.

Antenna

Snorkel
Tube used to renew the air inside the submarine.

Bow plane

HOW SONAR WORKS

1. The sonar emits waves.

2. When a wave strikes an object, it returns to the sonar.

3.The sonar analyzes the wave and determines the distance.

Ballast
Consists of tanks that fill with water to submerge and are emptied for surfacing.

Control room

Sonar
Sonar works by emitting waves and then analyzing how they bounce back. It detects any possible obstacle or object under the water.

Batteries

Crew berths

Torpedo room
These can contain torpedoes of different classes: e.g. antiship or antisubmarine.

Sonar room and radio room

▲ **F-14 Tomcat**
A squadron of U.S. Navy F-14 Tomcat fighter-bombers
during Operation Desert Storm (Gulf War, 1991).

CHAPTER 3
AIR

▲ **P-51 Mustang**
Manufactured by North American Aviation, the Mustang was one of the main Allied fighter aircraft of World War II.

INTRODUCTION

Although aviation and its use in the military has a history of little more than a hundred years, in this short time span development has been as fast as it has been breathtaking. As long ago as the early sixteenth century, the writings and sketches in Leonardo da Vinci's *Codice sul volo degli uccelli* (1505) described how to build a flying machine, and in the seventeenth and eighteenth centuries successful experiments were carried out with hot-air balloons. It was not until after 1900, however, that the skies were truly conquered. The first flying machines were designed and built in the early twentieth century. Capable of being piloted over long distances and based on the same flying principles as the aerostats, they incorporated a propeller and cabin, or gondola, and were known as "airships." Their use in warfare began in 1912, when the Italian army used them for monitoring the Turkish lines. Although they were soon to carry bombs and firearms, their effectiveness as war machines was rapidly eclipsed by developments in aviation. In fact, in the same conflict, airplanes had already been used in 1911, but it was not until three years later, at the outbreak of the Great War, that the first air combat would take place. Among the emerging air forces of the time, these battles came to be known as "dogfights," owing to the absence of rules or tactics. Pilots like the German Oswald Boelcke (1891–1916) or the British Edward Mannock (1887–1918) were the first to develop manuals for aerial combat, which included such recommendations as: only firing at close range and when the opponent is squarely in your sights; not letting yourself be deceived by ruses; or keeping the sun behind you.

By the end of World War I in 1918, the fuselage, size, and armament of airplanes were already being adapted to different activities, and shortly after, different models of bombers, fighters, and reconnaissance aircraft began to appear. Among the first of these were the so-called "dive-bombers," such as the English Swordfish Mk I or the German Ju 87-B Stuka, which carried torpedoes and large bombs for attacking ships and ground targets like gun emplacements or armored vehicles.

In the period between the two world wars, the idea spread among the ruling powers that strategic bombing would prevent a repeat of the horrific butchering caused by trench warfare from 1914 to 1918. Its proponents asserted that the effects bombing would have on civilian populations would force leaders to bring fighting to a swift end. At the time, technology was moving forward in leaps and bounds: aircraft were now metal monoplanes with engine capacities that tripled maximum speeds, and there were notable increases in service ceilings, ranges, and payloads. Air forces were formed among the major powers, which put new machines to the test, like the German Messerschmitt Bf 109, Junkers Ju 52, and Heinkel He 111 and He 51, used to bomb Spanish cities during the Civil War between 1936 and 1939. These strategies would soon be employed on a much larger scale by those countries involved in World War II, which had already begun to manufacture large bombers with between two and four engines, like the United States's B-17 and B-29, the British Avro Lancaster, or the German Junkers Ju 88, capable of dropping several tons of explosives.

After World War II, air forces became an essential element of all armies, and these machines for aerial warfare once again brought changes to military strategy. Attack aircraft, bombers, fighters, as well as cargo or reconnaissance planes, all developed at an astounding pace in just a few years, during which time the idea of air supremacy was based on the effectiveness of the "flying artillery" and its firepower. While dive-bombers

supported the advance of ground troops, in the air the first fighter planes fought one another in great battles that captured the world's attention, like those between the German Messerschmitt 109 and the British Hawker Hurricane during the Battle of Britain. Among the most remarkable aircraft of World War II were the English Supermarine Spitfire, the Japanese Mitsubishi A6M2 Zero fighter planes (used by the kamikaze pilots, literally "divine wind"), and certain bomber escort planes, like the American P-51 Mustang.

After the war was over, during the conflict between the United States and the USSR known as the Cold War—when advanced missile systems could be fitted with nuclear warheads and research was being conducted into atomic aircraft—fewer bombers and more fighter planes were manufactured. The latter became multirole aircraft, designed for air combat as well as ground attacks, like the Soviet MiG, the U.S. F-4 Phantom, or the French Mirage III, and they reached previously unimaginable combat radii, ranges, and flight ceilings. Furthermore, technological changes paved the way for rapid developments in systems

of communication, detection, surveillance, and radar, as well as weapons and aircraft guidance systems. Rather than coming to an end, the unbridled race for air supremacy that began in World War I was stepped up in the 1950s and 1960s and continues to this day.

Warplanes and helicopters—which brought a new dimension to air mobility and very quickly became crucial in aerial deployment—incorporated laser sensors in the 1970s, inertial navigation systems in the 1980s, GPS in the 1990s, and fire and flight control systems after 2000. They are now also equipped with stealth technology (radar-absorbent materials) and signal-jamming systems, and their structures, which were previously made of heavy materials and metals, are now composed of lightweight alloys, fiberglass, and carbon fibers. Today, aircraft like the 2003 Eurofighter Typhoon—which has thrust-vectoring capability and reaches supersonic speeds—or machines like the US V-22 Osprey—a multirole, tilt-rotor aircraft

combining helicopter and turboprop technology, which entered service in 2007—have already incorporated these materials into their structures. Today, with most societies unaccepting of total war and civilian casualties, nations are reformulating the role of air power and developing systems for operating unmanned craft, the so-called "drones" or UAVs (Unmanned Aerial Vehicles), controlled in real time from remote terminals. In recent years, models like the MQ-1C Predator or MQ-9 Reaper have been used in countries such as Bosnia, Iraq, Afghanistan, Yemen, and Pakistan.

▲ **F/A-18 Hornet**
Developed in the 1970s, the F-18 Hornet is a multirole carrier-based fighter of the U.S. Navy and U.S. Marine Corps.

Chronology

In little more than a century, war machines for air combat have developed at a pace as dizzying as the speeds these aircraft can reach today. From the Zeppelin that sailed across the skies of Europe in the first decades of the twentieth century to the state-of-the-art defense systems and air armaments of the twenty-first century, armies and military leaders have seen air supremacy as one of the keys of modern warfare strategy and tactics.

1911
Manufacturing begins of the Gnome Lambda internal combustion rotary engine, which was to be used in World War I.

1934
The first air surveillance radar systems are put to the test.

1921
The Italian general Giulio Douhet publishes the book *The Command of the Air*, which establishes the theory of "strategic bombing."

1942
The Eighth Air Force of the United States arrives in Britain.

1940
Battle of Britain. The first battle waged in the air.

1935
Hitler orders the creation of a new and powerful air force.

1943
Work begins on the first air-to-air missiles: the German Ruhrstahl X-4, which were not used, and the V-2 rockets.

1944
Battle of Leyte Gulf, which sees the first organized kamikaze attacks.

1914
World War I. First bombings by German airships.

1924
Military aircraft from the United States visit 61 cities, thus completing the world's first aerial circumnavigation.

1937
Bombing of Guernica (Spanish Civil War), involving the German Messerschmitt Bf 109, Heinkel He 51, and Junkers Ju 52 warplanes.

The German passenger airship, *Hindenburg*, catches fire in New Jersey.

1941
Japanese attack on the United States naval base at Pearl Harbor.

The first jet engines are built for British aircraft.

1900
First flight of the German airship, Luftschiff Zeppelin LZ 1.

1917
First flight of the German fighter triplane, the Fokker Dr.1.

1929
The German airship, LZ127 Graf Zeppelin, flies around the world.

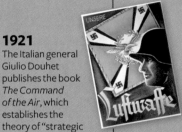

1945
Atomic bombs are dropped on Hiroshima and Nagasaki by B-29 bombers.

1900

"To have a true understanding of the movement of birds in the air we must first understand the wind, which we can do by observing the movements of water. This delicate science will be the key for us to gain an understanding of the volatile relation between the air and the wind."

Leonardo da Vinci, *Codice sul volo degli uccelli* **(1505)**

1950
Korean War, characterized by combat between jet fighters and missiles.

1956
First air-assault operation by the British Army during the Suez Crisis.

1964
The U.S. Congress approves the intervention of the United States in the Vietnam War.

1982
The armed forces of the United Kingdom use Harrier jets during the Falklands War against Argentina.

1995
Entry into service of one of the first UAVs (Unmanned Aerial Vehicles), or combat drone: the MQ-1 Predator.

2007
The first tilt-rotor military aircraft—the Bell-Boeing V-22 Osprey—enters service in the United States.

2011
French, British, and U.S. aircraft begin bombing Libya under the auspices of the United Nations.

1957
The Soviet Union successfully launches *Sputnik 1*, the first artificial satellite to orbit the Earth.

1999
The United States begins to deploy the new Milstar-2 system of military satellites.

Operation Allied Force in Yugoslavia. From May to June, NATO carries out the systematic bombing of Yugoslavian military installations in Kosovo and Serbia.

2013
North American B-2 Spirit bombers take part in maneuvers in South Korea, amid rising tensions with North Korea.

1965
B-52s of the USAF begin the massive bombardment of North Vietnam in Operation Rolling Thunder. The campaign lasts three years.

1990
Gulf War, in which the allied air forces fly over 100,000 sorties.

1959
Discoverer 14 is launched into space, the first spy satellite of the USAF (United States Air Force).

2010

Flying Aces

The term "Ace" was popularly used in France during World War I, when newspapers used it to refer to the pilot Adolphe Pégoud, who was the first to shoot down five German warplanes. Although the methods for assigning victories to air force pilots have changed dramatically since then, the current list of "Flying Aces" includes over 300 pilots who have shot down 20 or more enemy aircraft in battle.

1891–1916

Oswald Boelcke

One of the first German fighter pilots and a brilliant strategist. Considered the father of the German Air Force, he won 40 victories, the first in 1915 with a Fokker E. 1, and created the *Dicta Boelcke*, containing eight rules for victory in aerial combat.

1892–1918

Manfred von Richthofen

Aboard an Albatros D. II and a Fokker Dr. 1 triplane, the world-famous "Red Baron" shot down 80 enemy planes between September 1916 and May 1918, when he was shot down in the north of France, giving him first place among the flying aces of World War I.

1887–1918

Edward "Mick" Mannock

A major in the RAF (Royal Air Force), he was credited with 61 victories in combat in 17 months, making him the best British pilot of World War I. Most of his victories were won in an SE5a fighter plane and he was the author of a manual containing 15 rules for combat.

1913–1985

Alexandr Ivanovich Pokryshkin

Hero of the Soviet Union on three occasions between 1943 and 1944. As well as a pilot he was also the great tactician of the Soviet Air Force during World War II. His contributions to air-combat tactics were fundamental and he reached the rank of Marshal. He shot down 59 enemy aircraft.

Oswald Boelcke

Manfred von Richthofen

Edward "Mick" Mannock

Alexandr Ivanovich Pokryshkin

"For good or for ill, air mastery is today the supreme expression of military power, and fleets and armies, however vital and important, must accept a subordinate rank."

Winston Churchill, Prime Minister of the United Kingdom, days after the end of the Battle of Britain.

1920–1944
Hiroyoshi Nishizawa
Nicknamed the "Demon of Rabaul," he was a lieutenant in the Imperial Japanese Navy Air Service and shot down 86 enemy aircraft, mostly from his Mitsubishi A6M-3 Zero, in just two years. He fought the F4F, six of which he shot down, along with the P-38, P-40, and Corsair. He was killed in a transport plane.

1921–1943
Lydia Litvyak
Recognized as Heroine of the Soviet Union, at 21 she was already the first woman on the list of flying aces, with 12 solo victories and four shared kills. They called her the "White Rose of Stalingrad," and she flew a Lavochkin La-5. She was shot down in the Battle of Kursk.

1922–1993
Erich "Bubi" Hartmann
Nicknamed the "Black Devil" by the Soviets, because of the black tulip painted on the nose of his Messerschmitt Bf 109, he was the commander of the first German jet-fighter squadron. He fought on the Eastern Front, won 352 victories, and went into combat on 825 occasions.

b 1923
Charles Elwood "Chuck" Yeager
Retired brigadier general of the United States Air Force, he was a P-51 Mustang fighter pilot in World War II and the first to break the sound barrier. He became "ace in a day" after shooting down five enemy aircraft in a single day.

Hiroyoshi Nishizawa | Lydia Litvyak | Erich "Bubi" Hartmann | Charles Elwood "Chuck" Yeager

▲ Sopwith Triplane
Between 1916 and 1917 over 140 units of this British fighter were manufactured. Despite its success, it was replaced by the Sopwith Camel.

THE FIRST AIRCRAFT

In the early twentieth century, a new idea spread among the major powers: victory in war would depend on achieving air supremacy. It was the golden age of the great airships, self-propelled, maneuverable aerostats, which had captured the attention of the world. Shaped like a spindle, they had a large metal-alloy cylindrical structure with separate cells filled with gas—at first hydrogen and then helium—a protective fabric envelope, and a "gondola" beneath for the crew. When a German aircraft of this kind— the Luftschiff Zeppelin LZ1— was first used in warfare in World War I, the British had already built a smaller model, the SS (Sea Scout) class airships, which were armed with three or five machine guns and could carry 220-lb (100-kg) bombs. In 1919, a British-made airship, the R-34, was the first to cross the Atlantic, and in 1923, in the United States, the first helium-filled rigid airship was built—the USS *Shenandoah* ZR-1—although by that time fighter planes had already begun to take to the skies, and history's first aircraft carrier had entered service in the United States Navy.

After 1917, an array of aircraft began to be incorporated into the air forces of their respective countries, initially for reconnaissance missions and later for bombing, air-to-air combat, and ground attacks. These included 320 German-manufactured Fokker Dr.1 triplanes, armed with two 0.311-in (7.92-mm) light machine guns, the French Spad S. VII, and the British Sopwith Camel, which had a nine-cylinder, 97kW rotary engine. The Sopwith Camel was probably the best warplane in World War I, although it was the German Albatros D.V biplane that would become the model that subsequent aircraft would follow until the 1940s.

In the late 1930s, aeronautical engineers made swift progress in the design and power of engines used in aviation. In 1937, the year of the *Hindenburg* disaster in New Jersey, the European skies were ruled by what would be the last biplane fighter and the first fighter with an enclosed cockpit: the British Gloster Gladiator, whose SS 37 model was in active service until 1944. In its first version, the MK I, a Mercury IV engine offered a maximum speed of 236 mph (380 km/h), and had two machine guns on the sides of the fuselage and another two drum-fed machine guns beneath the wings. A carrier-based adaptation— called the Sea Gladiator—was specially designed for naval use, and traveled aboard the HMS *Courageous* aircraft carrier in 1939. By that time, however, five years had passed since the inaugural flights of the first monoplane fighters, like the Boeing P-26 Peashooter—the first all-metal production fighter in the United States—or the Soviet Polikarpov I-16, the first with cantilever wings and retractable landing gear, which were introduced in 1934 and withdrawn in 1943, although in some countries, like Spain, they were used until 1952.

Airships

Originally developed toward the end of the nineteenth century, these giants of the skies were first used in warfare during World War I. Germany built an entire fleet of Zeppelin airships, which were used to bomb Britain and France between 1915 and 1917. Although highly vulnerable and not very accurate, when the Zeppelins appeared in the sky they struck fear in the hearts of their enemies. Airships, however, were found to be of better use as reconnaissance aircraft and for naval protection, and were used to such ends by Germany, Great Britain, Italy, France, and the United States.

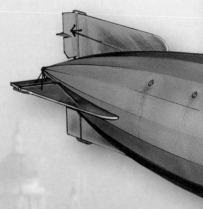

▲ Schütte-Lanz SL 11
This German airship was built from wood and wire. It dropped incendiary and explosive bombs on Britain on September 3, 1916, before being shot down by British planes.

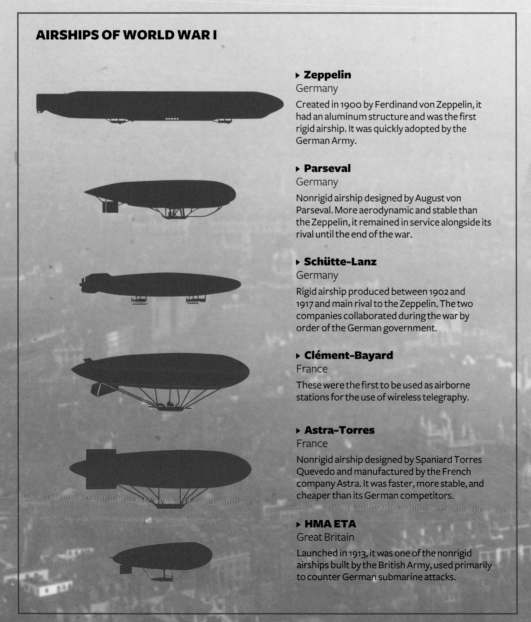

AIRSHIPS OF WORLD WAR I

▸ **Zeppelin**
Germany

Created in 1900 by Ferdinand von Zeppelin, it had an aluminum structure and was the first rigid airship. It was quickly adopted by the German Army.

▸ **Parseval**
Germany

Nonrigid airship designed by August von Parseval. More aerodynamic and stable than the Zeppelin, it remained in service alongside its rival until the end of the war.

▸ **Schütte-Lanz**
Germany

Rigid airship produced between 1902 and 1917 and main rival to the Zeppelin. The two companies collaborated during the war by order of the German government.

▸ **Clément-Bayard**
France

These were the first to be used as airborne stations for the use of wireless telegraphy.

▸ **Astra-Torres**
France

Nonrigid airship designed by Spaniard Torres Quevedo and manufactured by the French company Astra. It was faster, more stable, and cheaper than its German competitors.

▸ **HMA ETA**
Great Britain

Launched in 1913, it was one of the nonrigid airships built by the British Army, used primarily to counter German submarine attacks.

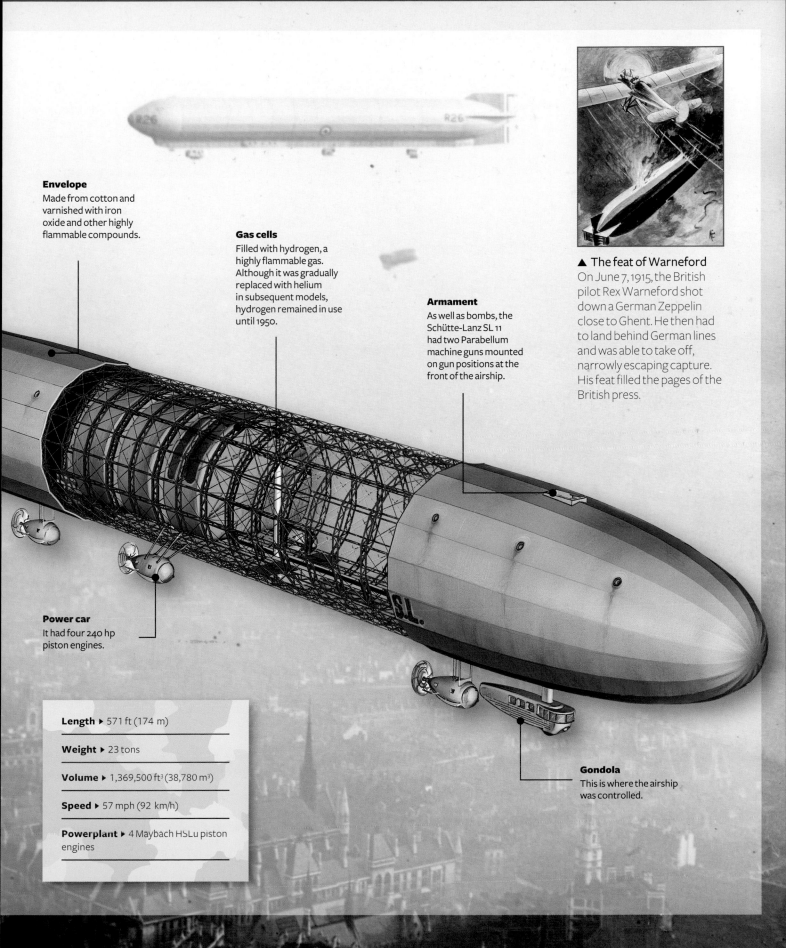

Envelope
Made from cotton and varnished with iron oxide and other highly flammable compounds.

Gas cells
Filled with hydrogen, a highly flammable gas. Although it was gradually replaced with helium in subsequent models, hydrogen remained in use until 1950.

Armament
As well as bombs, the Schütte-Lanz SL 11 had two Parabellum machine guns mounted on gun positions at the front of the airship.

▲ **The feat of Warneford**
On June 7, 1915, the British pilot Rex Warneford shot down a German Zeppelin close to Ghent. He then had to land behind German lines and was able to take off, narrowly escaping capture. His feat filled the pages of the British press.

Power car
It had four 240 hp piston engines.

Gondola
This is where the airship was controlled.

Length ▸ 571 ft (174 m)	
Weight ▸ 23 tons	
Volume ▸ 1,369,500 ft³ (38,780 m³)	
Speed ▸ 57 mph (92 km/h)	
Powerplant ▸ 4 Maybach HSLu piston engines	

Fokker Dr.1

Using a Sopwith triplane captured from the British, the Germans developed their own version: the Fokker Dr.1. The first two were delivered in August 1917 to the squadron of Manfred von Richthofen (known by the Allies as the "Red Baron"), who took one as his personal plane. The other Fokker went to Werner Voss, who shot down 20 planes in 24 days. Its exceptional maneuverability made it ideal for the kind of air combat—dog fighting—that was being waged at the time on the Western Front.

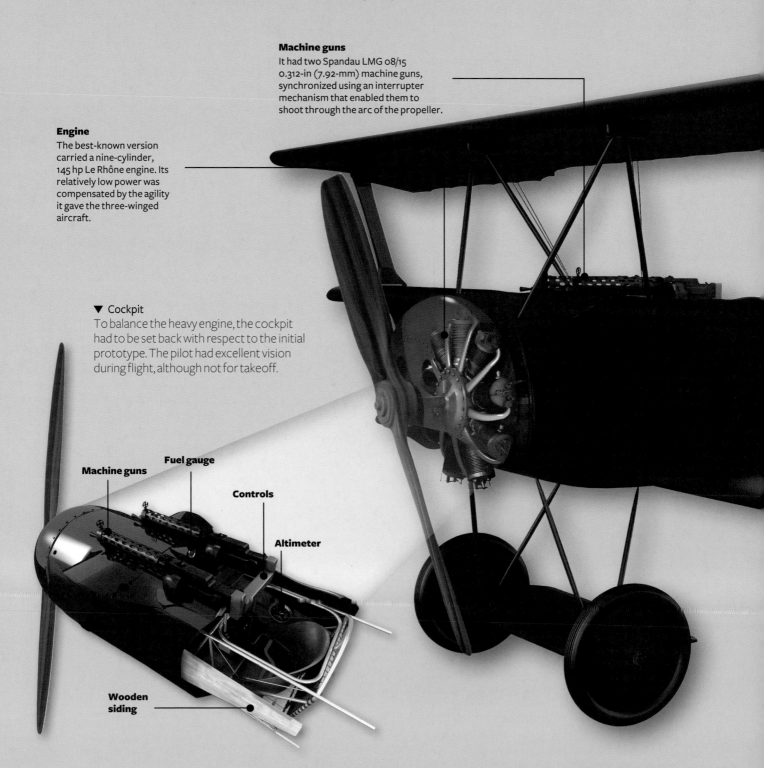

Machine guns
It had two Spandau LMG 08/15 0.312-in (7.92-mm) machine guns, synchronized using an interrupter mechanism that enabled them to shoot through the arc of the propeller.

Engine
The best-known version carried a nine-cylinder, 145 hp Le Rhône engine. Its relatively low power was compensated by the agility it gave the three-winged aircraft.

▼ Cockpit
To balance the heavy engine, the cockpit had to be set back with respect to the initial prototype. The pilot had excellent vision during flight, although not for takeoff.

Fuel gauge

Machine guns

Controls

Altimeter

Wooden siding

Manufacturer ▶ Fokker-Flugzeugwerke, from the design of Reinhold Platz

First flight ▶ August 21, 1917

Entry into service ▶ October 1917

Units built ▶ 318

Crew ▶ 1

Empty weight ▶ Approx. 893 lb/405 kg (depending on the model)

Maximum weight at takeoff ▶ 1,290 lb/ 585 kg (depending on the model)

Service ceiling ▶ 20,000 ft (6,100 m)

Top speed ▶ 115mph (185 km/h) at sea level

Cruising speed ▶ 1,100 ft/min (335 m/min)

Combat radius ▶ 185 miles (300 km)

Range ▶ 1 hour 20 minutes

Powerplant ▶ 1 Oberursel UR II; SHIII; GOE III; UR III or Le Rhône engine (depending on the model)

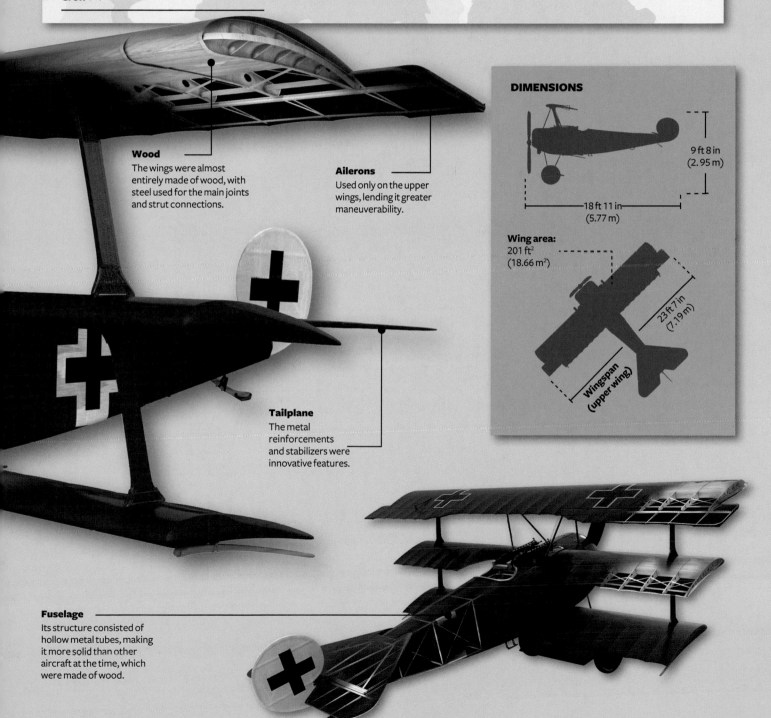

Wood
The wings were almost entirely made of wood, with steel used for the main joints and strut connections.

Ailerons
Used only on the upper wings, lending it greater maneuverability.

DIMENSIONS

9 ft 8 in (2.95 m)

18 ft 11 in (5.77 m)

Wing area:
201 ft² (18.66 m²)

23 ft 7 in (7.19 m)

Wingspan (upper wing)

Tailplane
The metal reinforcements and stabilizers were innovative features.

Fuselage
Its structure consisted of hollow metal tubes, making it more solid than other aircraft at the time, which were made of wood.

Sopwith Camel

Considered by many to be the best Allied fighter plane of World War I, the Sopwith Camel quickly became the aircraft of choice for many flying aces, though its features made it difficult for novice pilots to handle. In the relatively short time it was in service, from July 4, 1917, to November 11, 1918, it brought down no fewer than 2,880 enemy aircraft, a far greater figure than any other plane throughout the conflict.

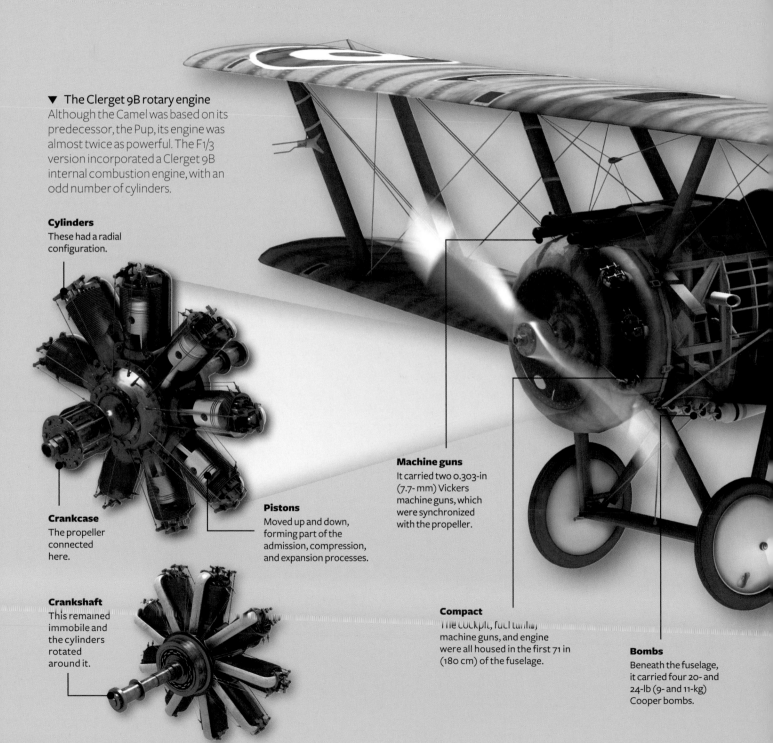

▼ **The Clerget 9B rotary engine**
Although the Camel was based on its predecessor, the Pup, its engine was almost twice as powerful. The F1/3 version incorporated a Clerget 9B internal combustion engine, with an odd number of cylinders.

Cylinders
These had a radial configuration.

Crankcase
The propeller connected here.

Crankshaft
This remained immobile and the cylinders rotated around it.

Pistons
Moved up and down, forming part of the admission, compression, and expansion processes.

Machine guns
It carried two 0.303-in (7.7- mm) Vickers machine guns, which were synchronized with the propeller.

Compact
The cockpit, fuel tanks, machine guns, and engine were all housed in the first 71 in (180 cm) of the fuselage.

Bombs
Beneath the fuselage, it carried four 20- and 24-lb (9- and 11-kg) Cooper bombs.

Manufacturer ▶ British Sopwith Aviation Co. from Herbert Smith's design

First flight ▶ February 1917

Entry into service ▶ July 4, 1917

Units built ▶ 5,940

Crew ▶ 1

Empty weight ▶ 928 lb/421 kg (depending on the model)

Maximum weight at takeoff ▶ 1,453 lb/ 659 kg (depending on the model)

Service ceiling ▶ 19,000 ft/5,790 m (F1 model)

Top speed ▶ 115 mph (185 km/h) at sea level

Rate of climb ▶ 1,093 ft/min (333 m/min)

Combat radius ▶ 290 miles (470 km)

Range ▶ 2 hours 30 minutes

Powerplant ▶ 1 x nine-cylinder Clerget (9B and Z); Le Rhône; GNOHE or BR1 rotary engine

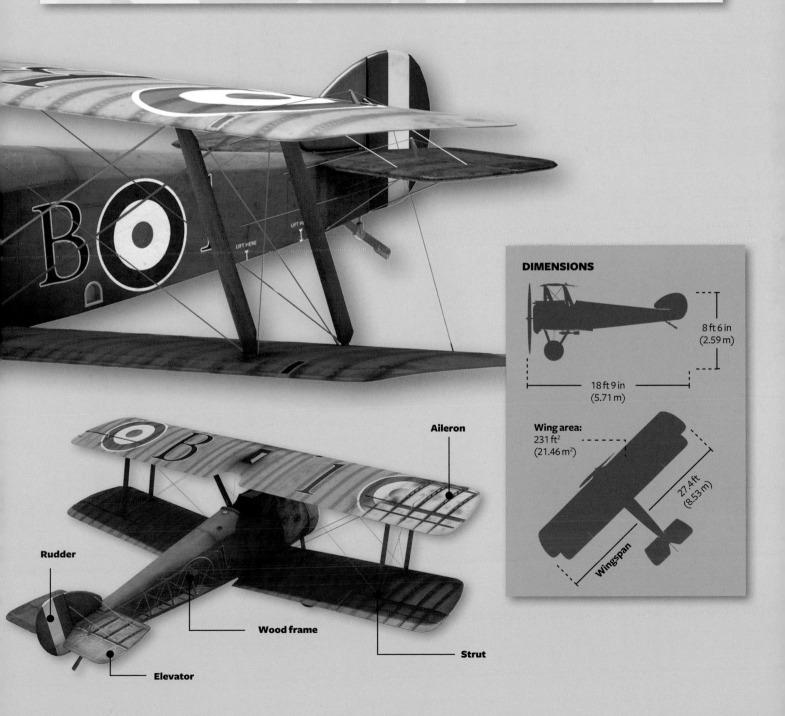

DIMENSIONS

8 ft 6 in (2.59 m)

18 ft 9 in (5.71 m)

Wing area: 231 ft² (21.46 m²)

27.4 ft (8.53 m)

Wingspan

Aileron

Rudder

Wood frame

Strut

Elevator

Gloster Gladiator

This was the last biplane fighter used by the Royal Air Force and the first to be armed with four fixed machine guns. It bridged the gap between the first biplanes and the new monoplanes that were starting to be developed. It entered service in 1937, and in less than a year it was being phased out by the Hurricane. The Gladiators equipped 24 squadrons, two of which were sent to France in 1939, where they were overwhelmed by the German attack of May 1940.

FOR THE SNOW
The wheels of the Gladiator could be replaced with skis for taking off and landing on snow.

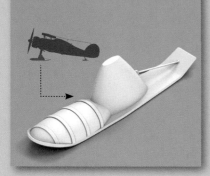

▼ **Bristol Mercury engine**
This nine-cylinder, air-cooled, radial engine could produce over 800 hp. It was the first British engine approved for use with variable-pitch propellers.

Cylinders

Crankshaft

Radial
This kind of internal combustion engine has cylinders in a radial configuration around the crankshaft.

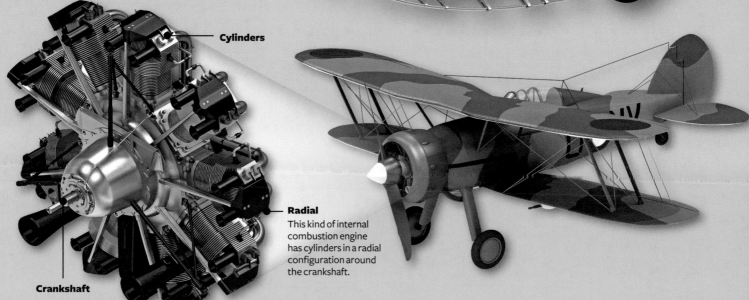

Propeller
On the Mk I version this was a wooden, two-bladed Watts propeller. For the Mk II version, it was changed for a three-bladed Fairey Reed.

Structure
The whole aircraft was built on a structure of metal tubes, which made it more lightweight. It had a canvas covering, with the exception of the metal panels at the front of the fuselage, which could be removed.

DIMENSIONS

11 ft 9 in (3.58 m)

27 ft 5 in (8.36 m)

Wing area: 323 ft² (30 m²)

32 ft 3 in (9.83 m)

Wingspan

Armament
From 1937, it was fitted with four 0.303-in (7.7-mm) Browning machine guns, two of which were mounted on the wings and the other two on the fuselage, unlike the first two versions, which were armed with 0.303-in (7.7-mm) Lewis and Vickers Mk V machine guns.

Manufacturer ▸ Gloster Aircraft Company

First flight ▸ September 12, 1934

Entry into service ▸ 1937

Retired from service ▸ 1953 (1944 from the RAF)

Units built ▸ 480 for the RAF; 216 for export; 60 Sea G versions

Crew ▸ 1

Empty weight ▸ 3,223 lb (1,462 kg)

Maximum takeoff weight ▸ 4,603 lb (2,088 kg)

Service ceiling ▸ 33,000 ft (10,060 m)

Top speed ▸ 235 mph (380 km/h) with Mercury IV engine

Cruise speed ▸ 209 mph (337 km/h)

Range ▸ 460 miles (740 km)

Powerplant ▸ 1 x Mercury radial engine (versions IV, VII, VIII, and IX)

*Data for MK I

Spad XIII C1

Developed from the Spad S. VII, which in itself was considered to be an excellent design, this aircraft performed so well in its test flights that it entered service almost immediately. Its advantages over its predecessor included a larger wingspan and greater firepower and a much more powerful engine. Its quality was appreciated not just by the French, but also by the British, Belgian, Italian, and United States air forces.

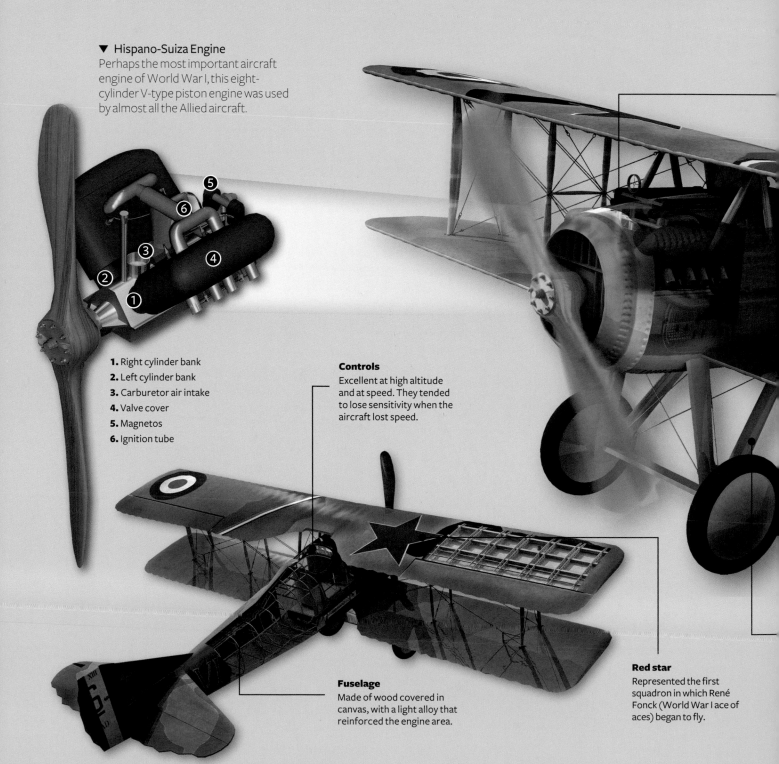

▼ Hispano-Suiza Engine
Perhaps the most important aircraft engine of World War I, this eight-cylinder V-type piston engine was used by almost all the Allied aircraft.

1. Right cylinder bank
2. Left cylinder bank
3. Carburetor air intake
4. Valve cover
5. Magnetos
6. Ignition tube

Controls
Excellent at high altitude and at speed. They tended to lose sensitivity when the aircraft lost speed.

Fuselage
Made of wood covered in canvas, with a light alloy that reinforced the engine area.

Red star
Represented the first squadron in which René Fonck (World War I ace of aces) began to fly.

Manufacturer ▸ Société Pour l'Aviation et ses Dérivés, from the design of Louis Béchéreau

First flight ▸ April 4, 1917

Entry into service ▸ May 1917

Units built ▸ 8,472 (until 1919)

Crew ▸ 1

Empty weight ▸ 1,246 lb (565 kg)

Maximum takeoff weight ▸ 1,814 lb (823 kg)

Service ceiling ▸ 21,815 ft (6,650 m)

Top speed ▸ 140 mph at 6,560 ft (225 km/h at 2,000 m)

Rate of climb ▸ 1,007 ft/min (307 m/min)

Combat range ▸ 171.5 miles (276 km)

Powerplant ▸ 1 x Hispano-Suiza 8-cylinder V-type engine (versions between 200 and 235 hp)

Armament
Fitted with two 0.303-in (7.7-mm) caliber Vickers machine guns, which could fire separately or together.

Stork
This was the insignia of "Les Cigognes," one of the best French fighter squadrons, commanded by René Fonck.

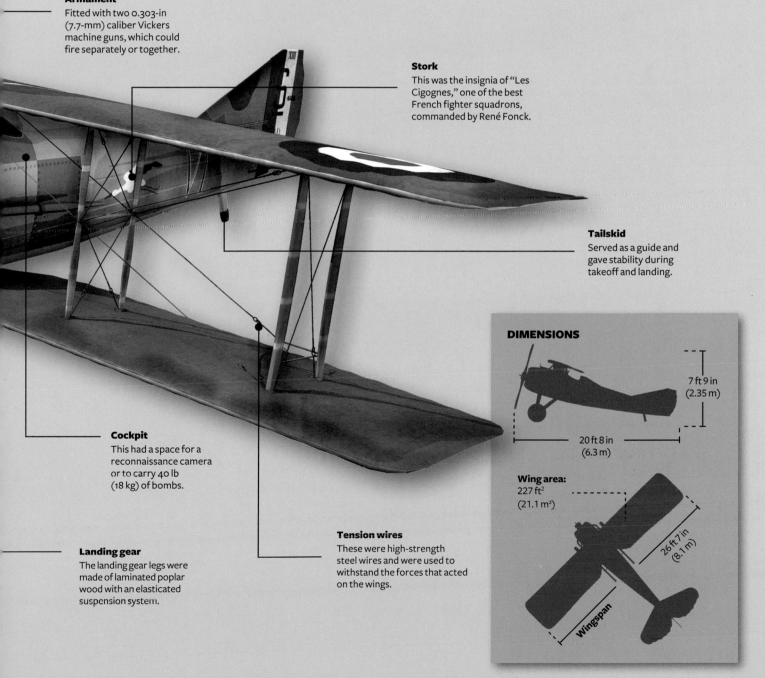

Tailskid
Served as a guide and gave stability during takeoff and landing.

Cockpit
This had a space for a reconnaissance camera or to carry 40 lb (18 kg) of bombs.

Landing gear
The landing gear legs were made of laminated poplar wood with an elasticated suspension system.

Tension wires
These were high-strength steel wires and were used to withstand the forces that acted on the wings.

DIMENSIONS

7 ft 9 in (2.35 m)

20 ft 8 in (6.3 m)

Wing area: 227 ft^2 (21.1 m^2)

26 ft 7 in (8.1 m)

Wingspan

Albatros D.V

At the beginning of 1916, the primary fighter of the German Air Force (*Luftstreitkräfte*), the Fokker E.III, had been surpassed by new Allied aircraft. To regain the initiative, in August of that year the Albatros was entered into action, and went on to become the backbone of the German Air Force. The first three models, D.I, D.II, and D.III, were fast, strong, and had greater firepower than their adversaries. They were followed by the D.IV, which did not enter service for technical reasons, the D.V, and the D.Va—these last two being the most aerodynamic aircraft of World War I.

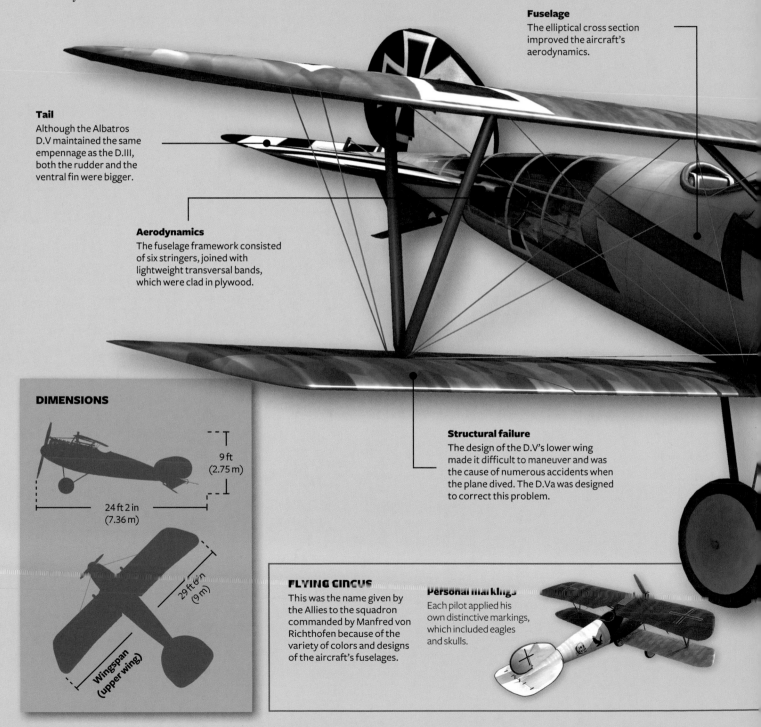

Fuselage
The elliptical cross section improved the aircraft's aerodynamics.

Tail
Although the Albatros D.V maintained the same empennage as the D.III, both the rudder and the ventral fin were bigger.

Aerodynamics
The fuselage framework consisted of six stringers, joined with lightweight transversal bands, which were clad in plywood.

DIMENSIONS

9 ft
(2.75 m)

24 ft 2 in
(7.36 m)

29 ft 6 in
(9 m)

Wingspan
(upper wing)

Structural failure
The design of the D.V's lower wing made it difficult to maneuver and was the cause of numerous accidents when the plane dived. The D.Va was designed to correct this problem.

FLYING CIRCUS
This was the name given by the Allies to the squadron commanded by Manfred von Richthofen because of the variety of colors and designs of the aircraft's fuselages.

Personal markings
Each pilot applied his own distinctive markings, which included eagles and skulls.

Manufacturer ▶ Ostdeutsche Albatros Werke	**Empty weight** ▶ 1,499 lb (680 kg)	**Combat range** ▶ 205 miles (330 km)
First flight ▶ April 1917	**Maximum takeoff weight** ▶ 2,017 lb (915 kg)	**Endurance** ▶ 2 hours
Entry into service ▶ May 1917	**Service ceiling** ▶ 18,700 ft (5,700 m)	**Powerplant** ▶ 1 x 6-cylinder Mercedes D IIIa engine, 180 hp
Units built ▶ 4,800 (of all versions)	**Top speed** ▶ 106 mph (170 km/h)	
Crew ▶ 1	**Rate of climb** ▶ 820 ft/min (250 m/min)	

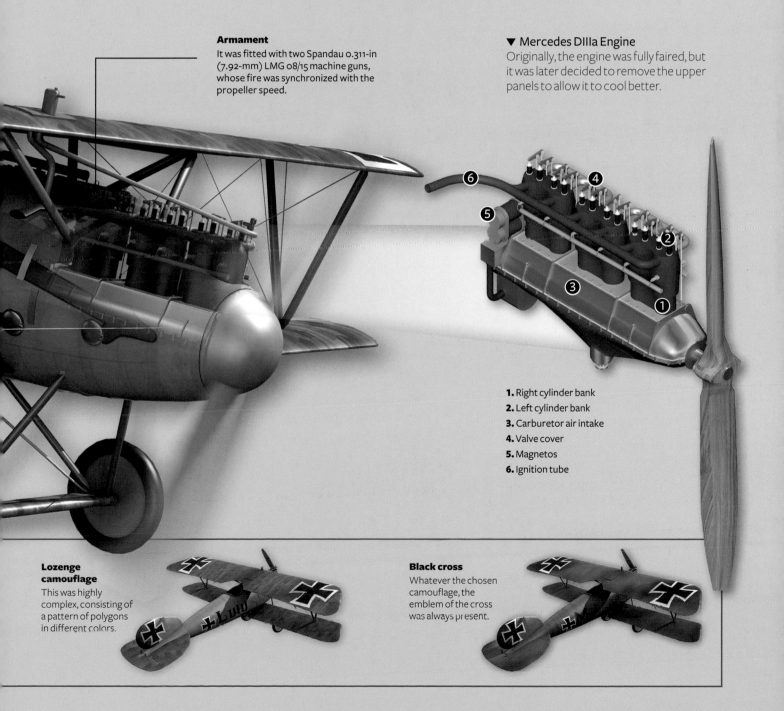

Armament
It was fitted with two Spandau 0.311-in (7.92-mm) LMG 08/15 machine guns, whose fire was synchronized with the propeller speed.

▼ Mercedes DIIIa Engine
Originally, the engine was fully faired, but it was later decided to remove the upper panels to allow it to cool better.

1. Right cylinder bank
2. Left cylinder bank
3. Carburetor air intake
4. Valve cover
5. Magnetos
6. Ignition tube

Lozenge camouflage
This was highly complex, consisting of a pattern of polygons in different colors.

Black cross
Whatever the chosen camouflage, the emblem of the cross was always present.

Aircraft against the Trenches

As World War I progressed, the armies on the Western Front found themselves stuck in a state of endless trench warfare. On these fronts, aircraft were used primarily for reconnaissance missions, and were crucial for revealing enemy troop movements, locating artillery, and directing their own fire.

▶ Air supremacy
The end aim of the air force was to achieve air supremacy, neutralizing enemy aircraft and thereby allowing military operations to progress without enemy interference.

Attacks
As the conflict advanced, reconnaissance planes started incorporating grenades and bombs.

Aerial photographs
Aircraft very soon incorporated cameras, which allowed them to capture aerial images and create a reliable map of enemy positions and movements.

Fighters
These escorted and protected reconnaissance planes while attempting to shoot down enemy aircraft.

Infantry support
Aircraft quickly began to incorporate more and better arms and were able to take part in offensive operations, providing support for ground troops.

▲ **Douglas SBD Dauntless**
Dive-bombers of the U.S. Navy in the Pacific theater, where they participated in several battles from 1941 until the end of the war.

BOMBERS

A century has passed since the first bomb was dropped from an aircraft on November 1, 1911, during the Italo-Turkish War, attributed to the pilot Giulio Gavotti. Since then, the offensive capabilities of these airborne war machines have been the focus of much attention. Their designs have varied to adapt to the changing needs and new demands contemplated in map rooms, on drawing boards, in engineers' workshops, and, of course, in the air, in the heat of battle, where pilots will always gain new knowledge of air combat.

Between 1910 and 1940—when the major nations unreservedly supported the theory of "strategic bombing," which proposed using aircraft to go beyond enemy lines and attack the civilian population directly—warplanes, which had already been used to attack trenches and tanks in World War I, now also became bombers. Four generations of these aircraft can be distinguished: those built between 1913 and 1927; 1928 and 1946; 1947 and 1969; and from 1970 up to the present day. There are also different categories: dive-bombers and light, medium, and heavy bombers. Among the most effective and agile from the second generation were the British Fairey Swordfish Mk I and Mk II, built between 1935 and 1944, which were fitted with a Pegasus III 3M engine and armed with an 18-in (457-mm), 1,612-lb (731-kg) torpedo, and the German Junkers JU-87 Stuka dive-bombers (1936–1944), of which 6,500 were manufactured. These were highly versatile two-seater planes, armed with two 0.311-in (7.92-mm) M617 machine guns on the wings, in which 3,968 lb (1,800 kg) of bombs could also be carried. These were still small aircraft, however, and nothing like the medium and heavy, twin-engine and four-engine bombers capable of carrying and dropping several tons of bombs, which were used by all armies during World War II. Among the most famous of these was the British heavy bomber—the Avro Lancaster, a four-engine bomber with a range of 2,860 miles (4,600 km), capable of carrying 14,000 lb (6,350 kg) of bombs. The Boeing B-29 Superfortress also stands out, the aircraft used most by the United States in the last years of World War II and in the Korean War, designed to fly at high altitudes and used to drop the bombs on Hiroshima and Nagasaki. The B-29 was followed by other versions (the B-47 and B-50), which were active until the end of the 1950s, when they were replaced by the subsonic, long-range, jet-powered strategic bomber: the B-52 Stratofortress.

In the 1970s, the major powers reassessed the role of air power and fewer bombers were built. The number of fighters and multirole aircraft increased, however, and other new and unusual planes were armed, like the Northrop Grumman B-2 Spirit. Introduced in 1997, this strategic, multirole, "invisible" bomber is capable of carrying up to 50,000 lb (23,000 kg) of conventional or nuclear bombs and has a range of more than 6,835 miles (11,000 km).

Fairey Swordfish Mk I and Mk II

The Swordfish was designed in the 1930s. Although obsolete and outdated in appearance, it transpired to be an excellent aircraft for its mission purpose. Its low speed, which made it vulnerable to attack, gave it great stability, allowing it to hold a steady course at low altitude, perfect for launching torpedo attacks while flying beneath the firing line of enemy ships. It was nicknamed the "Stringbag" (after the bags used by British women to do their shopping) because of its capacity to carry a wide variety of armaments.

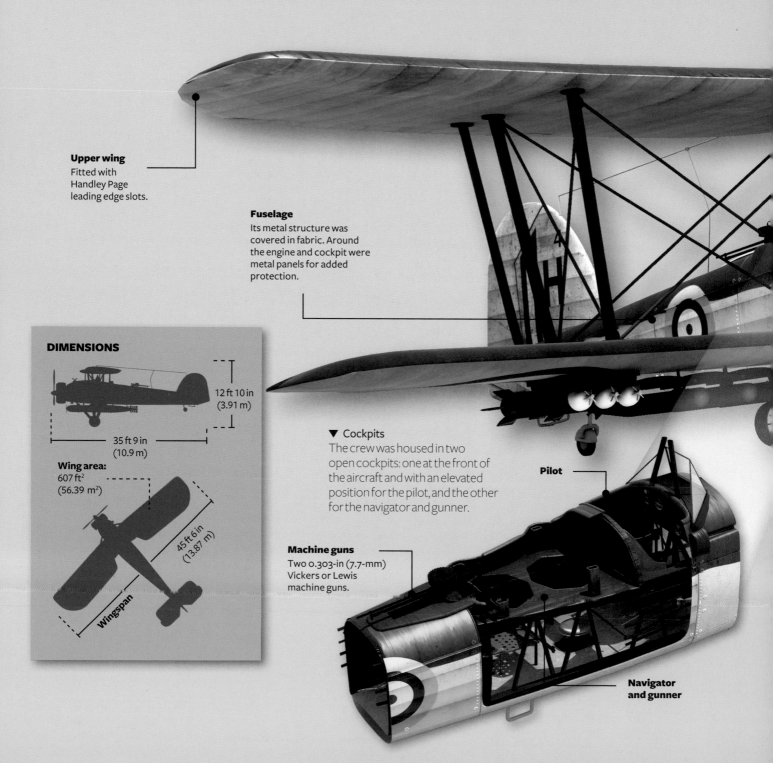

Upper wing
Fitted with Handley Page leading edge slots.

Fuselage
Its metal structure was covered in fabric. Around the engine and cockpit were metal panels for added protection.

DIMENSIONS

12 ft 10 in (3.91 m)

35 ft 9 in (10.9 m)

Wing area: 607 ft² (56.39 m²)

45 ft 6 in (13.87 m)

Wingspan

▼ Cockpits
The crew was housed in two open cockpits: one at the front of the aircraft and with an elevated position for the pilot, and the other for the navigator and gunner.

Pilot

Machine guns
Two 0.303-in (7.7-mm) Vickers or Lewis machine guns.

Navigator and gunner

Manufacturer ▸ Fairey Aircraft Co. Ltd./ Blackburn Aircraft Co. Ltd. from the design of Marcel Lobelle.

First flight ▸ April 17, 1934

Entry into service ▸ July 1936

Units built ▸ 2,391

Crew ▸ 3

Empty weight ▸ 5,200 lb (2,358 kg)

Maximum takeoff weight ▸ 9,248 lb (4,195 kg)

Service ceiling ▸ 15,000 ft (4,570 m)

Top speed ▸ 139 mph (224 km/h)

Rate of climb ▸ 548 ft/min (167 m/min)

Range ▸ 546 miles (879 km)

Endurance ▸ 6 hours

Powerplant ▸ 1 x Bristol Pegasus Mk3 engine, 690 hp, or a Pegasus XXX engine, 750 hp.

Lower wing
Reinforced with metal cladding. On the Mk II this allowed it to carry eight 3-in (76-mm) rockets.

Torpedo Mark XII
It weighed 1,612 lb (731 kg) and was activated when it touched the water. It had contrarotating propellers to allow it to hold a steady course.

Fuel tank
The main 186-gal (705-liter) tank was at the front of the fuselage, with a drop tank housed in front of the cockpit.

▶ **Floatplane version**
Unlike the Mk II, the Mk I had fixed landing gear that could be replaced by two floats.

Junkers Ju-87 Stuka

Their strange and threatening appearance, together with the peculiar howling of their engines, made the Stukas a fearsome presence in the Polish and French skies during the first two years of World War II. The world had already witnessed their power during the Spanish Civil War, when the A and B models were used by the Condor Legion. The Stuka was able to attack even small and moving targets with great precision.

Lever for opening the bombsight window

▶ **Cockpit**
Its two tandem seats were for the pilot-bomber and signaler-gunner. The bomber had a bombsight window in the floor.

Fuselage
Strong and robust, it had an oval cross section and metal structure, consisting of two reinforced sections.

Pilot

Radio equipment

Gunner

Machine guns
Fitted initially with a 0.311-in (7.92-mm) MG-15 machine gun, it later carried an MG-17, and after the D version, two Mauser MG 81Z.

Wings
The inverted gull wings were fitted with air brakes.

Machine guns
It was fitted with a 0.311-in (7.92-mm) Rheinmetall-Borsig MG-17 on each wing, which were later replaced by 0.787-in (20-mm) Mauser MG 151/20 cannons.

Bomb racks
Beneath the wings, its original capacity was for 1,102 lb (500 kg) of bombs, which later increased to 3,968 lb (1,800 kg) in the D and G series.

DIMENSIONS (JU 87B)

12 ft 10 in (3.9 m)

37 ft 9 in (11.5 m)

Wing area: 362.64 ft² (33.69 m²)

49 ft 3 in (15 m)

Wingspan

Manufacturer ▶ Junkers Flugzeugwerke AG from the design of Hermann Pohlmann

First flight ▶ September 17, 1935

Entry into service ▶ 1936

Units built ▶ Approx. 6,000

Crew ▶ 2

Empty weight ▶ 6,085 lb (2,760 kg)

Maximum takeoff weight ▶ Over 8,820 lb (4,000 kg)

Service ceiling ▶ Approx. 26,575 ft (8,100 m)

Top speed ▶ 239 mph at 13,450 ft (385 km/h at 4,100 m)

Rate of climb ▶ 9,850 ft (3,000 m) in 8 min.

Range ▶ 370–500 miles (600–800 km) depending on the load

Powerplant ▶ 1 x Junkers Jumo 211Da engine, 1,200 hp

* Data for JU-87 BII

Fuel
On the wings were two main tanks, each with a capacity of 127 gal (481 liters), and another two 79-gal (300-liter) drop tanks.

Camouflage
This model was used in the French campaign in 1940 and the Balkans campaign in 1941.

Propeller
This was a VS 5 or VS 11, made from plywood. It had three dual-position blades.

Engine
The engine was held to the fuselage by a cantilevered section formed by two high-strength metal beams.

Landing gear
This was fixed with fairing, oleo-pneumatic shock absorbers, and individual brakes.

Jericho Trumpet
This device emitted a sound similar to that of a siren. It was activated at the beginning of a dive and had a psychological impact on enemy troops.

Ventral pylon
A Siemens ETC 500/A for a SC 500 1,102 lb (500-kg) bomb tilted forward and launched the bomb in the desired direction.

Dive-bombers

The height of development for this class of bomber was during World War II, when they were widely used as close support for land troops and the navy. They were designed to be launched at great speed toward a target—military installations, bridges, ships, or tanks—and drop bombs with great precision, exposing themselves briefly to antiaircraft fire.

OTHER WORLD WAR II DIVE-BOMBERS

▸ **Douglas SBD Dauntless**
US–1940

Dive-bomber of the U.S. Navy, it had a major role in the Pacific. It could carry 1,603 lb (727 kg) of bombs under its fuselage and two 324-lb (147-kg) bombs under the wings.

▸ **Aichi D3A**
Japan–1940

Known as "Val" by the Allies, it operated from Japanese aircraft carriers and participated in a large number of operations in the first months of the war, including the attack on Pearl Harbor.

▸ **Yokosuka D4y Suisei**
Japan–1942

The Suisei ("kite" in Japanese), nicknamed "Judy" by the Allies, was known for its speed (max. 343 mph/552 km/h)

▸ **North American A-36 Apache**
US–1942

Known as "Invader," this was the dive-bomber version of the Mustang. It took part in the Italian Campaign and in India.

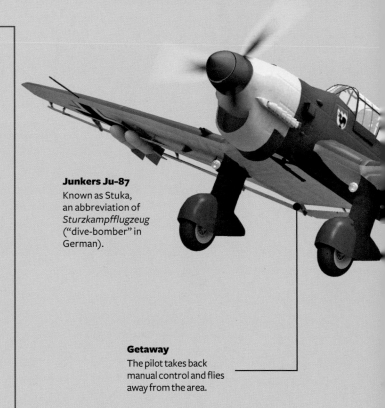

Junkers Ju-87
Known as Stuka, an abbreviation of *Sturzkampfflugzeug* ("dive-bomber" in German).

Getaway
The pilot takes back manual control and flies away from the area.

◂ *Blitzkrieg*
In the invasions of Poland, France, and the Netherlands, the Nazis used the *Blitzkrieg* ("lightning war") tactic, in which the Stukas were crucial.

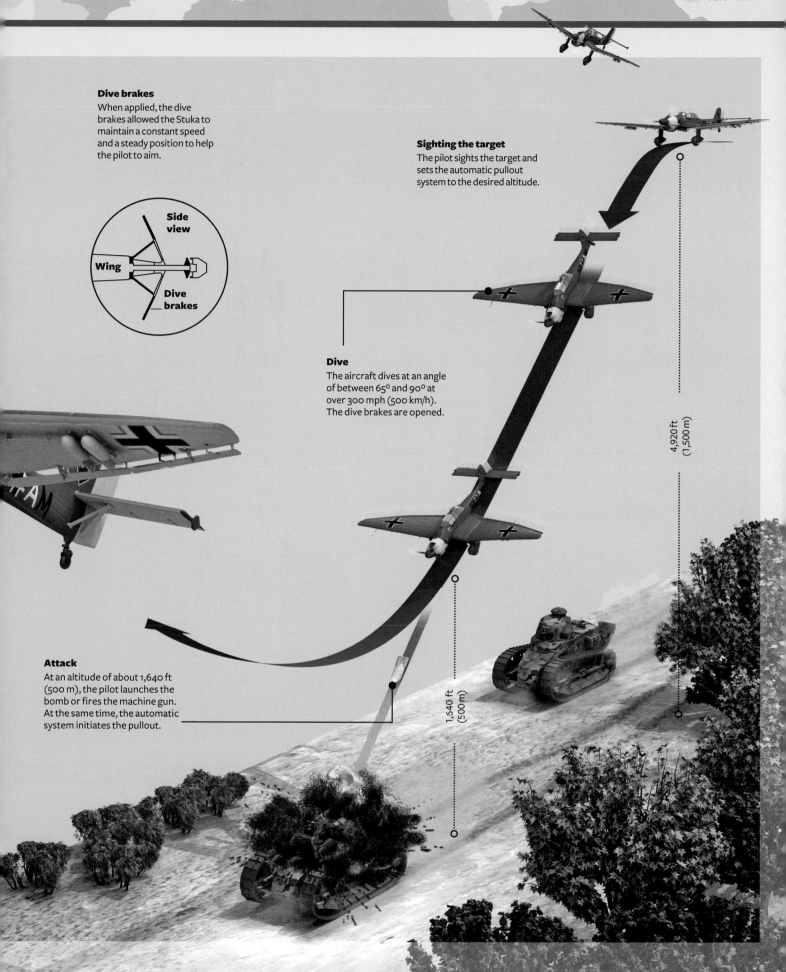

Dive brakes
When applied, the dive brakes allowed the Stuka to maintain a constant speed and a steady position to help the pilot to aim.

Side view

Wing

Dive brakes

Sighting the target
The pilot sights the target and sets the automatic pullout system to the desired altitude.

Dive
The aircraft dives at an angle of between 65° and 90° at over 300 mph (500 km/h). The dive brakes are opened.

Attack
At an altitude of about 1,640 ft (500 m), the pilot launches the bomb or fires the machine gun. At the same time, the automatic system initiates the pullout.

4,920 ft (1,500 m)

1,540 ft (500 m)

Northrop Grumman B-2 Spirit

This aircraft, the most expensive ever built, is a long-range strategic stealth bomber capable of entering enemy territory without being detected. Thanks to its advanced low-visibility technology it can attack heavily fortified targets. Its 136 flight computers are crucial for its automatic stabilization, as it has no tail fin. Designed in the United States during the Cold War for bombing targets in the Soviet Union, it was first used in combat in the Kosovo War in 1999.

DIMENSIONS

Wing area:
5,005 ft²
(465 m²)

17 ft
(5.1 m)

69 ft
(20.9 m)

Wingspan
171 ft
(52.12 m)

Wings
The wing contains most of its structural volume. The wing edges are extremely convex and contribute to the "invisibility" of the B-2.

Wheels
It incorporates three sets of retractable wheels.

▼ General Electric F118 engine
The four engines are mounted on the fuselage in pairs, on both sides of the bomb bays. They were developed especially for the B-2 from the F110 engine.

Nonafterburning
It has no afterburner to avoid heat detection.

Cockpit
Accommodates a pilot and mission commander, with the option of a third crew member. The pilot sits on the port side and the commander on the starboard.

Landing gear
Tricycle landing gear, adapted from the Boeing 757/767. There are four wheels on the main landing gear and two at the front.

Manufacturer ▶ Northrop Grumman Corp	**Empty weight** ▶ 160,000 lb (72,575 kg)	**Cruise speed** ▶ 475 mph (764 km/h)
First flight ▶ July 17, 1989	**Maximum takeoff weight** ▶ 336,500 lb (152,634 kg)	**Combat radius** ▶ 5,965 miles (9,600 km) without refueling; 11,508 miles (18,520 km) with one aerial refueling
Initial operating capability ▶ April 1997	**Service ceiling** ▶ 50,000 ft (15,240 m)	
Units built ▶ 21 (20 operative)	**Top speed** ▶ 569 mph (915 km/h)	**Endurance** ▶ Up to 50 hours
Crew ▶ 2		**Powerplant** ▶ 4 x General Electric F118-GE-100 turbofan engines

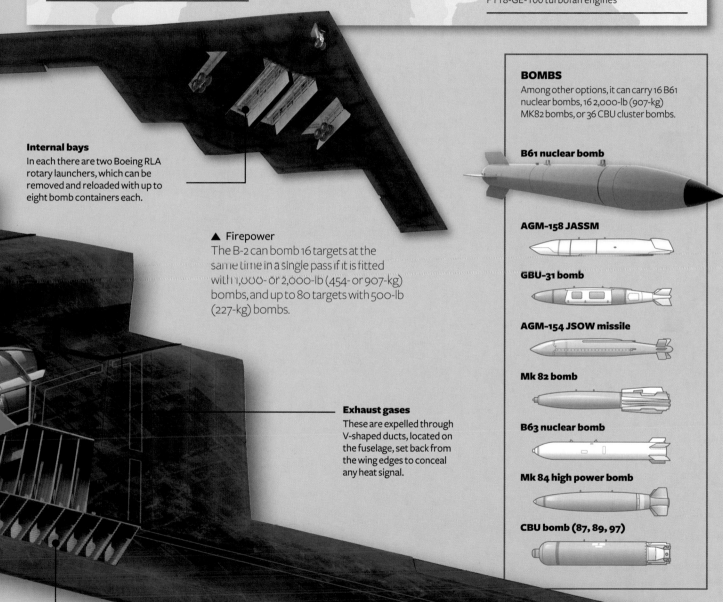

Internal bays
In each there are two Boeing RLA rotary launchers, which can be removed and reloaded with up to eight bomb containers each.

▲ **Firepower**
The B-2 can bomb 16 targets at the same time in a single pass if it is fitted with 1,000- or 2,000-lb (454- or 907-kg) bombs, and up to 80 targets with 500-lb (227-kg) bombs.

Exhaust gases
These are expelled through V-shaped ducts, located on the fuselage, set back from the wing edges to conceal any heat signal.

Structure
To absorb radar waves, the B-2 makes particular use of carbon-graphite composite materials in its structure.

BOMBS
Among other options, it can carry 16 B61 nuclear bombs, 16 2,000-lb (907-kg) MK82 bombs, or 36 CBU cluster bombs.

B61 nuclear bomb

AGM-158 JASSM

GBU-31 bomb

AGM-154 JSOW missile

Mk 82 bomb

B63 nuclear bomb

Mk 84 high power bomb

CBU bomb (87, 89, 97)

Strategic bombers

Strategic bombers sought to destroy the enemy's capacity to stay in the war. Their targets therefore were not only military facilities but also the enemy's infrastructure, industry, and even its cities, with the aim of destroying morale, too. Examples of this were the World War II bombings on Germany and occupied Europe after 1942, which involved thousands of British and U.S. bombers, including the B-17 of the Eighth Air Force of the USAAF (U.S. Army Air Force, predecessor of the USAF).

B-17 Flying Fortress
This was a four-engine heavy bomber, one of the most famous of the USAAF and also used by the RAF. Its powerful defensive armament (up to 13 .50-caliber machine guns) gave it the name "Flying Fortress."

▲ **Formation flying**
The B-17 flew in formation, in close proximity to one another, to give mutual support. The groups could consist of hundreds of planes.

THE USAAF IN BRITAIN
The U.S. Eighth Air Force, including B-17 bombers, arrived in Britain in 1942 to join the British Royal Air Force in the air campaigns against Germany and occupied Europe. In 1943, the Allied Combined Bomber Offensive was put into operation, which set the targets for the Allied strategic bombers. The aircraft of the RAF bombed at night and the USAAF during the day.

Preparations
The crew of a B-17 F in a base in Britain prepares the bombs for the next attack, in October 1942.

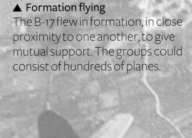

Crew
It carried 10 crew members including the pilot, copilot, radio operator, navigator, and gunners.

Engines
Four 1200-hp Wright radial engines with turbosuperchargers enabled it to fly at high altitudes without losing power.

Nose
Included a compartment for the bomber, who, thanks to the Plexiglas cover, had excellent visibility.

Bombs
The last of the B-17 models could carry almost 17,640 lb (8,000 kg) of bombs. The USAAF dropped over 1.5 million tons of bombs on Germany, 700,000 of which were dropped by the B-17.

▼ Escort
Despite its name, the B-17 was shot down on numerous occasions at the hands of German fighters. It was soon given a fighter escort, which was most often the P-47 Thunderbolt.

Manufacturer ▶ Boeing	
Production ▶ 1935–1945	
Units built ▶ 12,726	
Top speed ▶ 287 mph (462 km/h)*	
Service ceiling ▶ 35,597 ft (10,850 m)*	

* Data for B-17 G

Boeing B-52

The B-52 was designed at the height of the Cold War. With 76 units of its most recent version, the B-52 H, still in operation and scheduled to remain active until 2040, it is set to become the longest-serving bomber of the USAF. Known officially as Stratofortress, the B-52 can carry 35 tons of nuclear or precision-guided conventional weapons, and is used for strategic attack, aerial interdiction, aerial counteroffensive, and maritime operations.

DIMENSIONS

40 ft 8 in
(12.4 m)

159 ft 4 in
(48.5 m)

Wing area:
4,004 ft² (372 m²)

185 ft
(56.4 m)

Wingspan

▶ **Cockpit**
This has two levels. On the upper level are the pilot and copilot (side by side) and the EWO (Electronic Warfare Officer), responsible for electronic defense. Until 1991, it also incorporated a gunner. On the lower level are the navigator and radar operator.

Engines
The B-52H incorporates eight low-fuel-consumption engines. It can also be refueled in flight, giving it a combat radius that is limited only by the crew's endurance.

▼ **Technological upgrades**
The B-52H had an electro-optical viewing system (EVS) to improve its low-level flight capability. Operational units incorporate a LITENING targeting pod (in the image).

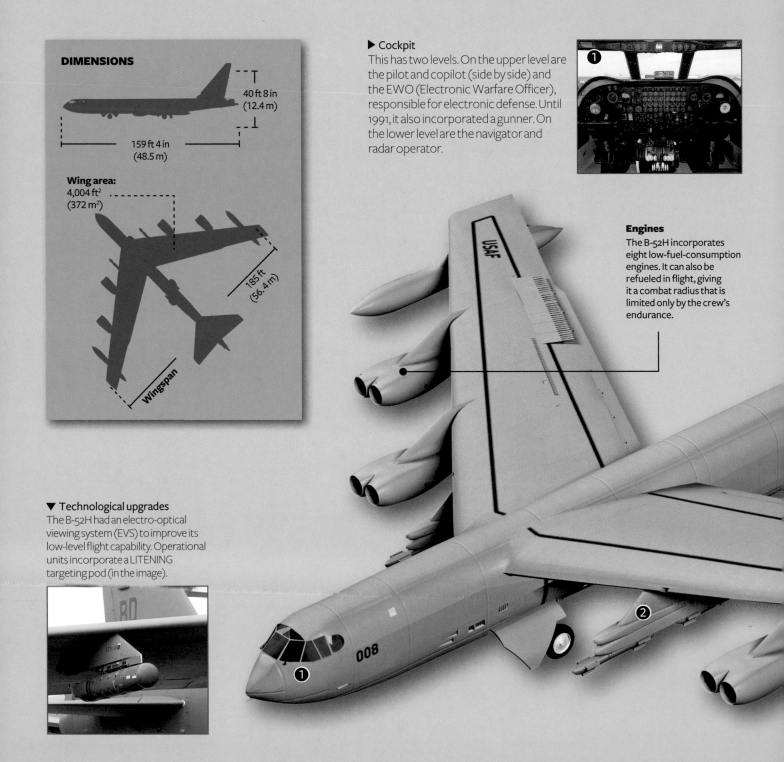

Manufacturer ▸ Boeing Military Airplane Co.

First flight ▸ April 15, 1952

Entry into service ▸ 1954

Production ▸ 1952 to 1962

Units built ▸ 744

Crew ▸ 5

Empty weight ▸ 185,000 lb (83,250 kg) approx.

Maximum takeoff weight ▸ 488,000 lb (219,600 kg)

Service ceiling ▸ 50,000 ft (15,166.6 m)

Top speed ▸ 650 mph/1,046 km/h (Mach 0.84)

Cruise speed ▸ 530 mph (853 km/h)

Combat radius ▸ 8,800 miles/14,080 km (without refueling)

Fuel capacity ▸ 312,196 lb (141,610 kg)

Powerplant ▸ 8 x Pratt & Whitney TF33-P-3/103 turbofans, with 17,000 lbf (76 kN) each (in the H version)

Tail turret
Version B-52 D was equipped with four 0.5-in (12.7-mm) caliber machine guns. These were later replaced with a 0.787-in (20-mm) remote-controlled gun, which was removed as of 1991, with version B-52 G.

▼ Armament
Located in internal bays and on underwing pylons. It can carry an extremely wide range of weapons (bombs, mines, and missiles), including 20 cruise missiles, in the case of the B-52 H.

②

Wings
The most recent version has 35° swept wings, designed to fly at high altitudes and speeds.

Landing gear
The main landing gear comprises four legs with two wheels on each and can be tilted up to 20° to facilitate crosswind landings.

▲ **AV-8 Harrier**
The Harrier II is an attack aircraft capable of vertical takeoff, used by the U.S. Marine Corps and Spanish and Italian navies.

ATTACK AND RECONNAISSANCE AIRCRAFT

After the Cold War, all attack aircraft were powered by jet engines. At that time, when ballistic missiles could reach across continents, armies understood that speed and altitude were no longer enough to protect the bombers. As a result, between the 1970s and 1980s, production began of highly maneuverable and heavily armed attack aircraft, which could fly at low altitudes and avoid radar detection, and also of reconnaissance aircraft, designed to monitor enemy activity. The latter included the long-range reconnaissance aircraft, the Lockheed SR-71 Blackbird, capable of reaching Mach 3, which was active between 1964 and 1998. With a titanium airframe and hybrid jet engine, this was the fastest manned aircraft and had the world's highest service ceiling, capable of flying at 85,000 ft (25,900 m) and surveying an area of 99,600 sq miles (258,000 km²).

The powerful A-10 Thunderbolt II, a twin-engine, straight-wing, jet aircraft developed in the United States in the early 1970s, was the best attack aircraft of the twentieth century, and is still active. Armed with a 1.18-in (30-mm) gun with seven rotating barrels, it incorporates air-to-surface missiles, laser-guided bombs, and rockets and has been upgraded on various occasions. In the 1980s, it incorporated a laser sensor and inertial navigation system; in 1999, a GPS; and in 2005, fire- and flight-control computers. They are scheduled to be phased out in 2028 and replaced by the F-35 Lightning II. An "invisible" attack plane was also developed in absolute secrecy in the 1970s in the United States, with a diamond-shaped fuselage. It was designed to penetrate enemy defense and radar systems and was capable of carrying out an initial attack on command centers, checkpoints, and missile launchers, thereby facilitating attacks by other bombers and fighter aircraft. This was the Lockheed F-117 Nighthawk, which flew for the first time in 1981, intervened in the Gulf War in 1990, and was retired in 2008. The McDonnell Douglas AV-8B Harrier II attack aircraft, which entered service in 1985, are still active and are capable of vertical takeoff and landing, fruit of a decades-long military cooperation between the United States and Great Britain.

The most recent reconnaissance and attack aircraft are the "drones," known in the military as UAVs (Unmanned Aerial Vehicles) or UCAVs (Unmanned Combat Aerial Vehicles). Among the first to be proven effective are the UAV RQ-2 Pioneer, which carried out surveillance missions in the Persian Gulf, Somalia, Bosnia, Kosovo, and Iraq, and the MQ-9 Reaper, loaded with missiles and used for the first time in Iraq, where they were also deployed in 2007. Based on the old Predator B (2001), each squadron has satellite monitoring systems and ground-control stations, as well as flight and maintenance crew, and incorporates several aircraft that can also be operated from aircraft carriers. The most recent designs have extended their range and destructive capability, as well as notably reducing their size.

Fairchild A-10 Thunderbolt II

This single-seat aircraft of the USAF was the first designed especially for close air support (CAS) missions for ground troops, capable of attacking armored vehicles and other low-level ground targets. It is highly maneuverable at low altitudes and can take off and land close to the front line and in poor conditions. It also has great firepower and is well protected against attack. It has operated in the Gulf War, the Bosnia and Kosovo Wars, and in Afghanistan.

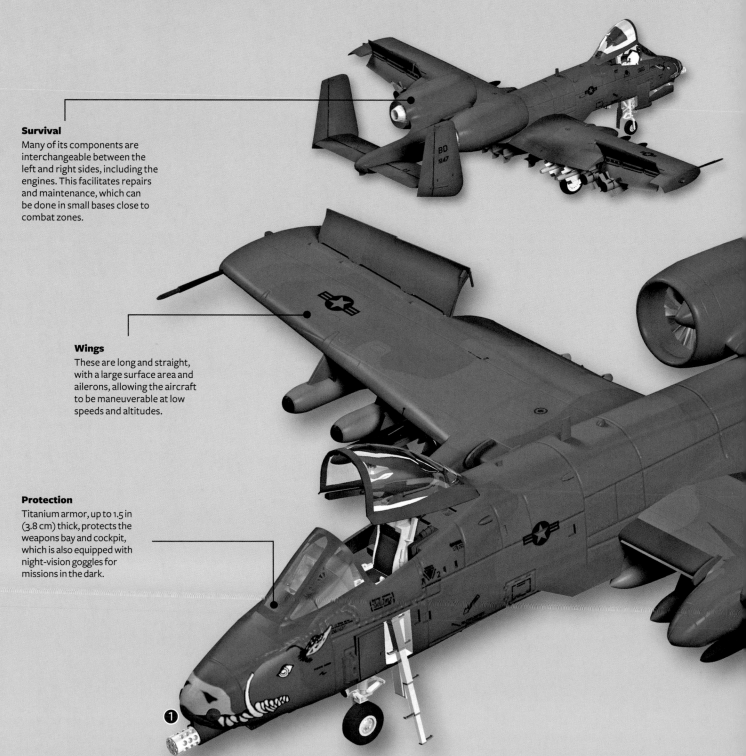

Survival
Many of its components are interchangeable between the left and right sides, including the engines. This facilitates repairs and maintenance, which can be done in small bases close to combat zones.

Wings
These are long and straight, with a large surface area and ailerons, allowing the aircraft to be maneuverable at low speeds and altitudes.

Protection
Titanium armor, up to 1.5 in (3.8 cm) thick, protects the weapons bay and cockpit, which is also equipped with night-vision goggles for missions in the dark.

①

Manufacturer ▶ Fairchild Republic Co.	**Empty weight** ▶ 29,000 lb (13,154 kg)	**Cruise speed** ▶ 335 mph (539 km/h)
First flight ▶ May 10, 1972	**Maximum takeoff weight** ▶ 50,600 lb (22,950 kg)	**Range** ▶ 2,580 miles (4,152 km)
Entry into service ▶ March 1976	**Service ceiling** ▶ 44,740 ft (13,636 m)	**Payload** ▶ 16,000 lb (7,257 kg)
Units built ▶ 715	**Top speed** ▶ 518 mph (833 km/h)	**Powerplant** ▶ 2 x General Electric TF34-GE-100A turbofans, 9,060 lbf (40.3 kN) each
Crew ▶ 1		

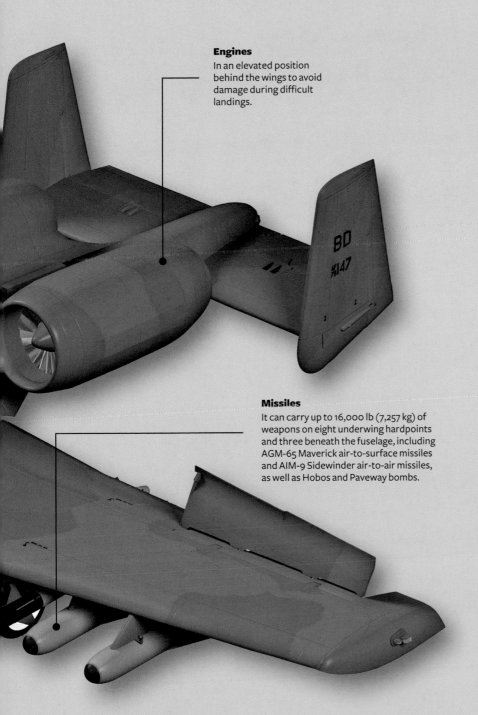

Engines
In an elevated position behind the wings to avoid damage during difficult landings.

Missiles
It can carry up to 16,000 lb (7,257 kg) of weapons on eight underwing hardpoints and three beneath the fuselage, including AGM-65 Maverick air-to-surface missiles and AIM-9 Sidewinder air-to-air missiles, as well as Hobos and Paveway bombs.

①

▲ Main weapon
It is equipped with a seven-barreled 1.18-in (30-mm) GAU 8/A Avenger Gatling cannon, capable of firing 4,000 rounds per minute.

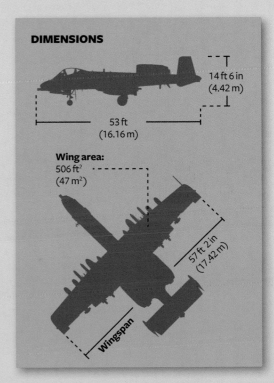

DIMENSIONS

14 ft 6 in (4.42 m)

53 ft (16.16 m)

Wing area:
506 ft² (47 m²)

57 ft 2 in (17.42 m)

Wingspan

Lockheed F-117 Nighthawk

In the late 1970s, the United States put into operation a program to develop an aircraft that was "invisible" to radar. This was how the F-117 came into being, whose development was kept secret until 1988. It was the world's first operational stealth aircraft, designed to penetrate enemy territory without being detected and attack ground targets with great precision. The F-117 served in Panama, the Gulf War, Kosovo, Afghanistan, and Iraq, but in 2008 it was retired because of its high costs and operational limitations.

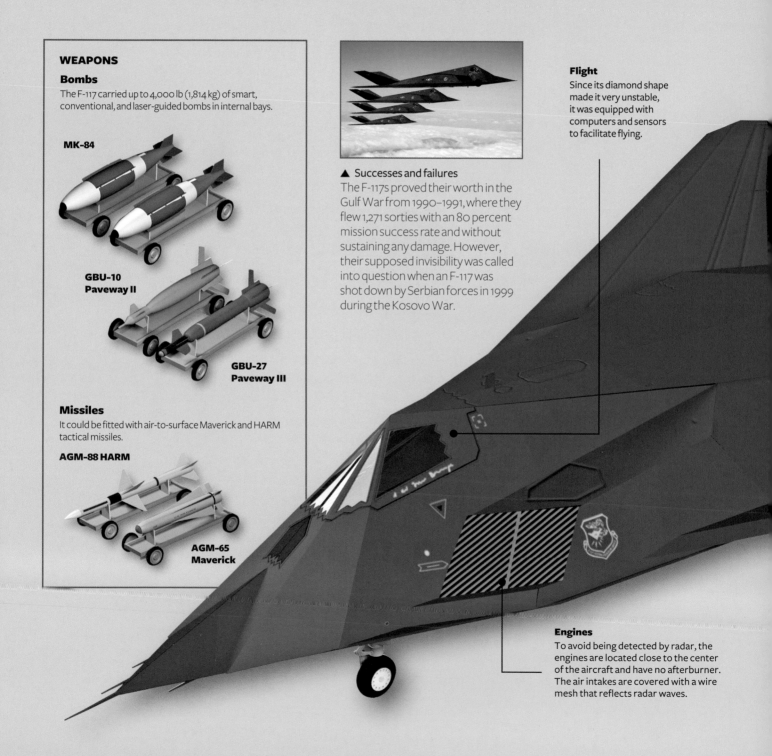

WEAPONS

Bombs

The F-117 carried up to 4,000 lb (1,814 kg) of smart, conventional, and laser-guided bombs in internal bays.

MK-84

GBU-10 Paveway II

GBU-27 Paveway III

Missiles

It could be fitted with air-to-surface Maverick and HARM tactical missiles.

AGM-88 HARM

AGM-65 Maverick

▲ Successes and failures

The F-117s proved their worth in the Gulf War from 1990–1991, where they flew 1,271 sorties with an 80 percent mission success rate and without sustaining any damage. However, their supposed invisibility was called into question when an F-117 was shot down by Serbian forces in 1999 during the Kosovo War.

Flight

Since its diamond shape made it very unstable, it was equipped with computers and sensors to facilitate flying.

Engines

To avoid being detected by radar, the engines are located close to the center of the aircraft and have no afterburner. The air intakes are covered with a wire mesh that reflects radar waves.

Shape
Faceted to deflect radar waves in different directions. All doors and panels have forward-facing serrated edges to reflect radar.

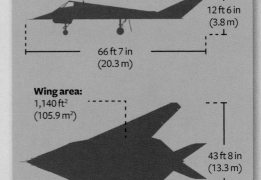

DIMENSIONS

12 ft 6 in (3.8 m)

66 ft 7 in (20.3 m)

Wing area: 1,140 ft² (105.9 m²)

43 ft 8 in (13.3 m)

Wingspan

Materials
Built in aluminum and titanium, its surface is clad in a radar-absorbing material (RAM).

Manufacturer ▸ Lockheed Martin Aeronautical Systems Co.

First model ▸ June 18, 1981

Entry into service ▸ October 1983

Retired ▸ April 22, 2008 (replaced by the F-22 Raptor)

Units built ▸ 64 (5 prototypes)

Crew ▸ 1

Empty weight ▸ 30,000 lb (13,608 kg)

Maximum takeoff weight ▸ 52,500 lb (23,814 kg)

Service ceiling ▸ 45,000 ft (13,716 m)

Top speed ▸ Supersonic

Cruise speed ▸ 684 mph (1,100.8 km/h)

Range ▸ Unlimited with inflight refueling

Powerplant ▸ 2 x General Electric F-404-F1D2 turbofans, 10,566 lbf (47 kN) each

Lockheed SR-71 "Blackbird"

The SR-71 is one of the most impressive spy planes in aviation history. Built for the USAF at the height of the Cold War, it flew faster (three times the speed of sound) and higher than any other reconnaissance aircraft during its almost 24 years in service. Equipped with sophisticated optical instruments, radars, and high-resolution cameras, the Blackbird, as it was popularly known, was capable of surveying 99,600 square miles (258,000 km²) of the Earth's surface per hour.

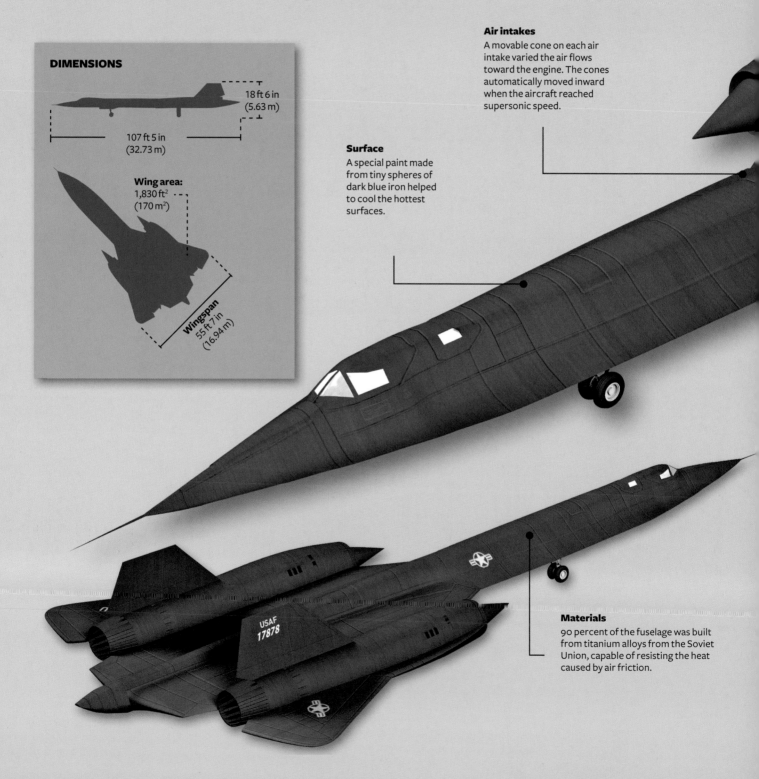

DIMENSIONS

18 ft 6 in
(5.63 m)

107 ft 5 in
(32.73 m)

Wing area:
1,830 ft²
(170 m²)

Wingspan
55 ft 7 in
(16.94 m)

Air intakes
A movable cone on each air intake varied the air flows toward the engine. The cones automatically moved inward when the aircraft reached supersonic speed.

Surface
A special paint made from tiny spheres of dark blue iron helped to cool the hottest surfaces.

USAF
17878

Materials
90 percent of the fuselage was built from titanium alloys from the Soviet Union, capable of resisting the heat caused by air friction.

Fuel
Stored in six large tanks in the fuselage and wings. The SR-71 used JP-7, a highly stable fuel that was difficult to ignite, thereby avoiding the aircraft exploding from the heat.

Pratt & Whitney J58 Turbojet
The engine of the SR-71 was designed to operate during long periods of time using its afterburner chamber. It was the first to be flight-qualified at Mach 3 by the USAF.

Fuselage
While on land, the fuselage panels did not fit perfectly together, as the heat generated by the aircraft's high speeds expanded the pieces during flight.

◀ Stealth design
The characteristic shape of the SR-71 and the radar-absorbing paint finish were meant to make the aircraft difficult for radar to detect. In practice, it was easily detected thanks to its exhaust plumes, although its ability to reach supersonic speeds enabled it to evade enemy fire.

Manufacturer ▶ Lockheed Martin Aircraft Corporation

First flight ▶ December 22, 1964

Entry into service ▶ January 1966

Retired ▶ 1998 (between 1990 and 1995 it was retired temporarily)

Units built ▶ 29

Crew ▶ 2

Empty weight ▶ 59,000 lb (26,762 kg)*

Loaded weight ▶ 140,000 lb (63,503 kg)*

Service ceiling ▶ 85,000 ft (25,900 m)*

Top speed ▶ 2,200 mph (3,220 km/h) (Mach 3)*

Combat radius ▶ 2,900 miles (4,667 km)*

Powerplant ▶ 2 x Pratt & Whitney J58 afterburning turbojets, 32,600 lbf (145 kN) each*

* Data for SR-71A

McDonnell Douglas AV-8B Harrier II

Fruit of a British and U.S. collaboration, the Harrier II replaced the HS Harrier, the first V/STOL (Vertical/Short Takeoff and Landing) aircraft. Ideal for use on a ship or forward operating bases, it can rise like a helicopter and then fly at subsonic speeds, carrying almost six tons of ordnance beneath its wings and fuselage. Its upgraded version, the Harrier II Plus, is used by the United States Marine Corps and the Spanish and Italian navies.

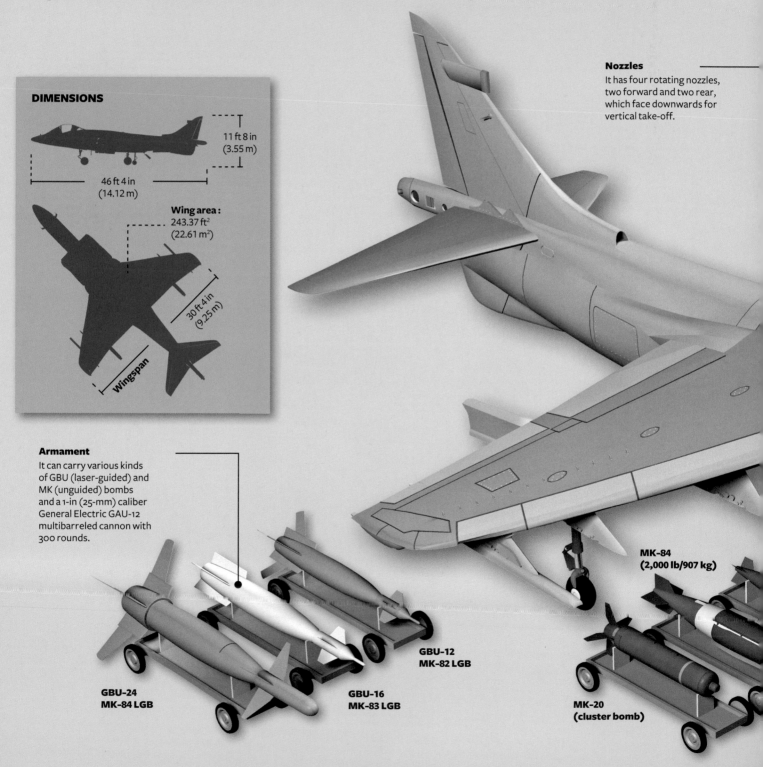

DIMENSIONS

11 ft 8 in
(3.55 m)

46 ft 4 in
(14.12 m)

Wing area :
243.37 ft²
(22.61 m²)

30 ft 4 in
(9.25 m)

Wingspan

Nozzles
It has four rotating nozzles, two forward and two rear, which face downwards for vertical take-off.

Armament
It can carry various kinds of GBU (laser-guided) and MK (unguided) bombs and a 1-in (25-mm) caliber General Electric GAU-12 multibarreled cannon with 300 rounds.

GBU-24
MK-84 LGB

GBU-16
MK-83 LGB

GBU-12
MK-82 LGB

MK-84
(2,000 lb/907 kg)

MK-20
(cluster bomb)

Manufacturer ▸ McDonnell Douglas and British Aerospace (now Boeing and BAE Systems)

First aircraft ▸ November 9, 1978

Entry into service ▸ January 12, 1985

Units built ▸ 500*

Crew ▸ 1

Empty weight ▸ 14,630 lb (6,636 kg)*

Maximum takeoff weight ▸ 31,000 lb (14,061 kg)*

Vertical takeoff weight ▸ 18,950 lb (8,596 kg)*

Service ceiling ▸ 50,000 ft (15,240 m)*

Top speed ▸ 662 mph (1,065 km/h) at sea level*

Maximum range ▸ 745 miles (1,200 km)*

Powerplant ▸ 1 x Rolls-Royce Pegasus F402-RR-408 vectored-thrust turbofan*

* Data for AV-8B Harrier II Plus

Engine
Developed especially for this aircraft, its more than 17,500 lb (8,000 kg) of thrust, in combination with the rotating nozzles, raises the aircraft vertically.

AIM-7 Sparrow

AIM-9 Sidewinder

AIM-120 AMRAAM

Missiles
Its armament includes Sidewinder heat-seeking missiles and AIM-120 AMRAAM missiles (a medium-range, advanced air-to-air missile).

MK-82 (500 lb/227 kg)

Air intakes
Its typical engine air intakes are next to the pilot's cockpit.

Unmanned Aerial Vehicles (UAV)

These state-of-the-art, unmanned aircraft are controlled by a ground crew located in military bases miles from the dangers of combat. They are capable of carrying out reconnaissance, attack, and support missions in the harshest of scenarios. Known popularly as "drones," UAVs came into military use in the 1990s.

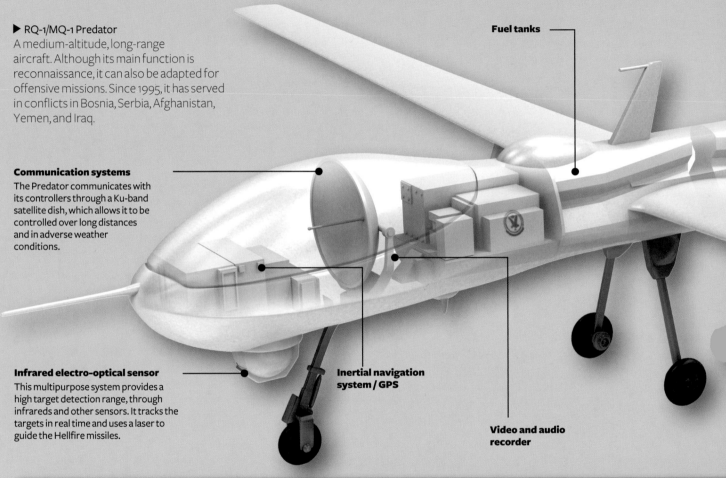

▶ RQ-1/MQ-1 Predator
A medium-altitude, long-range aircraft. Although its main function is reconnaissance, it can also be adapted for offensive missions. Since 1995, it has served in conflicts in Bosnia, Serbia, Afghanistan, Yemen, and Iraq.

Fuel tanks

Communication systems
The Predator communicates with its controllers through a Ku-band satellite dish, which allows it to be controlled over long distances and in adverse weather conditions.

Infrared electro-optical sensor
This multipurpose system provides a high target detection range, through infrareds and other sensors. It tracks the targets in real time and uses a laser to guide the Hellfire missiles.

Inertial navigation system / GPS

Video and audio recorder

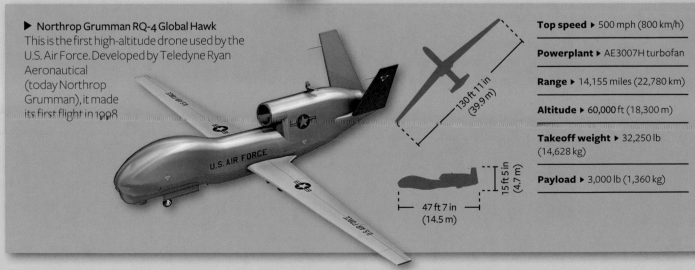

▶ Northrop Grumman RQ-4 Global Hawk
This is the first high-altitude drone used by the U.S. Air Force. Developed by Teledyne Ryan Aeronautical (today Northrop Grumman), it made its first flight in 1998.

130 ft 11 in (39.9 m)

15 ft 5 in (4.7 m)

47 ft 7 in (14.5 m)

Top speed ▶ 500 mph (800 km/h)

Powerplant ▶ AE3007H turbofan

Range ▶ 14,155 miles (22,780 km)

Altitude ▶ 60,000 ft (18,300 m)

Takeoff weight ▶ 32,250 lb (14,628 kg)

Payload ▶ 3,000 lb (1,360 kg)

Manufacturer ▸ General Atomics

First flight ▸ July 1994

Entry into service ▸ Summer 1995

Units built ▸ 360

Crew ▸ 0

Empty weight ▸ 1,800 lb (816 kg)

Maximum takeoff weight ▸ 2,550 lb (1,157 kg)

Service ceiling ▸ 25,000 ft (7,620 m)

Top speed ▸ 135 mph (217 km/h)

Cruise speed ▸ 80 mph (130 km/h)

Combat radius ▸ 685 miles (1,100 km)

Endurance in combat ▸ 40 hours

Powerplant ▸ 1 x Rotax 914 turboprop engine

Powerplant
The four-stroke and four-cylinder engine gives it 100 hp at 5,500 rpm.

Materials
Carbon fibers interwoven with aramid fibers are used for the construction of the fuselage and wings. The interior structure is formed from carbon fiber and aluminum ribs.

Armament
Under the wings it carries two air-to-surface AGM-114 Hellfire guided missiles (above) or two air-to-air AIM-92 Stinger missiles.

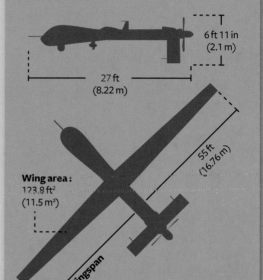

DIMENSIONS

6 ft 11 in (2.1 m)

27 ft (8.22 m)

Wing area : 123.8 ft² (11.5 m²)

55 ft (16.76 m)

Wingspan

▸ **Northrop Grumman X-47B**
Created by Northrop Grumman, its first flight was in 2011. It was designed to operate from aircraft carriers and in 2013 became the first drone to land on one.

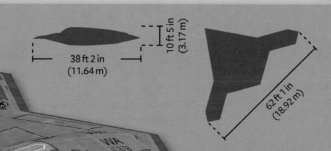

10 ft 5 in (3.17 m)

38 ft 2 in (11.64 m)

62 ft 1 in (18.92 m)

Top speed ▸ High subsonic

Powerplant ▸ Pratt & Whitney F100-PW220u turbofan

Range ▸ 2,417 miles (3,890 km)

Altitude ▸ 40,000 ft (12,190 m)

Weight ▸ 44,000 lb (19,958 kg)

Payload ▸ 5,000 lb (2,040 kg)

▲ Eurofighter Typhoon
This European-manufactured multirole fighter is equipped with the most advanced avionics and armament systems.

FIGHTERS

Of all military aircraft, the fighters, created for air-to-air combat against other aircraft, are responsible for contributing most to achieving air superiority in the twentieth century. Although World War I saw the first generation triplanes and biplanes, fitted with light armaments, it was not until World War II that they became crucial in battle. Small, maneuverable, fast, powerful, and fitted with highly efficient weapons, some of these aircraft were the undisputed leaders of the war in the air: the 1944 German Messerschmitt Me 262A, for example, the world's first jet fighter, powered by two Junkers Jumo 004B-1 turbojets; or the first British monoplane fighter, the Hawker Hurricane, designed for the RAF in the 1930s, which revealed its qualities in the Battle of Britain.

Other World War II fighters included the American P-51 Mustang, the perfect bomber escort; the Russian MiG-3 and the Yakovlev Yak-3—the former a transitional fighter from 1940, and the latter a low-wing, single-engine aircraft from 1944; and the Japanese Mitsubishi A6M2 Zero, the carrier-based aircraft with the best range and maneuverability of its time. Armed with two machine guns on the engine and two guns on the wings, this Japanese fighter could also incorporate a fixed 550-lb (250-kg) bomb for kamikaze attacks. However, one of the fastest fighter planes, and the only aircraft produced by the Allies throughout the whole of World War II, was the British Supermarine Spitfire. In service between 1938 and 1955, more than 20,000 units and 24 models were manufactured, including a host of variants. A few years later, fighter aircraft incorporated new armaments like automatic cannons, improved their air-to-air missile and radar systems, and some were designed as multirole aircraft, serving as bombers as well as fighters. One of the most effective was the McDonnell Douglas F-4 Phantom II, a long-range USAF fighter-bomber that set 16 speed and altitude records after entering service in 1961 and was used in the Vietnam War, where 16 squadrons were deployed between 1965 and 1973. It carried 18,695 lb (8,480 kg) of missiles and bombs in nine hardpoints, although the 1974 Grumman F-14 Tomcat would surpass it, being equipped with AIM-54 Phoenix long-range missiles capable of reaching targets 125 miles (200 km) away. It was heavy, but its variable-geometry wings and great ordnance capacity made it perfect for defending the large aircraft carriers. In those same years, the Mikoyan MiG-29 was designed in the Soviet Union; known as the Fulcrum by NATO, it entered service in 1983. Created for air superiority, this is a pure, highly maneuverable fighter aircraft, which, after 18 versions, is still operational as the current MiG-35.

One of the most modern multirole fighters, designed and built by a consortium of European businesses, is the Eurofighter Typhoon, which has been in service since 2003. Only 15 percent of its structure is composed of metals (titanium and light alloys); the rest is made from carbon and glass fiber, which makes it extremely light and agile.

Messerschmitt Me 262A-1a "Schwalbe"

This was the world's first jet-powered fighter. Its development could have allowed Germany to recover its air supremacy, had it not been for its late introduction and the extremely high level of maintenance the aircraft required. Development began in 1939, but it was not until 1944 that it entered combat. The Me 262 was superior to any other aircraft of its time, although it proved to be vulnerable during takeoff and landing maneuvers.

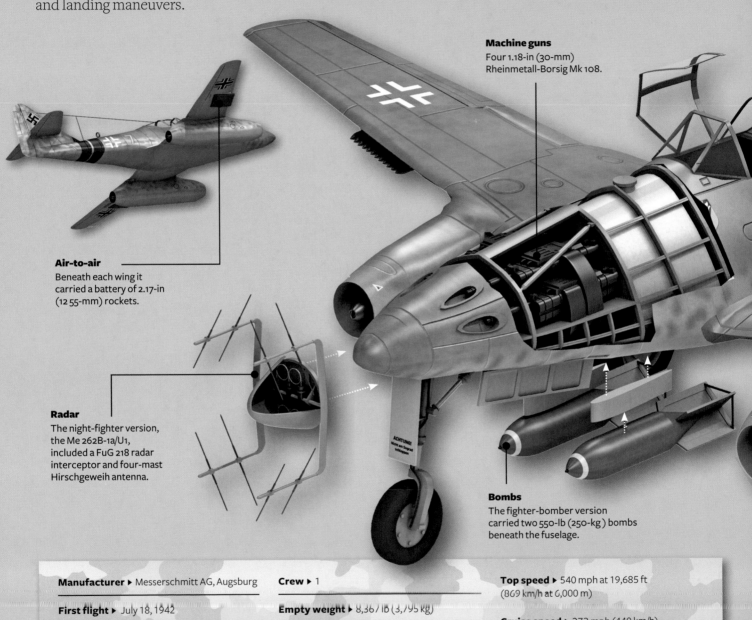

Machine guns
Four 1.18-in (30-mm)
Rheinmetall-Borsig Mk 108.

Air-to-air
Beneath each wing it
carried a battery of 2.17-in
(12 55-mm) rockets.

Radar
The night-fighter version,
the Me 262B-1a/U1,
included a FuG 218 radar
interceptor and four-mast
Hirschgeweih antenna.

Bombs
The fighter-bomber version
carried two 550-lb (250-kg) bombs
beneath the fuselage.

Manufacturer ▸ Messerschmitt AG, Augsburg	**Crew** ▸ 1	**Top speed** ▸ 540 mph at 19,685 ft (869 km/h at 6,000 m)
First flight ▸ July 18, 1942	**Empty weight** ▸ 8,367 lb (3,795 kg)	**Cruise speed** ▸ 273 mph (440 km/h)
Entry into service ▸ 1944	**Maximum takeoff weight** ▸ 14,080 lb (6,387 kg)	**Range** ▸ 652 miles at 29,530 ft (1,050 km at 9,000 m)
Retired ▸ 1945 (for Germany)	**Service ceiling** ▸ 40,000 ft/12,190 m (version 1A)	**Powerplant** ▸ 2 x Junkers Jumo-004 turbojets
Units built ▸ More than 1,400		

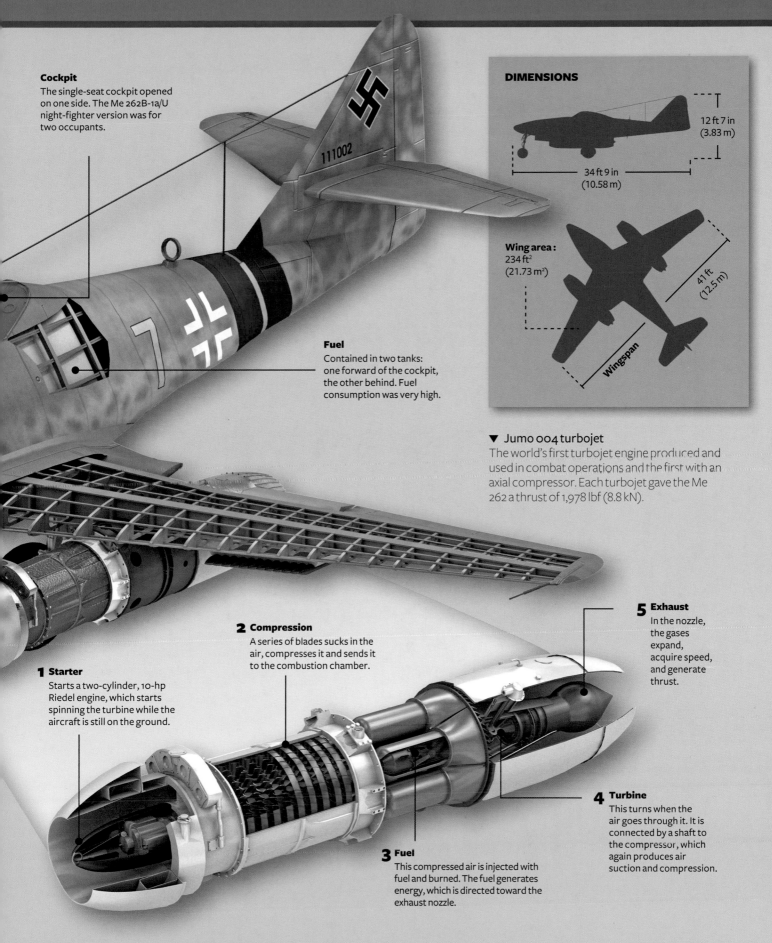

Cockpit
The single-seat cockpit opened on one side. The Me 262B-1a/U night-fighter version was for two occupants.

Fuel
Contained in two tanks: one forward of the cockpit, the other behind. Fuel consumption was very high.

DIMENSIONS

12 ft 7 in (3.83 m)

34 ft 9 in (10.58 m)

Wing area: 234 ft² (21.73 m²)

41 ft (12.5 m)

Wingspan

▼ Jumo 004 turbojet
The world's first turbojet engine produced and used in combat operations and the first with an axial compressor. Each turbojet gave the Me 262 a thrust of 1,978 lbf (8.8 kN).

2 Compression
A series of blades sucks in the air, compresses it and sends it to the combustion chamber.

5 Exhaust
In the nozzle, the gases expand, acquire speed, and generate thrust.

1 Starter
Starts a two-cylinder, 10-hp Riedel engine, which starts spinning the turbine while the aircraft is still on the ground.

3 Fuel
This compressed air is injected with fuel and burned. The fuel generates energy, which is directed toward the exhaust nozzle.

4 Turbine
This turns when the air goes through it. It is connected by a shaft to the compressor, which again produces air suction and compression.

Hawker Hurricane

Solid, reliable, tough, and versatile, the Hurricane was the first monoplane fighter to enter service for the RAF. It became the air force's backbone during the Battle of Britain, where it destroyed more enemy aircraft than all the other defense systems together. During the war, it also saw action in the Mediterranean theater of operations in successful ground attack missions.

Propeller
The first Hurricane had a two-blade propeller, which was replaced by a constant-speed, three-blade propeller.

Cockpit
It was the first RAF monoplane with an enclosed cockpit.

Engine
The first engine was a Merlin II, which was successively replaced by the Merlin III and Merlin XX. The latter notably increased its capabilities.

Fuel
It had two tanks in the wings, and another as a reserve.

▼ Firepower
The Hurricane I and II were armed with eight 0.303-in (7.7-mm) Browning machine guns, which gave it low firepower. This was increased in the MK IIB to twelve machine guns and in the MK IIC with four 0.787-in (20-mm) Hispano-Suiza HS.404 cannons.

Air-cooled barrel

Ammunition belt

Browning .303
One of the most versatile heavy machine guns ever produced.

Navigation lights
These were key for the frequent nighttime interception missions.

Manufacturer ▸ Hawker Aircraft Ltd., from the design of Sydney Camm

First flight ▸ November 6, 1935

Entry into service ▸ December 1937

Units built ▸ More than 14,000

Crew ▸ 1

Empty weight ▸ 5,800 lb (2,631 kg)*

Maximum takeoff weight ▸ 8,100 lb (3,674 kg)*

Service ceiling ▸ 35,600 ft (10,850 m)*

Top speed ▸ 328 mph at 19,685 ft (528 km/h at 6,000 m)*

Rate of climb ▸ 2,195 ft/min (669 m/min)*

Combat radius ▸ 460 miles (740 km)*

Endurance ▸ 3 hours*

Powerplant ▸ 1 x linear 12-cylinder Rolls-Royce V-12 Merlin XX, 1,280 hp

*Data for the Mk IIC

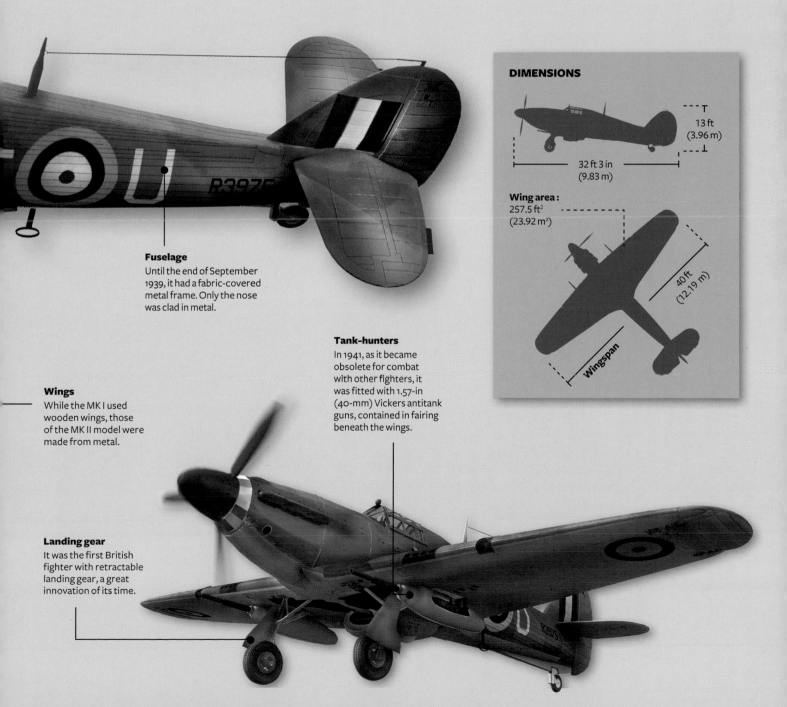

Fuselage
Until the end of September 1939, it had a fabric-covered metal frame. Only the nose was clad in metal.

Wings
While the MK I used wooden wings, those of the MK II model were made from metal.

Tank-hunters
In 1941, as it became obsolete for combat with other fighters, it was fitted with 1.57-in (40-mm) Vickers antitank guns, contained in fairing beneath the wings.

Landing gear
It was the first British fighter with retractable landing gear, a great innovation of its time.

DIMENSIONS

13 ft (3.96 m)

32 ft 3 in (9.83 m)

Wing area :
257.5 ft^2 (23.92 m^2)

40 ft (12.19 m)

Wingspan

North American P-51 Mustang

Considered by many to be the best fighter aircraft of World War II, it was originally designed at the request of the Royal Air Force, which received 620 units in 1940. When the United States entered the conflict, this aircraft became the main fighter of the USAAF, and proved to be fast, maneuverable, and solid. As a long-range aircraft it became useful for escorting bombing missions deep inside German territory, reaching as far as Berlin.

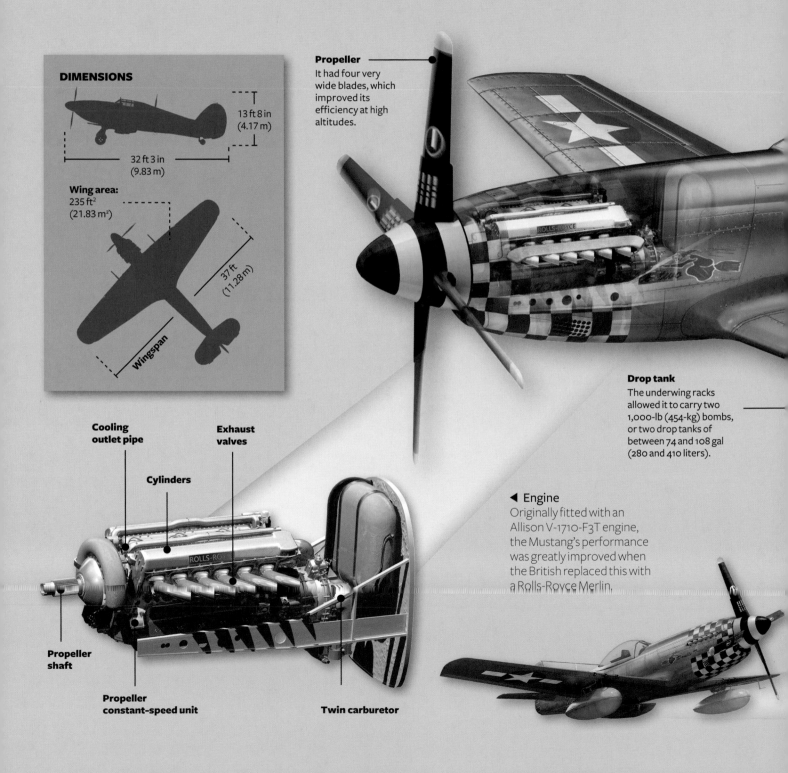

DIMENSIONS

13 ft 8 in (4.17 m)

32 ft 3 in (9.83 m)

Wing area: 235 ft² (21.83 m²)

37 ft (11.28 m)

Wingspan

Propeller
It had four very wide blades, which improved its efficiency at high altitudes.

Drop tank
The underwing racks allowed it to carry two 1,000-lb (454-kg) bombs, or two drop tanks of between 74 and 108 gal (280 and 410 liters).

◄ **Engine**
Originally fitted with an Allison V-1710-F3T engine, the Mustang's performance was greatly improved when the British replaced this with a Rolls-Royce Merlin.

Cooling outlet pipe

Exhaust valves

Cylinders

Propeller shaft

Propeller constant-speed unit

Twin carburetor

Manufacturer ▶ North American Aviation, from the design of Louis Wait, Ray Rice, and Edgar Schmued

First flight ▶ October 26, 1940

Entry into service ▶ 1941 (RAF) and 1942 (USAAF)

Units built ▶ More than 15,000 (of all versions)

Crew ▶ 1

Empty weight ▶ 7,639 lb (3,465 kg)*

Maximum takeoff weight ▶ 10,097 lb (4,580 kg)*

Service ceiling ▶ 41,700 ft (12,710 m)*

Top speed ▶ 370 mph at 14,990 ft (595 km/h at 4,570 m)*

Rate of climb ▶ 2,800 ft/min (853 m/min)*

Combat radius ▶ 1,712 miles/2,755 km (with drop tanks)*

Endurance ▶ 4 hours*

Powerplant ▶ 1 x 12-cylinder Packard Rolls-Royce Merlin V-1650-7 engine, 1,490 hp*

* Data for the P-51 K

Machine guns
The number of 0.5-in (12.7-mm) machine guns on the P-51D and P-51K models rose from four to six.

Wings
Being straight, with rectangular edges and wide flaps, gave the Mustang great maneuverability.

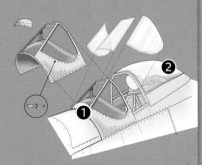

▼ The "bubble" version
On the P-51 D model, the height of the rear part of the fuselage was reduced to replace the cockpit with a "bubble" canopy, which provided the pilot with all-round visibility.

1. Bullet-proof windscreen
2. Sliding canopy with all-round visibility

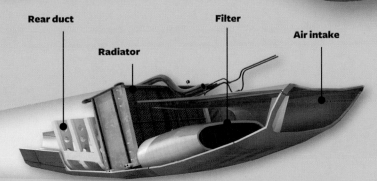

Rear duct

Radiator

Filter

Air intake

◀ Radiator
This was installed in a duct beneath the fuselage. The air that entered through it was heated through the radiator and expanded. The hot-air outlet through the rear duct contributed to the aircraft's thrust.

Yakovlev Yak-3

When the Nazis launched the invasion of the Soviet Union, "Operation Barbarossa," in 1941, the Soviets had three types of fighter—Yak-1, MiG-1, and LaGG-3. All were inferior to the German fighters, but they fought heroically to stop the invasion. By the middle of 1942, the Soviet aeronautic industry had developed new versions of the original trio of fighters. One of them was the Yak-3, recognized as the most efficient and agile fighter of the whole war, among other reasons, because of its minimal weight and size.

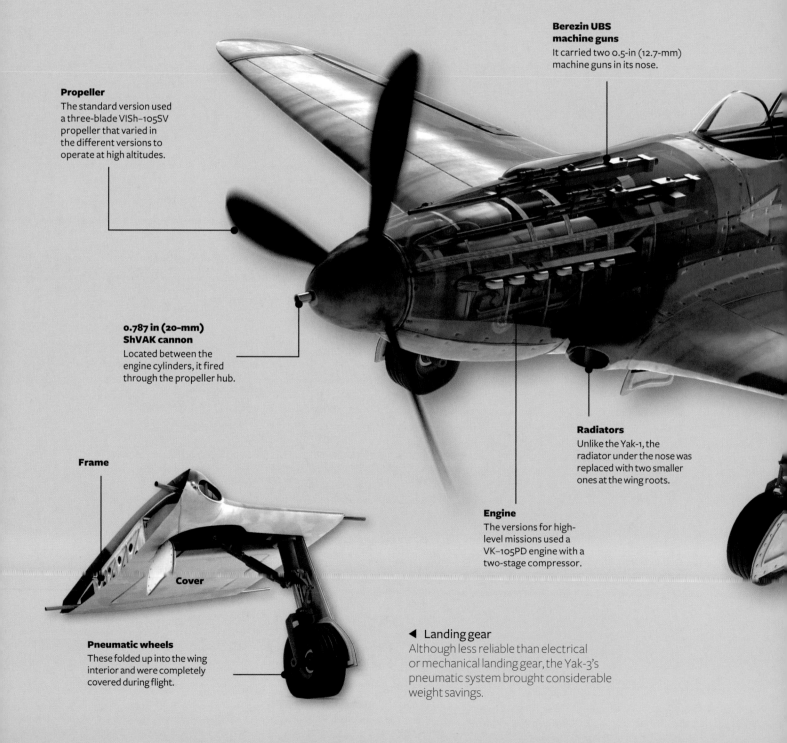

Berezin UBS machine guns
It carried two 0.5-in (12.7-mm) machine guns in its nose.

Propeller
The standard version used a three-blade VISh–105SV propeller that varied in the different versions to operate at high altitudes.

0.787 in (20-mm) ShVAK cannon
Located between the engine cylinders, it fired through the propeller hub.

Radiators
Unlike the Yak-1, the radiator under the nose was replaced with two smaller ones at the wing roots.

Frame

Engine
The versions for high-level missions used a VK–105PD engine with a two-stage compressor.

Cover

Pneumatic wheels
These folded up into the wing interior and were completely covered during flight.

◀ Landing gear
Although less reliable than electrical or mechanical landing gear, the Yak-3's pneumatic system brought considerable weight savings.

Manufacturer ▸ Yakovlev, from the design of Alexander Sergeyevich Yakovlev

First flight ▸ April 12, 1941

Entry into service ▸ 1944

Units built ▸ More than 4,000

Crew ▸ 1

Empty weight ▸ 4,641 lb (2,105 kg)

Maximum takeoff weight ▸ 5,952 lb (2,700 kg)

Service ceiling ▸ 35,695 ft (10,880 m)

Top speed ▸ 447 mph at 19,685 ft (720 km/h at 6,000 m)

Rate of climb ▸ 60.7 ft/s (18.5 m/s)

Combat radius ▸ 559 miles (900 km)

Endurance ▸ 3 hours

Powerplant ▸ 1 x Klimov VK-107A linear engine, 1,700 hp (for the Yak-3TK version)

Tail
The tail rudder had a hinged groove specially adapted to the structural resistance.

Windscreen

Control panel

Radio compartment

Pedals

▲ Cockpit
Located on the fuselage, farther forward than on the Yak-1, its bubble canopy offered excellent visibility and was designed to facilitate flying for the pilot.

Wings
Smaller than those of the Yak-1, they offered the Yak-3 less resistance and greater maneuverability.

Camouflage
The model corresponds to the aircraft used by General Georgi Zakharov, commanding officer of the 303rd Fighter Division.

DIMENSIONS

7 ft 11 in (2.42 m)

28 ft (8.55 m)

Wing area: 160 ft² (14.85 m²)

30 ft 2 in (9.2 m)

Wingspan

Mikoyan-Gurevich MiG-3

This fighter was designed to remedy issues that dogged its predecessor, the MiG-1. Although changes were introduced to the wings and the fuselage (the MiG-1's biggest problems), the MiG-3 was designed for high-altitude combat and therefore proved difficult to handle, since most dogfights with German fighter aircraft were carried out at low levels. Its impaired performance was partly offset by the Soviet pilots' attempts to fly at high altitudes and launch surprise attacks before quickly making their getaway.

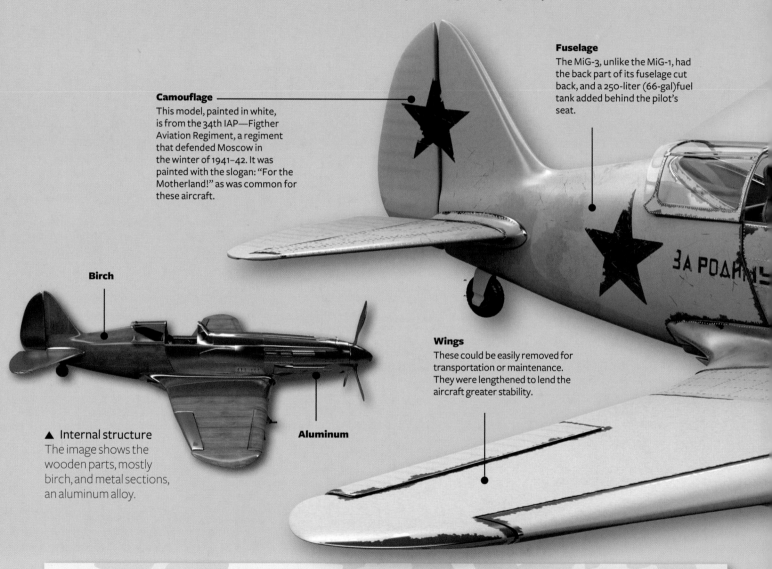

Fuselage
The MiG-3, unlike the MiG-1, had the back part of its fuselage cut back, and a 250-liter (66-gal)fuel tank added behind the pilot's seat.

Camouflage
This model, painted in white, is from the 34th IAP—Figther Aviation Regiment, a regiment that defended Moscow in the winter of 1941–42. It was painted with the slogan: "For the Motherland!" as was common for these aircraft.

Birch

Wings
These could be easily removed for transportation or maintenance. They were lengthened to lend the aircraft greater stability.

Aluminum

▲ **Internal structure**
The image shows the wooden parts, mostly birch, and metal sections, an aluminum alloy.

Manufacturer ▸ Mikoyan-Gurevich, from the design of Artem Mikoyan and Mikhail Gurevich	**Crew** ▸ 1	**Top speed** ▸ 398 mph (640 km/h)
First flight ▸ October 1940	**Empty weight** ▸ 5,950 lb (2,699 kg)	**Rate of climb** ▸ 2,894 ft/min (882 m/min)
Entry into service ▸ December 20, 1940	**Maximum takeoff weight** ▸ 7,397 lb (3,355 kg)	**Combat radius** ▸ 510 miles/820 km (depending on the load)
Units built ▸ More than 3,000	**Service ceiling** ▸ 37,730 ft (11,500 m)	**Powerplant** ▸ 1 x 12-cylinder, liquid-cooled Mikulin AM-35A linear engine, 1,130 hp, and later 1,350 hp

▶ **Cockpit**
The pilot's seat had a 0.35-in (9-mm) thick armored plate. The front glazing of the canopy was also armored.

Nose
This was lengthened with respect to the MiG-1, to be able to move the engine and bring the center of gravity farther forward.

Armament
A 0.5-in (12.7-mm) Berezin UBS machine gun and two 0.3-in (7.62-mm) ShKAS were located in the nose.

Engine
Moved forward 3.9 in (10 cm) inside the fuselage, although it kept the same powerplant as the MiG-1.

Machine guns
Modifications for different campaigns included two 0.3-in (7.62-mm) ShKAS located in underwing fairings.

DIMENSIONS

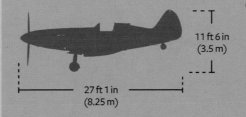

11 ft 6 in (3.5 m)

27 ft 1 in (8.25 m)

Wing area: 187.7 ft² (17.44 m²)

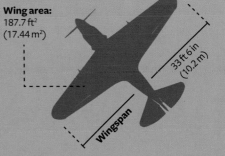

33 ft 6 in (10.2 m)

Wingspan

Morane-Saulnier MS 406

When the Nazis began their offensive on France in 1940, the Morane-Saulnier was the backbone of the Armée de l'Air's fighter force. However, it was soon apparent that its performance was inferior to that of the German fighters. Despite the bravery and skill of the French pilots, who shot down 175 aircraft, some 400 MS 406 were destroyed in combat or on the ground during the Battle of France. After France fell, they were used by the Vichy government in Indochina and Palestine.

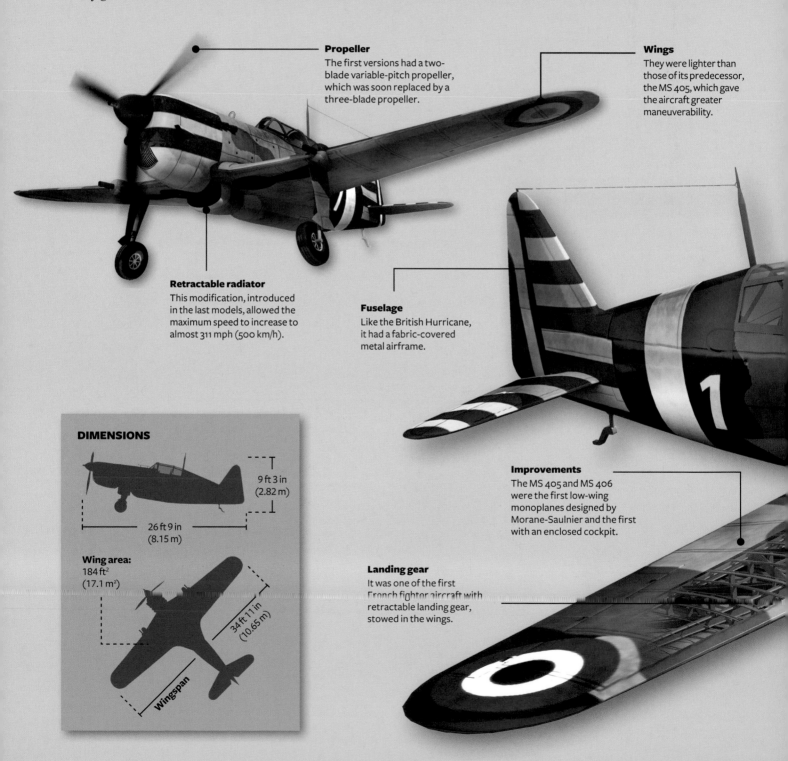

Propeller
The first versions had a two-blade variable-pitch propeller, which was soon replaced by a three-blade propeller.

Wings
They were lighter than those of its predecessor, the MS 405, which gave the aircraft greater maneuverability.

Retractable radiator
This modification, introduced in the last models, allowed the maximum speed to increase to almost 311 mph (500 km/h).

Fuselage
Like the British Hurricane, it had a fabric-covered metal airframe.

Improvements
The MS 405 and MS 406 were the first low-wing monoplanes designed by Morane-Saulnier and the first with an enclosed cockpit.

Landing gear
It was one of the first French fighter aircraft with retractable landing gear, stowed in the wings.

DIMENSIONS

9 ft 3 in (2.82 m)

26 ft 9 in (8.15 m)

Wing area:
184 ft^2 (17.1 m^2)

34 ft 11 in (10.65 m)

Wingspan

Manufacturer ▸ Morane-Saulnier	**Empty weight** ▸ 4,173 lb (1,893 kg)	**Rate of climb** ▸ 2,165 ft/min (660 m/min)
First flight ▸ August 8, 1935	**Maximum takeoff weight** ▸ 5,952 lb (2,700 kg)	**Combat radius** ▸ 560 miles (900 km)
Entry into service ▸ 1938	**Service ceiling** ▸ 32,316 ft (9,850 m)	**Endurance** ▸ 2 hours
Units built ▸ More than 1,000	**Top speed** ▸ 302 mph (486 km/h)	**Powerplant** ▸ 1 x Hispano-Suiza 12Y-31 (V-12) liquid-cooled engine, 860 hp
Crew ▸ 1		

▸ Cannon

The 0.787-in (20-mm) Hispano-Suiza HS.404 was located in the "V" formed by the engine cylinders, and fired through the propeller hub. It had a tendency to jam, leaving the pilot with just the machine guns.

1. Flash suppressor and muzzle brake

2. Recoil spring

3. Front mounting bolt and spring adjustment

4. Barrel

5. Rear support

6. Ammunition drum

Cockpit
A three-piece canopy offered good visibility despite being located behind the wings.

Armament
This was quite weak as it was reduced to a 0.787-in (20-mm) cannon and two 0.295-in (7.5-mm) MAC 1934 machine guns on the wings.

SWISS AND FINNISH VARIANTS

The aircraft performed better in versions developed by the Swiss and Finnish. The latter changed the engine and armament and used it with great success against the Russians.

Fighters EFW D-3800 and D-3801—Switzerland

J-270

Mörkö-Morane—Finland

MS-63

Supermarine Spitfire

This was undoubtedly the best British fighter aircraft of World War II. As many as 24 different basic models were manufactured, used by various countries during and after the war. Fast, maneuverable, and easy to fly, its reputation was forged during the Battle of Britain (July—October 1940), where it proved to be one of the few fighters capable of challenging the German Messerschmitt Bf 109. It was also successfully used in reconnaissance missions and as a fighter-bomber.

▲ **Iconic**
Its elliptical wings and decisive role in the Battle of Britain made the Supermarine Spitfire a British icon of World War II.

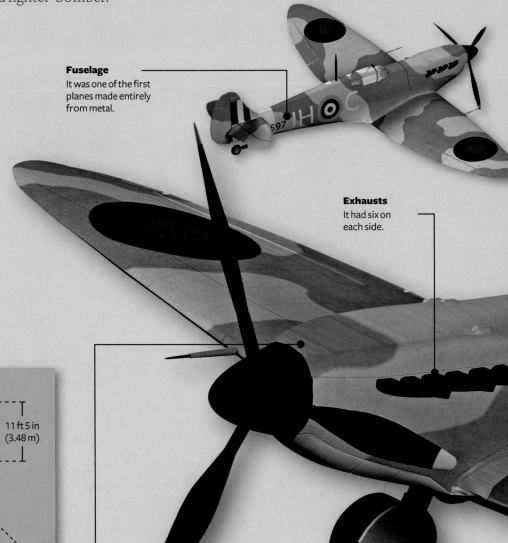

Fuselage
It was one of the first planes made entirely from metal.

Exhausts
It had six on each side.

DIMENSIONS

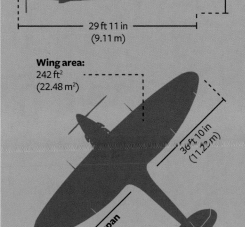

11 ft 5 in
(3.48 m)

29 ft 11 in
(9.11 m)

Wing area:
242 ft²
(22.48 m²)

36 ft 10 in
(11.22 m)

Wingspan

Engine
These varied from the first Rolls-Royce PV12 engines (later known as Merlin) of little more than 1,000 hp, to the 2,375 hp Griffon, used in the MK XXII.

Armament
The Mk IA carried eight 0.303-in (7.7-mm) machine guns beneath the wings. In versions like the VB these were replaced by two 0.787-in (20-mm) Hispano cannons and four 0.303-in (7.7-mm) Vickers machine guns.

Manufacturer ▸ Supermarine (subsidiary of Vickers-Armstrong)	**Units built** ▸ More than 20,000 (of all versions)	**Top speed** ▸ 374 mph at 12,992 ft (602 km/h at 3,960 m)*
First flight ▸ March 5, 1936	**Crew** ▸ 1	**Combat radius** ▸ 470 miles (756 km)*
Entry into service ▸ Summer 1938	**Loaded weight** ▸ 6,199 lb (2,812 kg)*	**Powerplant** ▸ 1 x Rolls-Royce Merlin 45 supercharged V12 engine, 1,440 hp*
Production ▸ 1938 to 1948	**Service ceiling** ▸ 37,000 ft (11,280 m)*	
Retired ▸ 1952 (from the RAF)		

*Data for the Mk VB

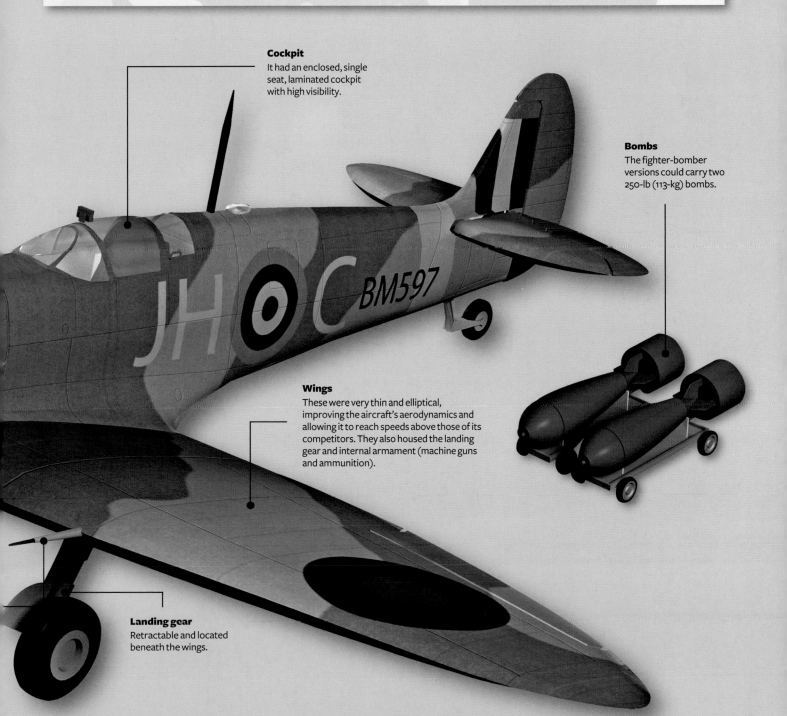

Cockpit
It had an enclosed, single seat, laminated cockpit with high visibility.

Bombs
The fighter-bomber versions could carry two 250-lb (113-kg) bombs.

Wings
These were very thin and elliptical, improving the aircraft's aerodynamics and allowing it to reach speeds above those of its competitors. They also housed the landing gear and internal armament (machine guns and ammunition).

Landing gear
Retractable and located beneath the wings.

Mitsubishi A6M Zero

Created in response to the Imperial Japanese Navy's need for a carrier fighter, the "Zero" or "Zeke" came to be the combat aircraft par excellence, not just for the carrier-based forces, but also for the Imperial Army. It was a superb aircraft, which, at the outset of World War II, excelled over many of its opponents. In service until the end of the war, its greatest virtues were its excellent maneuverability, its rate of climb, and its incomparable range.

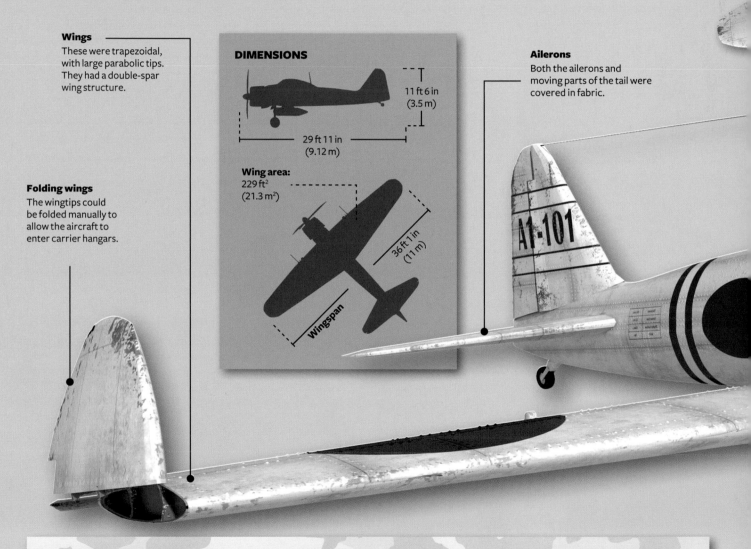

Wings
These were trapezoidal, with large parabolic tips. They had a double-spar wing structure.

Folding wings
The wingtips could be folded manually to allow the aircraft to enter carrier hangars.

DIMENSIONS

11 ft 6 in (3.5 m)

29 ft 11 in (9.12 m)

Wing area: 229 ft² (21.3 m²)

36 ft 1 in (11 m)

Wingspan

Ailerons
Both the ailerons and moving parts of the tail were covered in fabric.

A1-101

Manufacturer ▶ Mitsubishi, from the design of Jiro Horikoshi

First flight ▶ April 1, 1939

Entry into service ▶ September 1940

Units built ▶ 11,000 (until 1945)

Crew ▶ 1

Empty weight ▶ 4,178 lb (1,895 kg)*

Maximum takeoff weight ▶ 6,025 lb (2,733 kg)*

Service ceiling ▶ 38,517 ft (11,740 m)*

Top speed ▶ 350 mph at 19,685 ft (564 km/h at 6,000 m)*

Combat range ▶ 1,930 miles (3,105 km)*

Powerplant ▶ 1 x Nakajima Sakae 21 radial engine, 1,130 hp*

* Data for the A6M5 M-52

▲ **Type 97 Machine guns**
In the engine cowling it carried two 0.303-in (7.7-mm) machine guns, each with 500 rounds.

Cannon
Each wing carried a 0.787-in (20-mm) Type 99-1 cannon, which could fire 125 rounds per barrel. Under the wings it could carry two 132-lb (60-kg) bombs.

Camouflage
The aircraft of the Imperial Navy were painted entirely in a very light gray, while those of the Army were olive green and gray.

Cockpit
This was narrow, but had excellent visibility. It was equipped with radio equipment and oxygen system.

Propeller
The shaft of the three-bladed constant speed propeller was contained inside a metal cap.

Landing gear
This was totally retractable, and the wheels were fitted with hydraulic brakes.

Drop tank
It could carry an 87-gal (330-litre) drop tank under the fuselage.

Engine
The two-row, radial 14-cylinder engine had a two-speed supercharger and 1,130-hp maximum power.

McDonnell Douglas F-4 Phantom II

Designed in 1958 for the U.S. Navy, this supersonic fighter-bomber was later adopted by the U.S. Marine Corps and the Air Force, whose version of the F-4C made its first flight in 1963. Loaded with more than 15,430 lb (7,000 kg) of weapons on external hardpoints, the F-4 was a versatile, multirole fighter with great air-to-air and air-to-surface combat capabilities. Used in the Vietnam War and the Gulf War, the aircraft was in service for the USAF until 1996 and remained active in other countries for several more years.

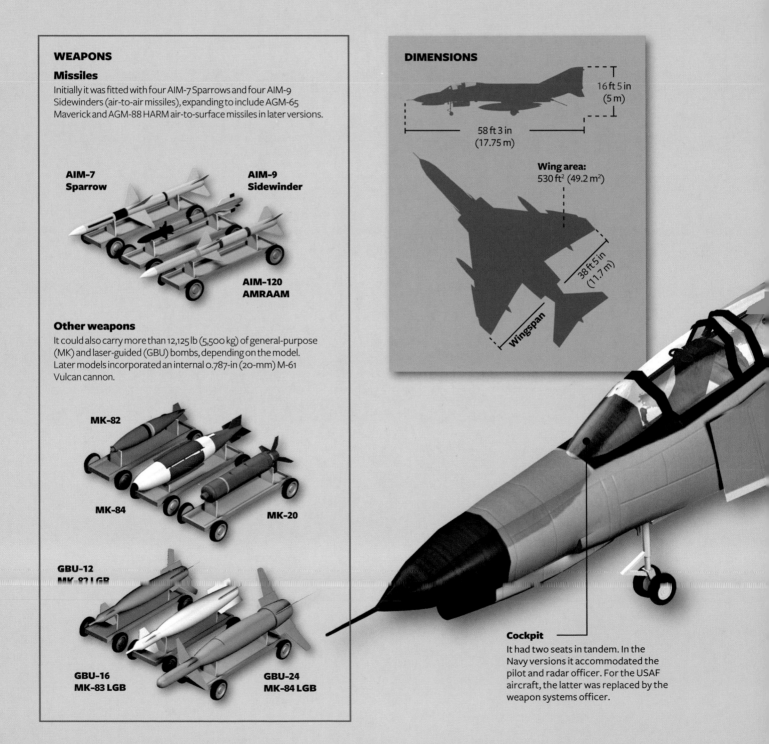

WEAPONS

Missiles

Initially it was fitted with four AIM-7 Sparrows and four AIM-9 Sidewinders (air-to-air missiles), expanding to include AGM-65 Maverick and AGM-88 HARM air-to-surface missiles in later versions.

AIM-7 Sparrow

AIM-9 Sidewinder

AIM-120 AMRAAM

Other weapons

It could also carry more than 12,125 lb (5,500 kg) of general-purpose (MK) and laser-guided (GBU) bombs, depending on the model. Later models incorporated an internal 0.787-in (20-mm) M-61 Vulcan cannon.

MK-82

MK-84

MK-20

GBU-12 MK-82 LGB

GBU-16 MK-83 LGB

GBU-24 MK-84 LGB

DIMENSIONS

16 ft 5 in (5 m)

58 ft 3 in (17.75 m)

Wing area: 530 ft² (49.2 m²)

38 ft 5 in (11.7 m)

Wingspan

Cockpit
It had two seats in tandem. In the Navy versions it accommodated the pilot and radar officer. For the USAF aircraft, the latter was replaced by the weapon systems officer.

Materials
One of the improvements introduced in later versions was the extensive use of titanium in the airframe.

Arresting hook
Located between the two engines, this mobile device served to decelerate the aircraft by automatically hooking onto a cable on the deck of the carrier during landing.

Fuel tanks
The F-4C incorporated two external fuel tanks, which could be dropped once empty.

Manufacturer ▶ McDonnell Douglas (now Boeing)

First aircraft ▶ May 27, 1958 (prototype)

Entry into service ▶ 1961

Production ▶ 1958 to 1979 (in U.S.) / 1981 (Japan)

Units built ▶ More than 5,000. (2,874 for the USAF and 1,200 for the U.S. Navy, the U.S. Marine Corps, and 11 other countries)

Crew ▶ 2

Empty weight ▶ 28,440 lb (12,900 kg)*

Maximum takeoff weight ▶ 55,596 lb (25,218 kg)*

Service ceiling ▶ 59,600 ft (18,166 m)*

Top speed ▶ 1,400 mph/2,253 km/h (Mach 2.1)*

Cruise speed ▶ 590 mph (950 km/h)*

Range ▶ 1,750 miles (2,816 km)*

Powerplant ▶ 2 x General Electric J-79-GE-15 turbojets, 17,000 lb (7,710 kg) of thrust each*

* Data for the F-4C

Mikoyan MiG-29 "Fulcrum"

Designed in the 1970s in response to the U.S. F-15 and F-16 fighters, this Soviet fighter aircraft combines efficiency in close-range air combat with ground-target attacks. Its performance in aerial combat improved with the incorporation of an integrated sighting system, the Shchel-3UM, which allows pilots to designate a target by just looking at it through a helmet-mounted display. In 1986, the first units were exported to India, and since then the different versions of the aircraft have sold to more than 30 countries around the world.

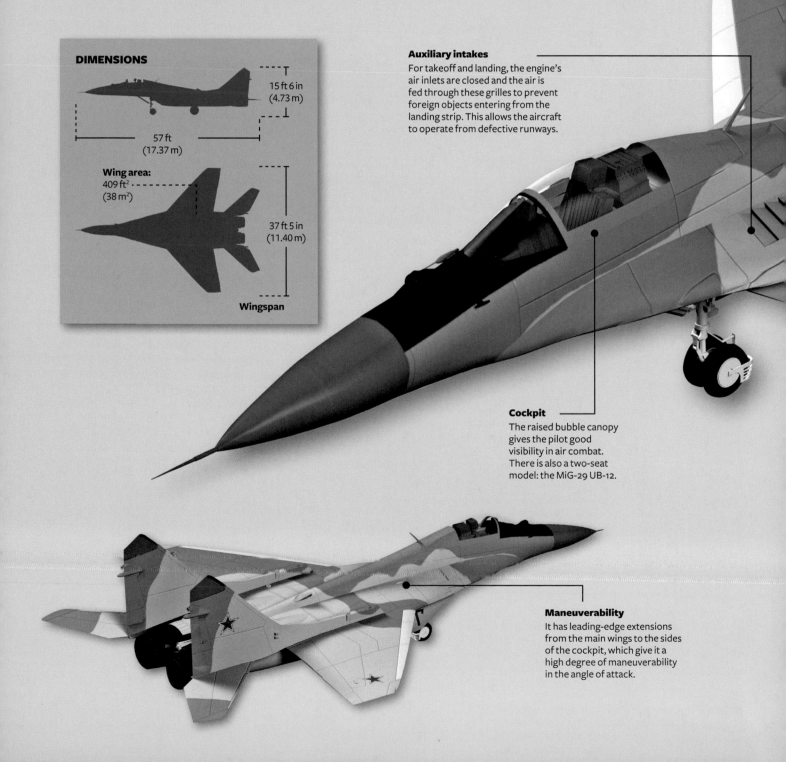

DIMENSIONS

15 ft 6 in
(4.73 m)

57 ft
(17.37 m)

Wing area:
409 ft²
(38 m²)

37 ft 5 in
(11.40 m)

Wingspan

Auxiliary intakes
For takeoff and landing, the engine's air inlets are closed and the air is fed through these grilles to prevent foreign objects entering from the landing strip. This allows the aircraft to operate from defective runways.

Cockpit
The raised bubble canopy gives the pilot good visibility in air combat. There is also a two-seat model: the MiG-29 UB-12.

Maneuverability
It has leading-edge extensions from the main wings to the sides of the cockpit, which give it a high degree of maneuverability in the angle of attack.

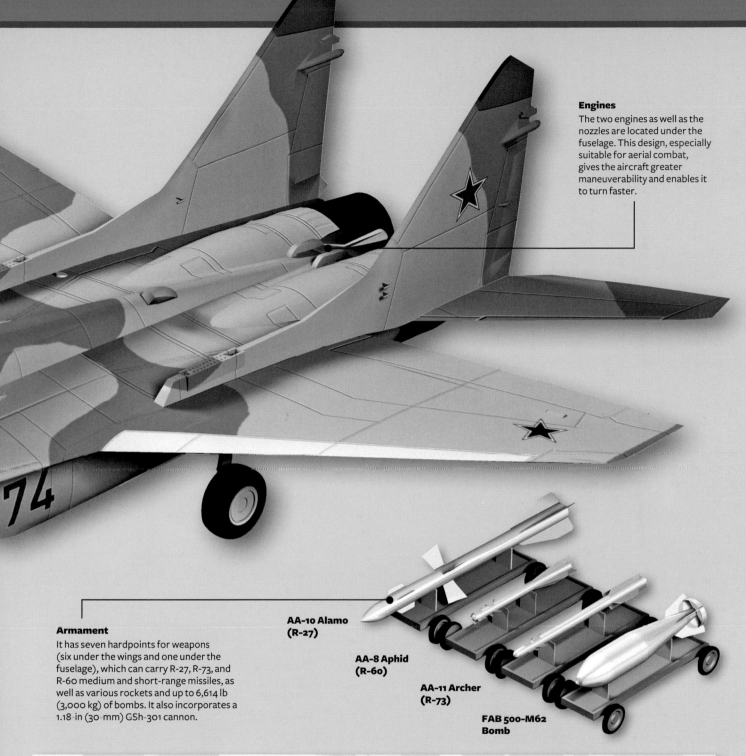

Engines
The two engines as well as the nozzles are located under the fuselage. This design, especially suitable for aerial combat, gives the aircraft greater maneuverability and enables it to turn faster.

Armament
It has seven hardpoints for weapons (six under the wings and one under the fuselage), which can carry R-27, R-73, and R-60 medium and short-range missiles, as well as various rockets and up to 6,614 lb (3,000 kg) of bombs. It also incorporates a 1.18-in (30-mm) GSh-301 cannon.

AA-10 Alamo (R-27)

AA-8 Aphid (R-60)

AA-11 Archer (R-73)

FAB 500-M62 Bomb

Manufacturer ▶ Mikoyan-Gurevich

First aircraft ▶ October 6, 1977

Entry into service ▶ August 1983

Production ▶ 1982 to present

Crew ▶ 1

Empty weight ▶ 24,250 lb (11,000 kg)

Maximum takeoff weight ▶ 39,683 lb (18,000 kg)

Fuel ▶ 1,057 gal (4,000 liters)

Service ceiling ▶ 59,054 ft (18,000 m)

Top speed ▶ 1,491 mph/2,400 km/h (Mach 2.3)

Cruise speed ▶ 932 mph (1,500 km/h)

Combat radius ▶ 930 miles (1,500 km)

Powerplant ▶ 2 x Klimov RD-33 afterburning turbofans, 18,300 lb (8,300 kg) thrust each.

Grumman F-14 Tomcat

Designed to replace the F-4 Phantom II, this supersonic, variable-sweep wing fighter-bomber of the U.S. Navy had advanced weapons control, navigation systems, and electronic countermeasures (ECM), and could carry almost 13,230 lb (6,000 kg) of missiles, rockets, and bombs. Designed for air superiority in all scenarios and weather conditions and for naval defense, it also performed ground-attack missions and tactical reconnaissance (with the incorporation of optical and infrared cameras).

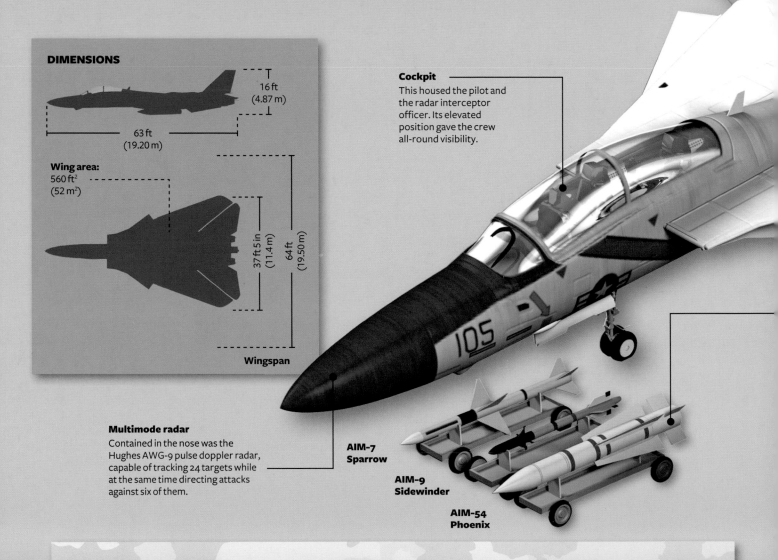

DIMENSIONS

16 ft
(4.87 m)

63 ft
(19.20 m)

Wing area:
560 ft² (52 m²)

37 ft 5 in
(11.4 m)

64 ft
(19.50 m)

Wingspan

Cockpit
This housed the pilot and the radar interceptor officer. Its elevated position gave the crew all-round visibility.

Multimode radar
Contained in the nose was the Hughes AWG-9 pulse doppler radar, capable of tracking 24 targets while at the same time directing attacks against six of them.

AIM-7 Sparrow

AIM-9 Sidewinder

AIM-54 Phoenix

Manufacturer ▸ Grumman/Northrop Grumman	**Crew** ▸ 2	**Top speed** ▸ 1,513 mph (2,434 km/h)*
First flight ▸ December 21, 1970	**Weight** ▸ 40,104 lb (18,191 kg)*	**Combat radius** ▸ 1,840 miles (2,963 km)*
Entry into service ▸ 1973	**Maximum takeoff weight** ▸ 59,714 lb (27,086 kg)*	**Powerplant** ▸ 2 x Pratt & Whitney TF-30P-414A afterburning turbofans, 20,900 lb (9,480 kg) of thrust each*
Retired ▸ September 22, 2006	**Service ceiling** ▸ more than 49,850 ft (15,200 m)*	

*Data for F-14A

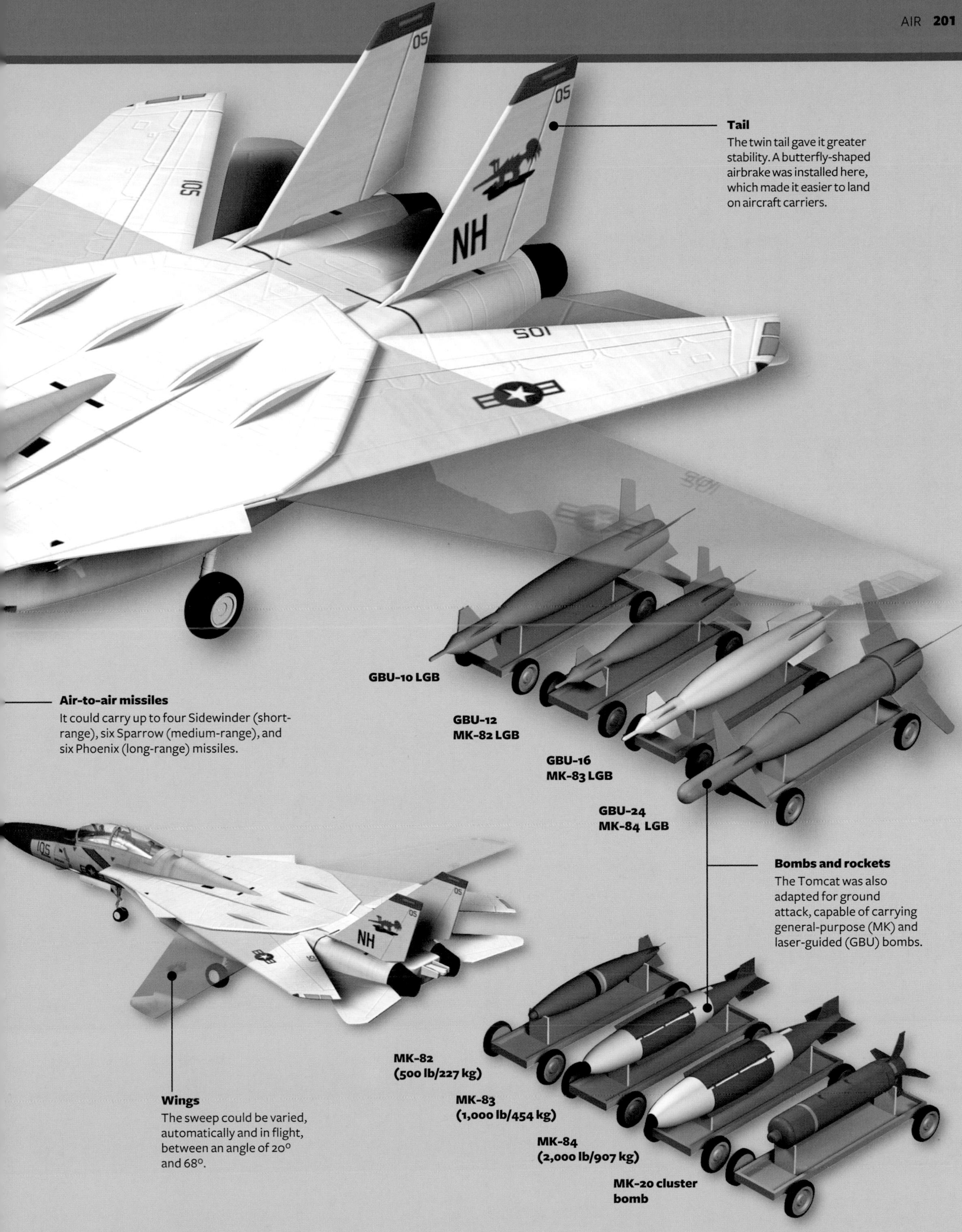

Tail
The twin tail gave it greater stability. A butterfly-shaped airbrake was installed here, which made it easier to land on aircraft carriers.

Air-to-air missiles
It could carry up to four Sidewinder (short-range), six Sparrow (medium-range), and six Phoenix (long-range) missiles.

GBU-10 LGB

GBU-12
MK-82 LGB

GBU-16
MK-83 LGB

GBU-24
MK-84 LGB

Bombs and rockets
The Tomcat was also adapted for ground attack, capable of carrying general-purpose (MK) and laser-guided (GBU) bombs.

Wings
The sweep could be varied, automatically and in flight, between an angle of 20° and 68°.

MK-82
(500 lb/227 kg)

MK-83
(1,000 lb/454 kg)

MK-84
(2,000 lb/907 kg)

MK-20 cluster bomb

Eurofighter Typhoon

In 1988, Germany, the United Kingdom, Italy, and Spain began development of a multirole fighter, capable of performing a wide range of operations, both in air-combat and ground-strike missions. The result was the Typhoon, a supersonic aircraft manufactured using state-of-the-art technologies and advanced materials, which provide it with a low radar profile and great strength. Aside from the air forces of the countries involved in its design, there are Typhoon units operating in Austria, Saudi Arabia, and Oman.

WEAPONS

The Typhoon can carry multiple combinations of armaments, which include short-range (ASRAAM) and long-range (AMRAAM) air-to-air missiles, Enhanced Paveway II laser-guided bombs, and more than 990 lb (450 kg) of general-purpose bombs. It also has a 1.06 in (27-mm) Mauser cannon.

Short- and medium-range air-to-air missiles

General-purpose bombs

Laser-guided bombs

DIMENSIONS

17 ft 4 in
(5.28 m)

52 ft 4 in
(15.96 m)

Wing area:
551 ft²
(51.20 m²)

35 ft 11 in
(10.95 m)

Wingspan

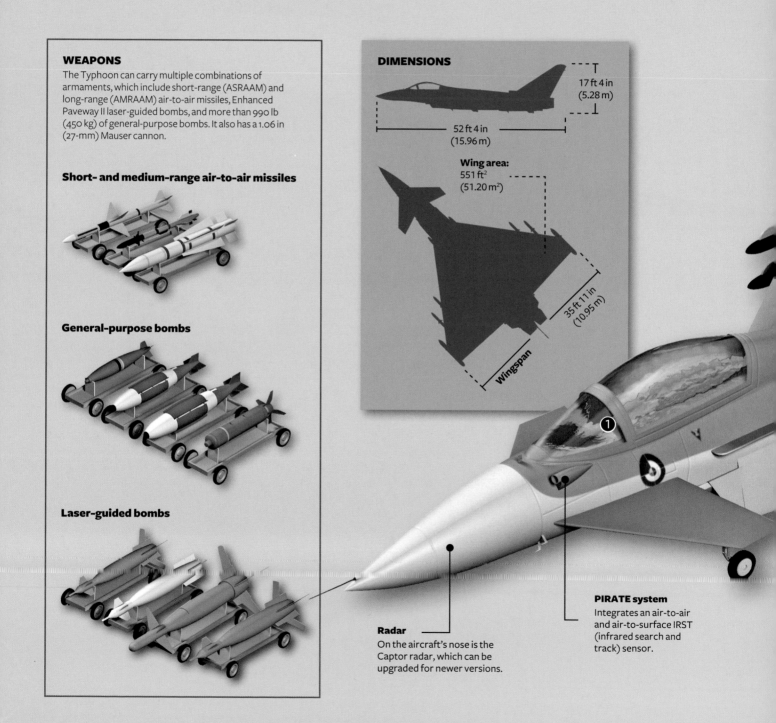

Radar
On the aircraft's nose is the Captor radar, which can be upgraded for newer versions.

PIRATE system
Integrates an air-to-air and air-to-surface IRST (infrared search and track) sensor.

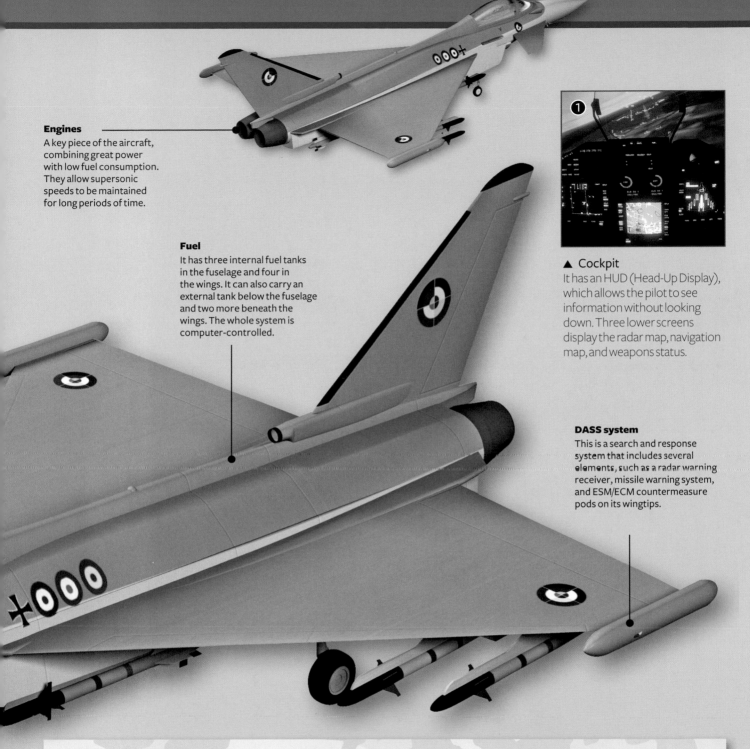

Engines
A key piece of the aircraft, combining great power with low fuel consumption. They allow supersonic speeds to be maintained for long periods of time.

Fuel
It has three internal fuel tanks in the fuselage and four in the wings. It can also carry an external tank below the fuselage and two more beneath the wings. The whole system is computer-controlled.

① ▲ Cockpit
It has an HUD (Head-Up Display), which allows the pilot to see information without looking down. Three lower screens display the radar map, navigation map, and weapons status.

DASS system
This is a search and response system that includes several elements, such as a radar warning receiver, missile warning system, and ESM/ECM countermeasure pods on its wingtips.

Manufacturer ▶ Eurofighter Company (a consortium of companies from Germany, the United Kingdom, Spain, and Italy)

First flight ▶ March 27, 1994

Entry into service ▶ 2003

Crew ▶ 1

Empty weight ▶ 24,250 lb (11,000 kg)

Maximum takeoff weight ▶ 51,809 lb (23,500 kg)

Service ceiling ▶ 55,003 ft (16,765 m)

Top speed ▶ 1,535 mph/2,470 km/h (Mach 2)

Cruise speed ▶ 652 mph/1,050 km/h (Mach 1)

Combat radius ▶ Aerial combat: 863 miles (1,389 km)

Range ▶ 2,175 miles (3,500 km)

Powerplant ▶ 2 x Eurojet EJ200 engines with 20,000 lb (9,072 kg) of thrust each.

▲ AH-64 Apache
The main attack helicopter of the U.S. Army, it has participated in the major conflicts of the last 20 years.

HELICOPTERS

Helicopters are a fundamental part of air forces today. These war machines, in just half a century, have reached such a high level of maneuverability that they are capable of doing almost anything in the air and in combat. Initially designed for tactical transport, reconnaissance, and combat search and rescue, they were not used by the military until World War II. Their development truly began in the 1970s, when the first turboshaft engines were produced. A case in point is the United States's Bell UH-1 Iroquois, nicknamed the "Huey," a two-blade transport helicopter, 7,000 of which were used in the Vietnam War, where they operated in pairs, armed with rocket and grenade launchers and machine guns. The AH-1G Cobra was also, for years, the backbone of the U.S. helicopter fleet, and over a thousand were manufactured between 1967 and 1973. The model that followed this in 1979—the tactical transport helicopter the UH-60 Black Hawk—had four blades and could be used for air assault missions, as its wing stubs were equipped with hardpoints for carrying missiles and antitank rockets.

The primary attack helicopter of the U.S. Air Force, however, was the AH-64 Apache, which entered service in 1982. To minimize combat damage it was fitted with two separate rotors, and the blades and different parts of its structure were armored to protect it against rounds of up to 0.906 in (23 mm). It was also one of the first to incorporate electronic

warfare systems, and could fire as many as 76 Hydra 70 rockets and 16 AGM-114 Hellfire missiles.

In the early 1960s, production began of an aircraft that today is one of the few of its era still manufactured in the United States: the heavy-lift transport helicopter, the CH-47 Chinook. This aircraft incorporated an innovative system consisting of two three-blade tandem rotors and two 2,200 hp engines. Fitted with a loading ramp and capable of transporting 28,000 lb (12,700 kg) of materiel and up to 55 men, more than ten versions have been made incorporating various improvements. One of the most recent—the CH-47F—is equipped with an advanced flight-control system. However, the most powerful and advanced long-range helicopter of the United States Air Force is the MH-53J Pave Low III, used until 2008 by U.S. special forces for performing combat search and rescue missions behind enemy lines. This armored aircraft was specially designed for night operations and fitted with highly complex tracking, navigation, and data-processing systems. One of today's most remarkable helicopters, thanks to its distinctive coaxial rotor system—rotors mounted one above the other on the same axis of rotation, thereby eliminating the need for a tail rotor—is the KA-50 Black Shark, designed and built by the Russian manufacturer Kamov. This "all-weather" reconnaissance and antitank aircraft is armored and fitted with two seats, both of which are fully ejectable.

Bell UH-1 Iroquois "Huey"

Manufactured in the 1950s for the U.S. Army by Bell Helicopter, the UH-1 Iroquois, best known as "Huey," gained its reputation from its involvement in the Vietnam War as a helicopter for medical evacuations, attack and reconnaissance missions, and for transporting soldiers, materiel, and arms. Since its introduction, more than 16,000 units have been produced of this model and its different variants, which have been exported to more than 40 countries, making it one of the most widely used and successful helicopters in history.

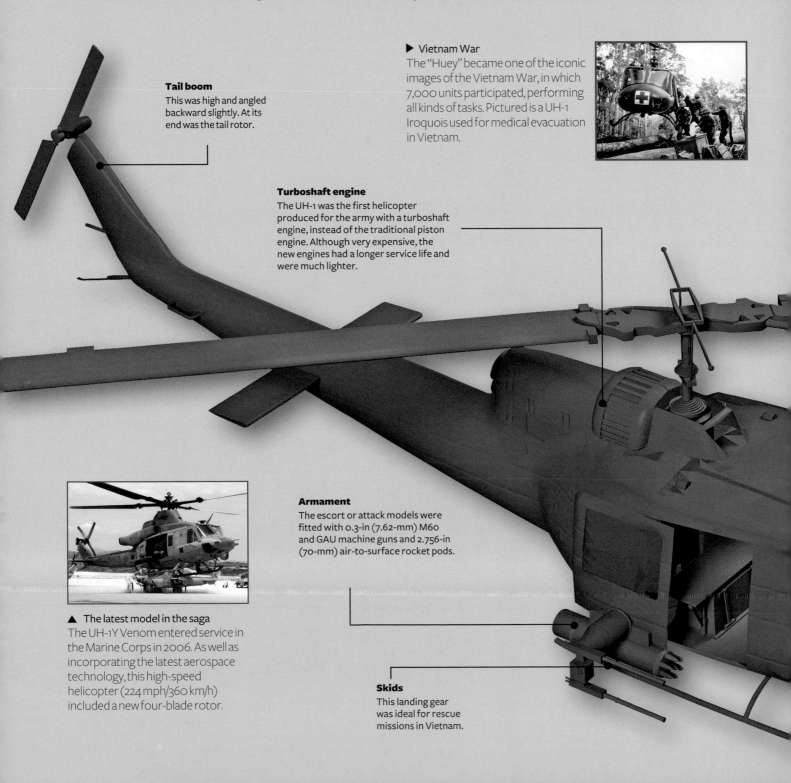

Tail boom
This was high and angled backward slightly. At its end was the tail rotor.

▶ Vietnam War
The "Huey" became one of the iconic images of the Vietnam War, in which 7,000 units participated, performing all kinds of tasks. Pictured is a UH-1 Iroquois used for medical evacuation in Vietnam.

Turboshaft engine
The UH-1 was the first helicopter produced for the army with a turboshaft engine, instead of the traditional piston engine. Although very expensive, the new engines had a longer service life and were much lighter.

Armament
The escort or attack models were fitted with 0.3-in (7.62-mm) M60 and GAU machine guns and 2.756-in (70-mm) air-to-surface rocket pods.

▲ The latest model in the saga
The UH-1Y Venom entered service in the Marine Corps in 2006. As well as incorporating the latest aerospace technology, this high-speed helicopter (224 mph/360 km/h) included a new four-blade rotor.

Skids
This landing gear was ideal for rescue missions in Vietnam.

Manufacturer ▸ Bell Helicopter Textron Inc.	**Empty weight** ▸ 5,210 lb (2,363 kg)	**Top speed** ▸ 137 mph (220 km/h)
First flight ▸ October 22, 1956	**Loaded weight** ▸ More than 8,820 lb/ 4,000 kg (depending on the version)	**Cruise speed** ▸ 127 mph (205 km/h)
Entry into service ▸ 1959	**Service ceiling** ▸ Up to 19,685 ft/6,000 m (depending on the version)	**Powerplant** ▸ 1 x Lycoming T53-L-13 turboshaft, 1,400 hp (model UH-1H)
Units built ▸ More than 16,000		
Crew ▸ 1–4	**Range** ▸ 318 miles (511 km)	

Cockpit
The UH-1, the military version of Bell's 204 commercial model, had, in its D model, capacity for two crew and six passengers or two stretchers.

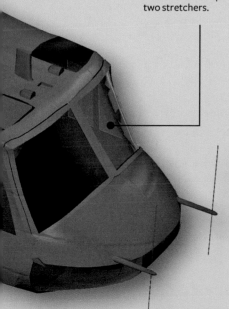

DIMENSIONS

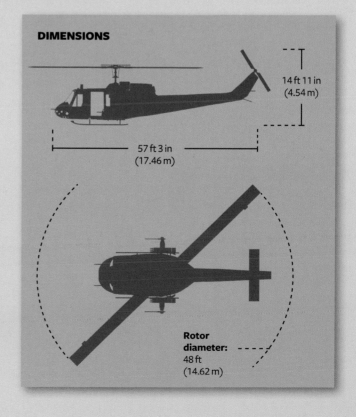

14 ft 11 in
(4.54 m)

57 ft 3 in
(17.46 m)

Rotor diameter:
48 ft
(14.62 m)

Sikorsky UH-60 Black Hawk

In light of its experience with the UH-1 in Vietnam, the United States Army decided to introduce new, more robust utility helicopters with greater capacity and less vulnerability to enemy fire. Sikorsky Aircraft won the UTTAS (Army Utility Tactical Transport Aircraft System) competition over Boeing's proposal, and in 1979 the UH-60 Black Hawk entered service as a tactical transport, medical evacuation, and air assault unit. It first served in conflict during the invasion of Grenada, in October 1983.

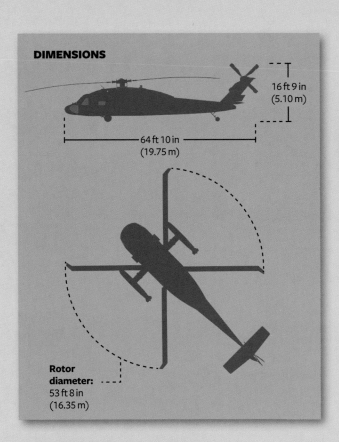

DIMENSIONS

16 ft 9 in (5.10 m)

64 ft 10 in (19.75 m)

Rotor diameter: 53 ft 8 in (16.35 m)

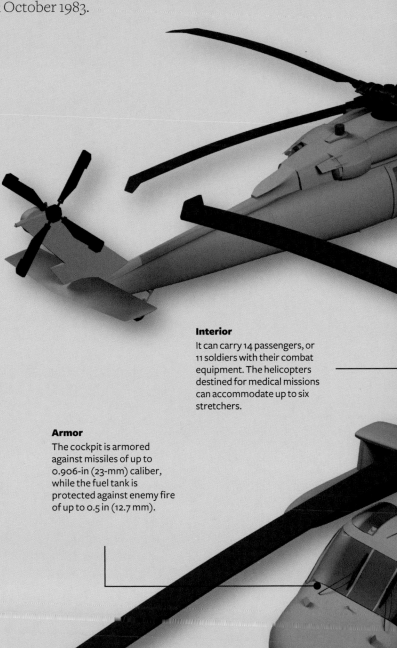

Interior
It can carry 14 passengers, or 11 soldiers with their combat equipment. The helicopters destined for medical missions can accommodate up to six stretchers.

Armor
The cockpit is armored against missiles of up to 0.906-in (23-mm) caliber, while the fuel tank is protected against enemy fire of up to 0.5 in (12.7 mm).

▲ VH-60N Marine One
Since 1989, this special version of the Sikorsky UH-60 has been one of the helicopters chosen by the U.S. Marine Corps for transporting the President of the United States.

Manufacturer ▸ Sikorsky Aircraft	**Empty weight** ▸ 10,582 lb (4,800 kg)	**Top speed** ▸ 183 mph (295 km/h)
First flight ▸ Autumn 1974	**Loaded weight** ▸ 23,150 lb (10,500 kg)	**Powerplant** ▸ 2 General Electric T700-GE-700 turboshaft engines, 1,410 hp (for the UH-60A version)
Entry into service ▸ June 1979	**Service ceiling** ▸ 19,000 ft/5,790 m / (depending on the version)	
Units built ▸ Around 3,000		**Fuel tank** ▸ 360 gal (1,360 liters)
Crew ▸ 4	**Range** ▸ 518 miles (834 km)	

▸ **Load capacity**
The interior can be loaded with up to 2,640 lb (1,200 kg), and an external cargo hook can also be fitted enabling it to carry 8,000 lb (3,630 kg).

Strength
The four blades of the main rotor and tail are made of titanium and fiberglass, allowing the aircraft to take big hits without being damaged.

Twin-engine
The most up-to-date version includes two T-70K turboshaft engines of 1,540 hp, which are cooled by particle-separating air inlets.

Structure for missiles
The UH-60 could be fitted with antitank, air-to-surface AGM 114-Hellfire missiles or 2.76-in (70-mm) Hydra rockets. They also had M240H (0.3 in/7.62 mm), M134 Minigun (0.3 in/7.62 mm), or GAU-19 (0.5 in/12.7 mm) machine guns.

Boeing AH-64 Apache

This is the United States Army's primary advanced attack helicopter. Thanks to its advanced avionics, with sophisticated sensor systems and a wide range of armaments, it can be used during the day or night on all kinds of attack, escort, and antitank missions. Since the mid-1980s, it has served in the invasion of Panama, the Gulf War, and the most recent conflicts in Afghanistan and Iraq. The United Kingdom, Israel, Japan, and Egypt, among other countries, also have this helicopter in their fleets.

◀ **Tandem seats**
In the armored cockpit, the copilot or gunner sits at the front and the pilot sits behind, 18.9 in (48 cm) higher to ensure perfect vision.

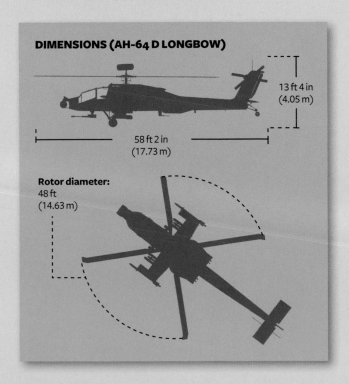

DIMENSIONS (AH-64 D LONGBOW)

13 ft 4 in (4.05 m)

58 ft 2 in (17.73 m)

Rotor diameter: 48 ft (14.63 m)

Sensors
Contained in the nose is the infrared TADS/PNVS (target acquisition and designation sights and pilot night vision system), which projects images in the pilot's helmet (IHADSS system).

Radome
The SH-64 Apache Longbow (which entered service in 1997) incorporates the AN/APG-78 Longbow radome on the main rotor shaft, which contains advanced radar systems.

Stabilizers
The large fins allow the aircraft to be controlled during low-level and low-speed flights.

Turboshaft engines
These occupy independent compartments on either side of the fuselage, far enough apart so that the helicopter is not destroyed if one of the engines is damaged in combat.

Armament
This varies depending on the mission and target. It carries a fixed automatic 1.18-in (30-mm) M230 gun, and its wings can be fitted with AGM-114 Hellfire laser-guided missiles, Hydra 70 rockets, AIM-92 Stinger or AIM-9 Sidewinder antiaircraft missiles, and AGM-122 Sidearm antiradar missiles, among others.

Manufacturer ▶ Boeing (previously Hughes Helicopters and McDonnell Douglas)

First flight ▶ September 30, 1975

Entry into service ▶ January 1984

Units built ▶ More than 1,800

Crew ▶ 2

Empty weight ▶ 11,795 lb (5,350 kg)*

Maximum takeoff weight ▶ 22,278 lb (10,105 kg)*

Service ceiling ▶ 21,000 ft (6,400 m)*

Range ▶ 255 miles (410 km)*

Top speed ▶ 169 mph (273 km/h)*

Powerplant ▶ 2 x General Electric T700-GE-701C turboshaft engines*

*Data for the AH-64D

Boeing CH-47 Chinook

Since it entered service more than 50 years ago, the CH-47 Chinook has been the primary transport helicopter of the United States Army. Different versions have been deployed since the Vietnam War, right up to recent operations in Iraq and Afghanistan. This twin-engine, tandem rotor, heavy-lift transport helicopter is used mainly to move troops, artillery, ammunition, fuel, water, and battlefield supplies and equipment.

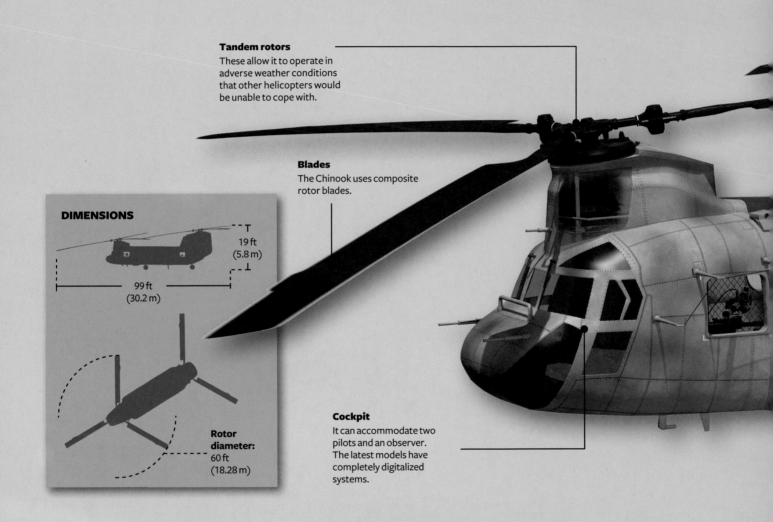

Tandem rotors
These allow it to operate in adverse weather conditions that other helicopters would be unable to cope with.

Blades
The Chinook uses composite rotor blades.

DIMENSIONS

19 ft
(5.8 m)

99 ft
(30.2 m)

Rotor diameter:
60 ft
(18.28 m)

Cockpit
It can accommodate two pilots and an observer. The latest models have completely digitalized systems.

Manufacturer ▸ Boeing Vertol / Boeing Rotorcraft Systems

First flight ▸ September 21, 1961

Entry into service ▸ 1962

Units built ▸ More than 1,000

Empty weight ▸ 22,454 lb (10,185 kg)

Crew ▸ 3 (pilot, copilot, flight engineer) + 3 gunners.

Maximum takeoff weight ▸ 50,000 lb (22,680 kg)

Service ceiling ▸ 18,500 ft (5,639 m)

Top speed ▸ 196 mph (315 km/h)

Rate of climb ▸ 25 ft/s (7.7 m/s)

Powerplant ▸ 2 x Textron Lycoming T55-L712 turboshaft engines

Combat range ▸ 460 miles (741 km)

Endurance ▸ 2.3 hours

◀ **Hold capacity**
The cargo capacity is 1,483 ft³ (42 m³) with a surface area of 226 ft² (21 m²). It can transport two Humvee vehicles or a Humvee and a 4.13-in (105-mm) howitzer.

Ramp

Armor
The hold is fitted with Kevlar armor plating to protect its occupants.

Hold
Able to transport between 33 and 55 soldiers, or 24 stretchers for medical missions.

Engines
It has enough power to lift a damaged aircraft or another Chinook.

Fuel tanks
These are mounted on the external fairing on the sides of the fuselage and have a capacity of 1,030 gal (3,900 liters).

UNITED STATES ARMY

Fire-control unit

Electric generator

▶ **Machine guns**
On the U.S. Army version it carries a 0.3-in (7.62-mm) M134 Minigun mounted on the forward position and two 0.3-in (7.62-mm) M60s, one on the rear position and another on the ramp.

Multiple cannons

M134 Minigun

LIFT CAPACITY
It has a triple-hook cargo system: the center hook can carry up to 26,455 lb (12,000 kg), and the other two, 16,535 lb (7,500 kg) each.

Sikorsky MH-53J Pave Low III

Successor of the CH-53 Sea Stallion "Jolly Green Giants" which operated in Vietnam, the MH-53J Pave Low III was, for more than two decades, the most powerful and sophisticated heavy-lift helicopter of the United States Air Force. Its main activity was the search, rescue, and supply of special forces behind enemy lines, in all kinds of conditions, making use of state-of-the-art radars, sensors, and GPS. In 2008, it was replaced by the CV-22B Osprey.

◀ External tanks
After the C version, the MH-53J was the option of being fitted with two large 450-gal (1,700-liter) tanks for long-range missions, which could be jettisoned to gain speed.

Cockpit
The crew was composed of two pilots (officers), two flight engineers, and two aerial gunners equipped with machine guns mounted on the sides.

Probe
Allows inflight refueling. The probe extended during refueling to avoid the rotor blades.

Manufacturer ▸ Sikorsky Aircraft	**Empty weight** ▸ 32,000 lb (14,515 kg)	**Cruise speed** ▸ 165 mph (265 km/h)
Entry into service ▸ 1968	**Maximum takeoff weight** ▸ 46,300 lb (21,000 kg)	**Range** ▸ 600 nautical miles (unlimited with inflight refueling)
Retired ▸ 2008	**Service ceiling** ▸ 16,000 ft (4,875 m)	**Powerplant** ▸ 2 x General Electric T64-GE-415 turboshaft engines, 4,330 hp
Crew ▸ 6	**Top speed** ▸ 196 mph (315 km/h)	

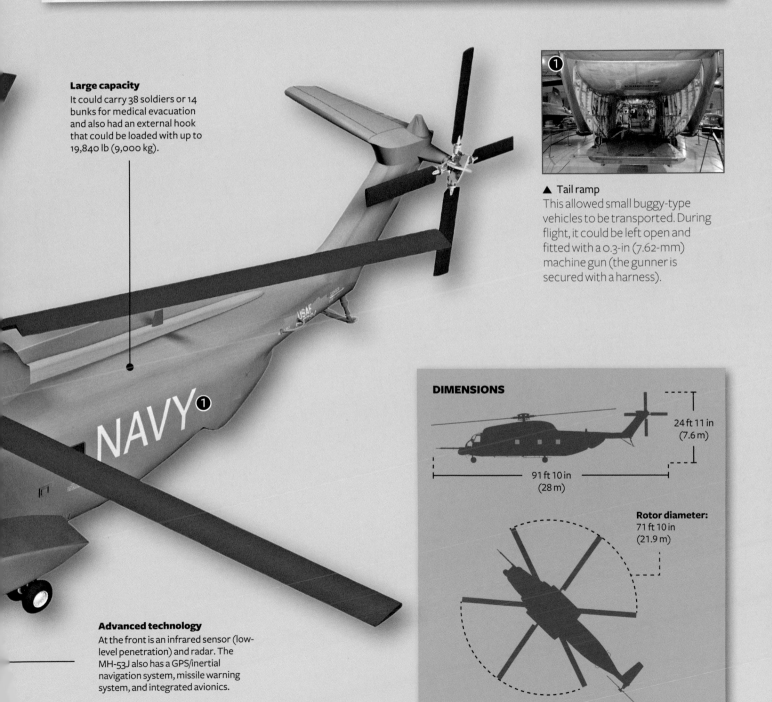

Large capacity
It could carry 38 soldiers or 14 bunks for medical evacuation and also had an external hook that could be loaded with up to 19,840 lb (9,000 kg).

①

▲ Tail ramp
This allowed small buggy-type vehicles to be transported. During flight, it could be left open and fitted with a 0.3-in (7.62-mm) machine gun (the gunner is secured with a harness).

NAVY **①**

DIMENSIONS

24 ft 11 in (7.6 m)

91 ft 10 in (28 m)

Rotor diameter:
71 ft 10 in (21.9 m)

Advanced technology
At the front is an infrared sensor (low-level penetration) and radar. The MH-53J also has a GPS/inertial navigation system, missile warning system, and integrated avionics.

Kamov Ka-50 Black Shark

This versatile single-seat attack helicopter made by Kamov was Russia's response to the successful Apache models manufactured by the United States in the 1980s. Equipped with inertial navigation systems, infrared sensors, tracking radar, and defensive electronic countermeasures, as well as a wide range of weapons, the Ka-50 is designed to destroy tanks and slow-moving air targets. In 2001, it was first used in combat in Chechnya, during the Russian attack on the rebel positions.

Coaxial rotor
The Ka-50 incorporates Kamov's characteristic contrarotating coaxial rotor, which provides great agility and maneuverability and renders a tail rotor unnecessary.

Ejection seat
This is the first helicopter to include this device for emergency situations. Before being activated, the rotor blades are blown away by explosive charges.

◀ Ka-52 Alligator
Kamov subsequently manufactured a two-seat version—the Ka-52 Alligator—with a wider cockpit and seats arranged side by side and not in tandem, as in most attack helicopters.

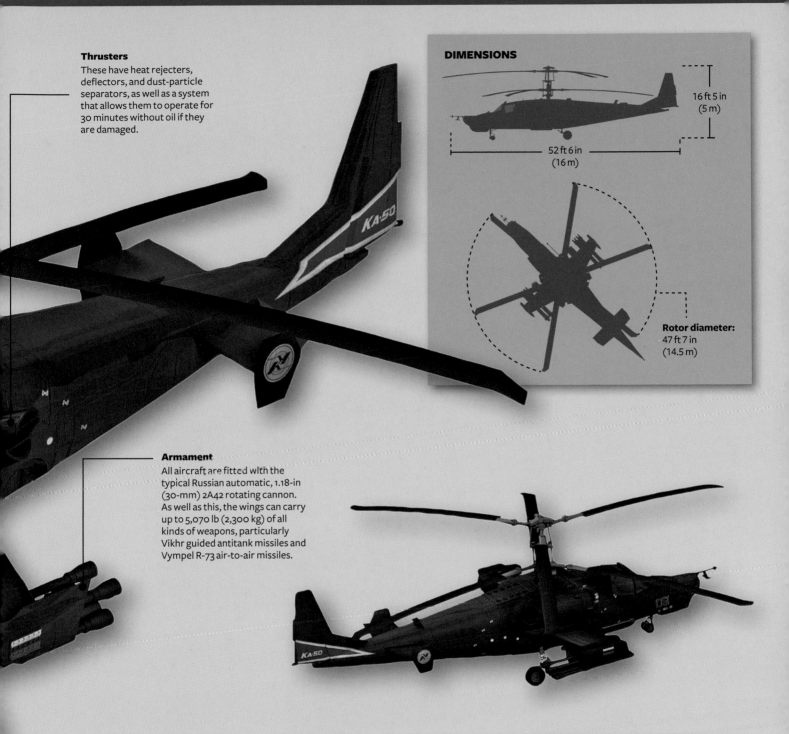

Thrusters
These have heat rejecters, deflectors, and dust-particle separators, as well as a system that allows them to operate for 30 minutes without oil if they are damaged.

DIMENSIONS

16 ft 5 in
(5 m)

52 ft 6 in
(16 m)

Rotor diameter:
47 ft 7 in
(14.5 m)

Armament
All aircraft are fitted with the typical Russian automatic, 1.18-in (30-mm) 2A42 rotating cannon. As well as this, the wings can carry up to 5,070 lb (2,300 kg) of all kinds of weapons, particularly Vikhr guided antitank missiles and Vympel R-73 air-to-air missiles.

Manufacturer ▸ Kamov Company	**Crew** ▸ 1	**Range** ▸ 572 miles (920 km)
First flight ▸ June 27, 1982	**Empty weight** ▸ 21,495 lb (9,750 kg)	**Top speed** ▸ 199 mph (320 km/h)
Entry into service ▸ August 28, 1995	**Maximum takeoff weight** ▸ 23,700 lb (10,750 kg)	**Cruise speed** ▸ 270 km/h (168 mph)
Variants ▸ KA-50 Sh and KA-50-2	**Service ceiling** ▸ 18,045 ft (5,500 m)	**Powerplant** ▸ 2 x Klimov TV3-117Vk turboshaft engines, 2,300 hp (1,640 kW)

INDEX

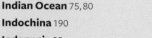

Based on an idea by Joan Ricart
Editorial coordination Marta de la Serna
Design María Nolis
Copy (supplied by) Federico Puigdevall
Editing Alberto Hernández, Mar Valls
Translation Jay Noden
Copy Editor Stuart Franklin
Guidance Llibreria Etcétera
Graphic Editor Alberto Hernández
Layout María Nolis, Clara Miralles
Infographics Sol90 Images
Photography
Aci: 48 (d/l), 53 (m/r), 53 (d/r), 55 (up), 65 (up), 70 (d), 80 (l, m, r), 126-127, 163 (d), 164 (d), 166-167
AGE fotostock: 6-7, 8-9, 10-11, 12-13, 16-17, 18 (up/l), 20 (l), 21 (l),26 (d), 41 (d/r), 42-43, 45 (d/l), 70 (m), 72-73, 78 (m), 81 (m/l), 82-83, 94-95, 102, 103, 132 (m), 133 (up), 134 (l), 136-137, 138-139 (background), 139 (up/r), 150 (m/l), 158 (up/l), 162-163(background), 165, 169, 170, 178-179, 203, 209
Album: 22-23, 30-31, 90, 134 (r)
Cordon Press/Corbis: 14-15, 204-205, 210
Cordon Press/TopFoto: 19 (d/l), 21 (m), 134 (m), 158 (d/l)
Cordon Press/Ullstein: 135 (m/r)
Getty Images: 18 (m/d, r/d), 19 (m/l, up, m/d), 20 (m/l, m/r), 21(up, m/r, r), 28, 36 (d), 58-59, 64-65 (background), 69 (d), 74-75, 76-77, 78 (m/d), 79 (m/l, m, r/up, r/d, up), 81 (l, m/r, r, up), 108, 110-111, 118-119, 130-131, 132 (m/l, up/r, m), 133 (l/up), 134 (m/l), 135 (up, m/l), 150 (d/l), 151 (d/r), 152-153, 162 (d/l, m), 164 (up/r), 173, 192, 206 (up/r), 210, 214
Thinkstock: 19 (up/l), 70 (up/r), 124-125 (background), 128-129, 133 (m, r)
Bundesarchiv: Bild 101I-782-0041-31 / Borchert, Erich (Eric) / CC-BY-SA 19 (m/up)
Budeswehr-Fotos: 65 (d/r)